# IN DANTE'S WAKE

# IN DANTE'S WAKE

READING FROM MEDIEVAL
TO MODERN IN THE
AUGUSTINIAN TRADITION

JOHN FRECCERO

*Edited by*

DANIELLE CALLEGARI AND MELISSA SWAIN

Fordham University Press   New York   2015

Fordham University Press has no responsibility for the persistence or accuracy of URLs for external or third-party Internet websites referred to in this publication and does not guarantee that any content on such websites is, or will remain, accurate or appropriate.

Fordham University Press also publishes its books in a variety of electronic formats. Some content that appears in print may not be available in electronic books.

Visit us online at www.fordhampress.com.

Library of Congress Cataloging-in-Publication Data

Freccero, John.
[Essays. Selections]
In Dante's wake : reading from medieval to modern in the Augustinian tradition / John Freccero ; edited by Danielle Callegari and Melissa Swain.
pages  cm
Includes bibliographical references and index.
ISBN 978-0-8232-6427-8 (hardback) — ISBN 978-0-8232-6428-5 (paper)
1. Dante Alighieri, 1265–1321. Divina commedia. 2. Dante Alighieri, 1265–1321—Criticism and interpretation. 3. Dante Alighieri, 1265–1321—Influence.
I. Callegari, Danielle, editor. II. Swain, Melissa, editor. III. Title.
PQ4390.F825   2015
851'.1—dc23
2014048475

Printed in the United States of America

17  16  15  5  4  3  2  1

First edition

# Contents

# Figures

*Preface*

As his lifetime of contributions to Dante studies has by now amply demonstrated, the work of John Freccero speaks for itself. With this in mind, the editors of this volume have preferred to let Freccero do the talking, working only to facilitate a comfortable reading experience and to accommodate a diverse audience. As the author submitted his essays to us, it was our goal to eliminate digression and frame each piece with clear language and a familiar apparatus, both with the newly presented but previously published articles and with his fresh contributions. The following essays have been revised to reflect preferred current styles of notation and references, translations have been inserted where in the past they were not provided, and phrasing has been occasionally retouched where necessary for clarity and with this wider audience in mind. The content remains otherwise unchanged from the author's original. It is our hope that *In Dante's Wake* will thus be equally enjoyable for scholars of Dante and those outside the field, and that it will spark new interest for those familiar with Freccero's work while engaging the uninitiated.

Those existing fans will immediately recognize this as only the second time Freccero has collected his work into a single volume, and, like *The Poetics of Conversion*, this book gathers independent pieces that combine to form a cohesive whole. Several of the essays included here have been published previously, but many of these have been substantially edited by the author, and two appear in print for the first time. This reshaping emphasizes Freccero's consistent methodology, in turn producing a tool that can guide the reader from medieval to modern. The chapters can be enjoyed individually without reference to their companions, and are self-contained in both their arguments as well as their references and notes. However, each of the pieces included here represents not only a distinctive element of the author's approach, but also a major, enduring preoccupation for Freccero. Furthermore, the ordering of the chapters is not exclusively chronological, but also an intentional reflection of Freccero's thought process and understanding of the canon. As a whole, the book highlights the threads that can be followed throughout Freccero's work and advances new connections and possibilities made visible through his interpretive lens.

This lens has always been trained on Dante but has often found traces of the poet by searching among the words of other authors. Though Freccero firmly maintains his focus on the poet and indeed rarely strayed from the *Commedia*, he has not always approached Dante head on. As the title of this volume implies, the scholar of Dante is forever swimming in the poet's wake, but so too are all those who followed, absorbing and reproducing him in their respective works. Reading Petrarch, Machiavelli, Donne, and Svevo has provided Freccero with the opportunity to understand Dante more intimately and to feel his presence in later literature, simultaneously drawing readers of other moments and traditions toward the medieval poetry that has so inspired him. Treading in Dante's wake, in these essays Freccero continues the rigorous effort to give liveliness and vibrancy to the conversation he first began more than fifty years ago, aiming to strengthen the existing community of students of Dante while giving blood to new members.

Danielle Callegari
Melissa Swain

## Author's Acknowledgments

I cannot easily find the space to thank the innumerable scholars and attentive readers who have offered me their thoughts and reflections on the ideas presented in this book. I limit myself here to expressing my sincere gratitude to my editors, Danielle Callegari and Melissa Swain. I am deeply saddened that I cannot share the final version of this book with my editor, Helen Tartar, an exceptional person whose passion for books was inspiring, and indeed gave life to this unexpected volume.

# Editors' Acknowledgments

The editors wish to thank first and foremost the tremendous efforts of the Fordham University Press editorial team, in particular Tom Lay, who remained patient and available to us through the long preparations of the manuscript and furthermore in the face of tragedy. We also owe thanks to the several previous publishers who granted permission for the republication of Professor Freccero's earlier essays, and the previous editors of those essays. Finally, to our friends and colleagues at New York University, who often served as sounding boards and provided fresh eyes when our own could no longer be trusted, our sincere thanks.

Some of the essays in this collection have previously appeared in print. The following is a list of the original titles, places, and dates of publication. These essays are reprinted with the kind permission of the publishers:

"The Epic of Transcendence." In *The Cambridge Companion to the Epic*, edited by Catherine Bates, 76–92. Cambridge: Cambridge University Press, 2010.

"The Portrait of Francesca. *Inferno* V," *MLN* 124, no. 5, Supplement (2009): S7–S38.

"Allegory and Autobiography." In *The Cambridge Companion to Dante: Second Edition*, edited by Rachel Jacoff, 161–80. Cambridge: Cambridge University Press, 2007.

"Medusa and the Madonna of Forlì: Political Sexuality in Machiavelli." In *Machiavelli and the Discourse of Literature*, edited by Albert Ascoli and Victoria Kahn, 161–78. Ithaca, N.Y.: Cornell University Press, 1993.

"The Eternal Image of the Father." In *The Poetry of Allusion: Virgil and Ovid in Dante's Commedia*, edited by Rachel Jacoff and Jeffrey T. Schnapp, 62–76. Stanford: Stanford University Press, 1991.

"The Fig Tree and the Laurel: Petrarch's Poetics." *Diacritics* 5, no. 1 (1975): 34–40.

"Donne's Valediction: Forbidding Mourning." *ELH* 30, no. 4 (December 1963): 336–76; first read at the Johns Hopkins Philological Association in January 1963.

"Zeno's Last Cigarette." *MLN* 77, no. 1 (1962): 3–23.

Most further references to John Freccero's earlier publications can be found in *Dante: The Poetics of Conversion*. Edited by Rachel Jacoff. Cambridge, Mass.: Harvard University Press, 1986.

This volume refers to the following editions of primary texts when not otherwise noted:

*La Commedia secondo l'antico vulgata*. Edited by Giorgio Petrocchi. 4 vols. Milan: Mondadori, 1966–67.

*La Divina Commedia*. Translated and commentary by Charles S. Singleton. 6 vols. Princeton, N.J.: Princeton University Press, 1973.

*Convivio*. Edited by Giorgio Inglese. Milan: Biblioteca Universale Rizzoli, 1993.

*The Banquet*. Edited and translated by Christopher Ryan. Saratoga, Calif.: Anma, 1989.

Augustine. *Confessions*. Edited and translated by Henry Chadwick. Oxford: Oxford University Press, 1991.

John Donne. *The Sermons of John Donne*, edited by George R. Potter and Evelyn M. Simpson. Berkeley: University of California Press, 1953.

Homer. *The Odyssey*. Translated by Robert Fitzgerald. New York: Vintage Books, 1990.

Niccolò Machiavelli. *The Prince*, translated by Robert M. Adams. New York: Norton, 1977.

Petrarch. *Petrarch's Lyric Poems: The "Rime Sparse" and Other Lyrics*. Edited and translated by Robert M. Durling. Cambridge, Mass.: Harvard University Press, 1976.

Plato. *Phaedo*. Translated by R. Hackforth. New York: Liberal Arts Press, 1955.

————. *Timaeus.* In *Timaeus, Critias, Cletiophon, Menexenus, Epistles.* Translated by R. G. Bury. Cambridge, Mass.: Harvard University Press, 1929.

————. *Plato Latinus IV: Timaeus a Calcidio translatus commentario-que instructus.* Edited by J. H. Waszink, vol. 4 of *Corpus Platonicum Medii Aevi.* Edited by R. Klibansky. 4 vols. London: Warburg Institute, 1940–1962.

Plotinus. *Plotinus.* 6 vols. Edited and translated by Hilary A. Armstrong. Cambridge, Mass.: Harvard University Press, 1978.

Italo Svevo. *La coscienza di Zeno.* Edited by Marziano Guglielminetti and Alberto Cavaglion. Brescia: La scuola, 1986.

————. *Confessions of Zeno.* Translated by Beryl de Zoete. New York: Vintage, 1930.

Virgil. *The Aeneid.* Translated by Robert Fitzgerald. New York: Random House, 1983.

# IN DANTE'S WAKE

# Shipwreck in the Prologue

I n a famous essay of 1920 entitled *The Theory of the Novel*, György Lukács drew a sharp distinction between ancient epic and the modern novel.[1] The genres both sought to represent concrete reality, he maintained, but their perceptions of it were very different. The world of the epic was experienced as homogeneous, a totality of which the hero was part, while in the novel, the world was experienced as fragmentary and, with respect to subjectivity, radically "other." The "blissful" world of Homeric epic was integrated and closed, bounded by the starry heaven, within which gods and humans felt equally at home, even as they struggled among themselves. The heroes of the epic lived through harrowing external adventures, but their inward security was such that their essence could never be seriously threatened. In the eternal world of the epic, the hero "was the luminous center," the passive, immobile point around which reality moved.

In contrast, the novel—the predominant genre of modernity—recounts an interior adventure, in which the solitary hero is alienated from a world that is no longer hospitable. He yearns for integration, but finds it perpetually out of the reach of his desire. The gods have grown silent and the "world of action loses contact with that of the self, leaving man empty and powerless, unable to grasp the real meaning of his deeds." The hero of the novel is alone; an unbridgeable gap separates him from all others, in a universe vastly expanded and no longer intelligible. The novel represents the "epic of a world from which God has departed."

Lukács's discussion of the contrast between the "Hellenic" epic and the "Western" novel unfolds brilliantly, if daringly, at the highest degree of generalization, with few textual citations and no historical detail. When he speaks of epic, he usually means Homer. Rome is largely ignored, except for Virgil, who is mentioned only once in passing, and then with a touch of condescension, for having "conjured up a reality that has vanished forever." To Lukács, Christianity seems directed to a utopian dream to substitute for the disappearance of the ancient *polis*, presumably the City of God. As for the novel, his primary concern, the earliest work that fits his definition of the genre is *Don Quixote*.

In this synoptic view of the two millennia and more that separate Hellenism from Cervantes, it was impossible to avoid Dante, but the poet's towering genius made it equally impossible to categorize his work as either epic or novel. Lukács concluded, therefore, that it should be thought of as the historical transition between the genres, a singular tour de force, which, for the first time in Western literature, represented real personality:

> In Dante there is still the perfect immanent distancelessness and completeness of the true epic, but his figures are already individuals, consciously and energetically placing themselves in opposition to a reality that is becoming closed to them, individuals who, through this opposition, become real personalities.[2]

It would follow from this observation (although he does not say so) that "real personality" in the poem is to be found only where there is the clash between the individual and reality, which is to say, only in Hell. In this chapter, it will be assumed that the sharp distinction between epic and novel has some validity, but I will ask how, specifically, Dante transformed a few key epic themes into autobiography. We shall see that Augustine, who described his inner life as a spiritual odyssey, was Dante's predecessor in that endeavor and provided the poet with a model for recounting his own spiritual struggle.

To speak of the epic in Dante inevitably recalls Virgil (to others if not to Lukács), and especially the revisionist Ulysses of *Inferno*, about whom every "Dantista" has had something to say. Ulysses is not only a character in Hell, but an icon in the poem: Unlike all other sinners, he has an "afterlife" in both *Purgatorio* and *Paradiso*. He is the only major speaker in Hell not a contemporary, or near contemporary, of the poet.

He is clearly a surrogate, perhaps for Guido Cavalcanti (Dante's friend and fellow poet) or for Dante himself, before he wrote the *Commedia*. The ancient hero is the archetype of the philosopher who believes in the sufficiency of human knowledge to reach secular happiness. In terms of the journey, Aeneas mediates between the pilgrim and the ancient mariner, as Virgil mediates between Dante and Homer. Our consideration of both Ulysses and of Virgil can be very brief, because they have been so thoroughly studied, and by some very well. David Thompson has written about Dante and the epic, with particular emphasis on Virgil, and Winthrop Wetherbee has extensively examined the influence of Roman epic in the *Commedia*.[3]

In this chapter, I will be primarily concerned with the prologue of the poem, where Odysseus is a submerged presence, ignored by most critics. I will discuss not only with the transformation of the epic into the novel, which is the essence of Dante's fictional account of Ulysses, but what Lukács calls the "retransformation" of the "novelistic" *Inferno* into the new epic of transcendence.[4] I will try to answer the unspoken historical question raised by Lukács's book concerning the provenance of Dante's representation of subjectivity, so foreign to the epic and essential in the novel. Augustine, Dante's exemplary forerunner, was something of a novelist himself. In fact, Phillip Cary has referred to him as the "inventor" (in the Latin sense of "discoverer") of the inner self.[5]

The novelistic quality of *Inferno* seems indisputable. Hell is an autonomous region, totally separate from deity, where there is no court, but only a monstrous, Kafkaesque bureaucrat, mechanically and implacably meting out sentences to the sinners. Most readers have found the damned to be more memorable than the blessed. In their epic integration, the blessed, like happy families, are all alike, while the souls in Hell are alone together. They are irreducibly individual, even when they are paired, as Francesca and Paolo, Ulysses and Diomede or, horribly, Ugolino and Ruggieri. It is this individuality and "loneliness" that Lukács takes for "real personality."

As in Lukács's reading of the novel, irony dominates in *Inferno*, both verbal, in the exchanges with the pilgrim, and situational: We have only the testimony of the sinners about the mitigating circumstances surrounding their downfall, but their protestations are silently undermined by infernal reality. It is as if their relative moral culpability were transformed metaphorically into physical weight and the depth of their immersion into the abyss infallibly determined by "specific grav-ity." This fiction, derived from Augustine's metaphor of the "pondus amoris," implies that one *is* what one loves and that sin, stripped of its allure and disguise, is therefore its own punishment (*Conf.* 13.8). In this immanent justice, God bears no responsibility for the sinners' torment, other than for having created Hell, as He created heaven and earth. This reality is clearly novelistic, the antithesis of the "blissful" world of the epic.

What is missing from this description of *Inferno* is the prologue scene, which establishes the autobiographical dimension of the *Comedy*, distinguishing it from both the epic and the novel, although it contains elements of both genres. It has no "real personalities," nor any of the "mimetic" quality for which Dante is famous, yet it is the only account we are given of the hero's alienation and aloneness when he sets out, lost in an interior landscape. It thus serves as the point of departure for this discussion.

Had the pilgrim begun his journey at the gates of Hell and ended it in utter defeat, *Inferno* by itself might have qualified as the first novel, albeit with a relatively passive protagonist. The journey begins with a prologue, which theorists of Dante's "realism" usually skip over when they read *Inferno*, finding its allegorism to be vague and even tiresome. Yet the *Commedia* is primarily autobiography and the prologue is all we are told in *Inferno* of his spiritual crisis. It is a prelude, a schematic map of a spiritual state, setting forth themes to which, from time to time, the poem will retrospectively refer—notably, the three beasts, of which only a child turning the pages of Dante's nineteenth-century illustra-tor, Gustave Doré, would ever be afraid. We should no more expect realism in those first two cantos than we would in an interior mono-logue or penitential meditation. The first explorer of this terrain, the "inner self," was Augustine, whom Lukács does not mention. Never-theless, the subsequent development of the novel of interiority seems inconceivable without his example.

As for the ending of *Inferno*, it is a new beginning, both in theme and in literary genre. In modern narrative, one might expect the defeat or even death of an alienated hero, but Dante survives this destructive first part of his journey to begin an ascent from a cave at the center of the universe. The descent into Hell is necessary simply to reach the cave, which for Plato, in the myth of the *Republic*, was the point of departure. Virgil and the pilgrim crawl down Satan's thigh through

Cocytus, the lake of ice, turn upside-down, and climb to the other side of the "mirror" of Hell. There, all dimensions are reversed: Down is up, left is right, and Satan, the Prince of this world, is buried upside-down with respect to heaven. Perhaps Lewis Carroll was remembering this grotesque passage through the lake of ice when he led Alice into another world, beyond the looking glass.

The end of *Inferno* is a rebirth and the beginning of a rehabilitation, as well as a return to the light that seemed unreachable in the prologue. The pilgrim is back where he started, this time in sharp focus, with a guide and no impediments. From the standpoint of the geometric imagination, it is literally a return. He has emerged from the vertex of the infernal cone to find himself at the circular base of a similar cone of immense volume, the mount of Purgatory, high enough so that its apex is beyond meteorological change.

In canto 34, we are told that the material of the mountain was formed ("forse" [perhaps] says Dante, anticipating incredulity) when the earth was displaced by Satan's fall into the southern hemisphere (124). Part of it rose up in the northern hemisphere to form the dry land, which previously had been covered with water (earth being heavier than water, in its "natural" state) and part rose up in the southern hemisphere to form the mountain. Geometrically speaking, again, it is as if the mountain were extracted from the mold of Hell, leaving behind its negative impression in the rock. The path of the ascent of the mountain, the outside of the cone, spirals to the right, while the infernal descent spirals left, but, because the travelers turned upside down at the center, their path is in the same absolute direction. Purgatory is Hell, turned inside out.

The bizarre myth of the similar shape of Hell and Purgatory is a physical representation of the theological doctrine of "Justification."[6] The word describes the action whereby a sinner is redeemed, or reborn. It is a continuous action, but it is logically two-fold: the destruction of a previous form (the sinful self, we might say) and the generation of a new self. Existentially, destruction and regeneration take place simultaneously—in life there can be no zero point. In the poem, however, Dante presents us with an "anatomy" of regeneration, a "living dissection," in which degrees of degradation in the realm of destruction correspond to degrees of elevation in the realm of generation. The zero point of the universe is a spiritual abstraction, the half-life of the soul, permitting Dante to say, "Io non mori' e non rimasi vivo" (I did not die and was not still living) (*Inf.* 34.25). The juxtaposition of the two other-worldly realms serves equally well as a spatial illustration of what Lukács refers to as the "re-transformation" of novelistic pessimism. An allegory of hope replaces infernal irony, its negative inversion, and is in turn replaced by ecstatic vision in an epic of transcendence.

To return to the question of infernal "subjectivity," its origin is doubtless to be found in the ultimate moral negation, which is sin, as it is represented in Scripture. The inexplicable gap in Lukács' discussion of "realism" is his exclusion of the Bible from consideration, a blind spot subsequently illuminated by Erich Auerbach, his contemporary, who used the Old Testament to contrast with Homeric realism in order to educe his own theory of "mimesis."[7] Conscience and consciousness (the Romance Languages have a single word for both terms) seem to create the interior distance separating the sinners in Hell from each other and from reality. Their isolation and solipsism is evident in virtually all of the dialogues of the damned, an estrangement first suffered by Cain and made explicit by Satan's words: "Which way I fly is Hell; myself is Hell" (*Paradise Lost* 4.75).

The themes of alienation and exile have mythic roots in Genesis and claim historicity in Exodus, the epic of liberation. St. Paul, the Roman citizen, for whom the theme of political liberation must have seemed somewhat remote, established a figural interpretation of the Exodus of more immediate and personal relevance. He reads it as a moral trope, applying it to himself and to his audience: "All these things were done as a figure for us" (I Cor. 10). The desert of Exodus thus became part of Paul's own experience and was thereafter universally accepted as the moral (or tropological) meaning of the desert in Christian exegesis. Augustine alluded to the desert of his inner life, referring to it with a Plotinian phrase: the "region of unlikeness." For Dante, Exodus became the dominant figure of *Purgatorio*, the middle ground between infernal Egypt and the Heavenly Jerusalem.[8] But the first allusion in the poem occurs in the prologue, with the pilgrim hobbling across a "piaggia diserta" (desert strand) (*Purg.* 1.29), halfway between the sun and the dark wood. These interior landscapes are bleak, but unlike King Lear's heath, they can, with difficulty, be traversed.

The journey of the Jews through the desert has its counterpart in the sea voyage of Odysseus. The medium and the vehicle could not be more different, of course, but the goal is the same: to return home. The circular path of Odysseus's journey, *nostos*, seemed to later Neoplatonists an admirable emblem for the souls' fall from the heavens and their return. Such allegorizations transformed Homer into a theologian, whose subsequent history in Western literature has been traced by Robert Lamberton.[9] A realistic verse from the *Iliad* will serve to illustrate how persistent such allegorizations became, no matter how wildly incongruous they may appear to us. In Agamemnon's ironic exhortation to his men, calculated to have the opposite effect from its ostensible meaning, he urges them to give up the siege of Troy and return to their ships: "Let us flee then to the beloved fatherland" (*Iliad* 2.140). Plotinus, the most influential of "Homeric theologians," wrenched the verse from its context, associated it with the Odyssey, and claimed to read into it the soul's return to the One:

> We shall put out to sea as Odysseus did [. . .] "Let us flee then to the beloved fatherland" [. . .] Our Fatherland is that whence we came, and the Father is there. What then is our journey, our flight? Not by feet is it to be accomplished; for feet carry one from here to there all over the earth. Nor should you procure a chariot or ship; you should leave all such things behind and not look, but close your eyes and awaken another sort of vision instead—a sort of vision which everyone possesses but few use.
>
> *Enneads* 1.6.8

As Paul "interiorized" the epic of the Jews, Plotinus "interiorized" the epic of the Greeks. In a sermon, Ambrose echoed this passage, exhorting the faithful to flee with their minds, "fugiamus animo," or with their "interior feet," as did Augustine, in the *City of God*: "Where is that Plotinus, when he says, 'Let us flee therefore, to that dearest homeland . . .' What is the ship or the flight? It is to make ourselves like God" (*Liber de Isaac et anima* 8.79; *De civitate Dei* 9.17). Homer's Agamemnon turns out to be the ultimate source of the verse in the first canto of *Inferno* describing the panic of the errant pilgrim:

> E come quei che con lena affannata,
>      uscito fuor del pelago a la riva
>        si volge a l'acqua perigliosa e guata,
> così *l'animo* mio, ch'ancor *fuggiva*,
>        si volse a retro a rimirar lo passo

che non lasciò già mai persona viva.
Poi che'èi posato un poco il corpo lasso,
ripresi via per la piaggia diserta,
sì che 'l piè fermo sempre era 'l più basso.

*Inf.* 1.22–30

And as he who with laboring breath has escaped from the deep to the
shore turns to look back on the dangerous waters, so *my mind* which
was still *fleeing* turned back to gaze upon the pass that never left anyone
alive.

I have cited these three *terzine* in order to provide the context for
the key phrase, *fugiamus animo* (in Ambrose's version). The tell-tale
word "animo" indicates that this is a flight of the mind, in the philosophical tradition of Plotinus, rather than of "anima," in the usual
theological sense. The choice of the word is also a premonition of the
subsequent failure; we shall see that a purely philosophical effort, on
one's own, is not enough for a Christian, in spite of Plotinus's assurance
that one needs no guide (*Enneads* 1.6.9). More than that, however, each
of the *terzine* alludes to a motif drawn from the tradition of "Homeric
theology": a near drowning, a mental flight, and a hobbling across a
desert. We shall see that the obscure lines that seemed tiresome to some
critics constitute a network of intertextuality transforming three epic
images into a drama of interiority.

Augustine explored his own interior landscape, the "caves" and
"mansions" of memory, in which he found himself to be utterly alone.
He compares his wandering in the desert with the story of the Prodigal
Son (Luke 15:11–35) as well as echoes of Plotinus:

> One does not go far away from you or return to you by walking or by
> any movement through space. The younger son in your Gospel did not
> look for horses or carriages or ships; he did not fly on any visible wing,
> nor did he travel along the way by moving his legs when he went to
> live in a far country and prodigally dissipated what you, his gentle
> father, had given him on setting out [. . .] To live there in lustful pas-
> sion is to live in darkness and to be far from your face.
>
> *Confessions* 1.18.28

James J. O'Donnell has remarked on the way Neoplatonic themes
are here synthesized with the parable of the Prodigal Son. In this text,

the key phrase, "in regionem longinquam" (in a far country) echoes the Plotinian, but ultimately Platonic "in regionem dissimilitudinis."[10]

Augustine alludes to Plotinus again at the moment of his conversion in the garden:

> To reach that destination [the covenant with God] one does not use ships or chariots or feet. It was not even necessary to go the distance I had come from the house . . . It was necessary to have the will to go . . . provided only that the will was strong and unqualified, not the twisting and turning first this way, then that, of a half-crippled will [*semisaucium*] struggling with one part rising up and the other falling down.
>
> *Conf.* 8.19

Attentive readers of the prologue will recognize the lower "firm foot" of the pilgrim in this description of the half-crippled will. These "vehicles" of the interior journey correspond to the fictive or metaphoric "vehicles" of the pilgrim's progress: the feet, then ship, then flight to God.

I have said that *Purgatorio* announces the transformation of the novelistic dead-end of *Inferno* into a new epic beginning. This may have seemed a generalization, but it is in fact exactly what the poet intended to convey. Not only does the *cantica* begin with a classical navigational metaphor, but it invokes Calliope, the muse of epic poetry, so that "dead poetry may rise again":

> Per correr miglior acque alza le vele
> omai la navicella del mio ingegno,
> che lascia dietro a sé mar sì crudele;
> e canterò di quel secondo regno
> dove l'umano spirito si purga
> e di salire al ciel diventa degno.
> Ma qui la morta poesì resurga,
> o sante Muse, poi che vostro sono;
> e qui Calïopè alquanto surga,
> Seguitando il mio canto . . .
>
> *Purg.* 1.1–10

To course over better waters the little bark of my genius now hoists her sails, leaving behind her a sea so cruel; and I will sing of that second realm where the human spirit is purged and becomes fit to ascend to Heaven. But here let dead poetry rise again, O holy Muses,

since I am yours; and here let Calliope rise somewhat, accompanying
my song . . .

Further evidence of the "re-transformation" of the novelistic dead-
end into an epic of redemption, if needed, can be gleaned from examin-
ing the difference between the opening of *Inferno* and the epic openings
of *Purgatorio* and *Paradiso*.

Nautical imagery was commonly used in Latin literature as a metaphor for the writing of poetry. The composition of an epic might be
compared to a seagoing voyage, while a lyric poem was more apt to be
a fragile bark. In the numerous examples studied by E. R. Curtius, sails
are unfurled in invocations and, after innumerable vicissitudes, lowered
at journey's end.[11] There is always the threat of shipwreck, but in spite
of reefs and storms, the outcome of such a voyage can never be in serious doubt, since the existence of the poem is proof of the success of the
undertaking. No matter how arduous the journey, every poet's ship
must come in, bearing its more or less golden fleece.

This is very different from the nautical imagery that served in
antiquity to describe intellectual or spiritual adventure. The quest for
truth was thought to be much more problematic than the search for
rhetorical effect. In the biography of a philosopher, shipwreck, real or
allegorical, was not merely a threat to the outcome of the undertaking,
but rather the obligatory point of departure for a journey to wisdom
and true happiness. The philosopher was described as a castaway, a
lonely survivor of the wreckage of the unexamined life. In his book
*Shipwreck with Spectator*, Hans Blumenberg cites Lucretius, to whose
work the title alludes, as well as many other ancients.[12] He concludes
that "shipwreck, as seen by a survivor, is the figure of an initial philosophical experience." In the modern world, as well, some philosophers
have thought of drowning, real or allegorical, as occasioning a review
of one's life in retrospect, an hypothesis sustainable, obviously, only
from the report of survivors.[13] We shall see that one of the initial similes
of the poem suggests that the near drowning is a prelude for staging
memories of Dante's life and times.

Like all great poets, Dante leaves no *topos* untouched, so that a
simple enumeration of its occurrences in his works, such as Curtius
provides, offers no hint of the complexity of his navigational imagery.
The complexity derives from the fact that the famous exordia of *Purgatorio* and of the final ascent in canto 2 of *Paradiso* erase the distinction

between conventional figures for the writing of poetry and the literal fiction of the journey. At the opening of *Purgatorio*, when he claims that the bark of his genius will now course over better waters and leave behind so cruel a sea, the theme and its vehicle seem inseparable. The *poeta theologus* uses the navigational vehicle to describe the progress of both his poem and his spiritual journey. His narrative creates a sequential illusion out of the logical distinction between the journey and its record, as though the experience preceded the writing of the story. In "real time," they are one.

In the second book of the *Convivio*, Dante's earlier philosophical work, which he abandoned one-third of the way through its projected length, he introduced a nautical image that was much admired by Curtius: "lo tempo chiama e domanda la mia nave uscir di porto; per che, dirizzato l'artimone della ragione all'òra del mio desiderio, entro in pelago con isperanza di dolce cammino e di salutevole porto" (conditions bid and command my ship to leave port. So, having set the sail [*artimone*] of reason to catch the breeze of my desire, I put out to sea [*pelago*] with hopes of a pleasant journey and of a safe and honorable arrival) (2.1). With erudite condescension, Curtius congratulates Dante on the use of the unfamiliar technical term "artimone," a Mediterranean type of foresail, not realizing, any more than did the poet, the ominous implications of the word. In Acts 27:40, it is precisely the "artimone" that drives Paul's ship to disaster off the island of Malta: "levato artemone secundum aurae flatum tendebant ad littus" (having hoisted the foresail to the wind, they made for shore). The *Convivio* met a similar fate. It was never finished, but foundered instead in the *pelago*, on which it had set forth with such optimism, and Dante was forced to abandon ship. When he began the *Commedia*, it was as a castaway, "uscito fuor dal pelago alla riva" (escaped from the deep to shore).

The journey of *Commedia* may be said to begin, metaphorically, with the wreck of the *Convivio*. The prologue of *Inferno* has its initial nautical metaphor, as do *Purgatorio* and *Paradiso*, but, as we have seen in the three terzine quoted previously, it is a metaphor of narrow escape from a near-drowning. The imagery has no descriptive function in the prologue scene, but rather serves to identify this moment as a philosophical conversion in ancient tradition. Dante's shipwrecked mariner may be traced back to the *Odyssey*. In particular, the figure of a castaway gasping for breath recalls the episode from the fifth book of the *Odyssey*, when Odysseus swims from the wreckage of his raft to the Phaeacian shore and his encounter with Nausicaa:

> Swollen from hand to foot he was, and seawater
> Gushed from his mouth and nostrils. There he lay,
> Scarce drawing breath, unstirring, deathly spent.
> In time, as air came back into his lungs
> And warmth around his heart, he loosed the veil [of Ino] . . .
>
> *Odyssey* 5.540–4

Homer may have inserted the physical details simply to heighten the realism of the episode (because they were *there*, as Auerbach says of Odysseus's scar), but allegorists read into those details significances never dreamt of by the poet. Felix Buffière studied the influence of Homeric myth on Greek thought and noted that Democritus, for example, read into Odysseus's gasping breath the presence of pneuma, the principle of the soul itself.[14] Dante's reference to the "lena affanata" is derived, by however circuitous a route, from the Homeric detail.

More important for our purposes is a passage from the *Phaedo*, where there are several allusions to the *Odyssey*. The subject is the imminent death of Socrates and the efforts of his friends to understand what happens after death. Simmias thinks it would be best to discover for oneself or, if this is impossible, one should "take the best and most irrefutable of human theories and let this be the raft upon which he sails through life—not without risk, as I admit, if he cannot find some word of God which will surely and safely carry him" (*Phaedo*, 85B–88B). This possible allusion to the raft of Odysseus—according to an acute hypothesis of Giovanni Reale—suggested to Augustine the wood of the cross:[15]

> It is as if one were able from afar to see the homeland, but were separated from it by the sea. He sees where he must go, but lacks the means of getting there . . . So [the Lord] has prepared for him the wood [*lignum*] enabling him to cross the sea. In fact, no one can cross the sea of this world unless he is carried by the cross of Christ [*nemo enim potest transire mare hujus saeculi, nisi cruce Christi portatus*].
>
> *In Ioannis evangelium* 2.2.2[16]

I do not know of a better gloss for the verse of *Inferno* 1.26–7: "lo passo / che non lasciò già mai persona viva" (the pass that no man ever left alive).

To return to the shipwreck and survival of Odysseus, it was widely allegorized in antiquity as a philosophical adventure. In the *Life of Plotinus*, which Augustine knew, Porphyry relates the supposed praise of Plotinus by the Delphic oracle in a passage filled with reminiscences of the fifth book of the *Odyssey*, especially the lines that describe Odysseus swimming swiftly:

> Spirit! Once just a man, but now nearing the diviner lot of a spirit, as the bond of human necessity has been loosed for you, and strong in heart, you swam swiftly from the roaring surge of the body to that coast where the stream flows strong, far apart from the crowd of the wicked, there to set your steps firm in the easy path of the pure soul . . . you were struggling to escape from the bitter wave of this blood-drinking life, from its sickening whirlpools, in the midst of its billows and sudden surges.
>
> *Life of Plotinus* 22

This oracle of Apollo may be taken as the paradigm for the ancient turning to the light. This form of philosophical salvation is an illumination, "a shaft of light," guidance out of the "crooked ways" to the "direct path" to immortality. Apollo promises Plotinus the company of Plato and Pythagoras and kinship with the most blessed, as well as the judges of the underworld. The presence of Rhadamanthus identifies this place as Elysium, where Homer placed him. In this drama, Plotinus is transported directly from near drowning to immortal love. In the *Convivio*, in the full flush of philosophical enthusiasm, Dante imagined Heaven as a "celestial Athens" much like this, where the ancient sages (including Epicureans!) would gather together to philosophize about God. He changed his mind in the *Commedia* and relegated them instead to a lugubrious Limbo, artificially illuminated, surrounded by the sighs of the unbaptized. Virgil, who is in their number, says: "sanza speme vivemo in disio" (without hope, we live in desire) (*Inf.* 4.42).

When William Butler Yeats rendered Porphyry's words about the oracle praising Plotinus, he intimated that it is not so easy to rinse away the bitter salt of the sea:

> Behold that great Plotinus swim,
> Buffeted by such seas;
> Bland Rhadamanthus beckons him,
> But the Golden Race looks dim,

Salt blood blocks his eyes.
Scattered on the level grass
Or winding through the grove
Plato there and Minos pass,
There stately Pythagoras
And all the choir of Love.[17]

The eyes of the philosopher are bloodshot, but it is his biographer who is sanguine. One is not so easily purged of the passions as to be acceptable to the clear-eyed judge. Yeats's arch critique is not very different from Augustine's, who insisted that tears of contrition were necessary for any such conversion. That is exactly what "Purgatory" is for.

One has only to contrast Plotinus's landscape of light with Dante's prologue scene to understand the difference between a philosophical conversion of the mind and spiritual conversion with the grace of God. As Augustine says at the end of Book 7 of the *Confessions*: "It is one thing from a wooded mountain-top (*de silvestre cacumine*) to see the homeland of peace and not to find the way to it, but vainly to attempt the journey along an impassible route, when one is beset . . . by the lion and the dragon, and quite another thing to hold to the way that leads there, defended by the protection of the heavenly emperor" (21.27).

Book 7 of the *Confessions* recounts Augustine's discovery of the "books of the Platonists" and his subsequent astonishment reading their "theology" to find their doctrine of the word similar in every respect to the Logos of the Gospel of John, save only the most crucial: "but that the word was made flesh and dwelt among us I did not read." His vain attempts to reach the Plotinian light led him to acknowledge that only through Christ would he reach salvation and "learn to discern the difference between presumption and confession, between those who see what the goal is but not how to get there and those who see the way which leads to the home of bliss . . ." He ends his meditation with a quotation from Matthew 11:25: "You have concealed these things from the wise and prudent and have revealed them to babes." The next book, 8, is his account of his conversion under the fig tree in the garden of Milan.

The extraordinary parallelism between his spiritual experience and Dante's, at roughly same age, even with comparable erotic distractions, would be exact, if it had been Neoplatonists rather than Aristotelians who led Dante to the overweening confidence in philosophy he seemed to share with Guido Cavalcanti, his "first friend." But by far the most striking similarity in the spiritual adventures of Augustine and Dante is that both chose to describe the crisis of the proud philosopher in terms of the Homeric allegory of Ulysses, although, as even the most casual reader of the poem knows, Dante's Ulysses dies in a shipwreck.

The return was the point of Homer's story, qualifying the *Odyssey* for the allegorization it was to receive for centuries. Dante's insistence on his revision of the story is too pointed to allow us to attribute it to his ignorance of Homer's text. The first canto of *Purgatorio* claims: "Venimmo poi in sul lito diserto, / che mai non vide navicar sue acque / omo, che di *tornar* / sia poscia esperto" (then we came on to the desert shore, that never saw any man navigate its waters who afterwards had experience of return) (*Purg.* 1.130–2). If there were any doubt about who such a man might be, it would be dispelled by the next sentence, when Virgil girds Dante with the rush of humility, "sì come altrui piacque" (as pleased another) (1.133). This is the same phrase that ends the canto of Ulysses. His ship is swallowed by the sea "com' altrui piacque" (*Inf.* 26.141). The contrast between the drowning of the proud philosopher and the humility of the penitent could not be more clear.

In the prologue of an early work on happiness, *De beata vita*, Augustine recapitulated the major events of his spiritual struggle, not in the realistic terms of the *Confessions*, but in the guise of a transparent and somewhat tedious allegorical navigation toward the port of philosophy, in a tempestuous sea.[18] There is no mention of Ulysses, but he does speak of turning his ship to avert the Sirens. There is little doubt that Odysseus was his model. Jean Pepin has written an exhaustive study of "The Platonic and Christian Ulysses," illustrating the great popularity of the figure in Augustine's day.[19] Robert J. O'Connell expressed his doubts that Augustine could have known all the Greek texts amassed by Pepin, but nevertheless concluded from innumerable examples that Augustine's "odyssey" was based on Homer's: "The Odyssey image of conversion manifests all the main features one would expect of it. We, meaning our souls, find ourselves on the stormy sea of this world, wandering away from our homeland, confronting dangers of shipwreck from mists, sinking stars, and tempests; we have forgotten the homeland we left, and yet, we guard a certain vague nostalgia for it which prompts us to 'look back' when we are given signals 'reminding' us of it."[20] There is good reason to believe that the odyssey of Dante's Ulysses was based on Augustine's.

Augustine's "sinking stars" might have suggested to Dante "tutte le stelle già de l'altro polo / vedea la notte, e 'l nostro tanto basso, / che non surgëa fuor del marin suolo" (the night now saw the other pole and all its stars and ours so low that it did not rise from the ocean floor) (*Inf.* 26.127–9) and Augustine's "totis velis, omnibus remis" might have inspired "de' remi facemmo ali al folle volo" (of our oars we made wings for the mad flight) (*Inf.* 26.125), although the words recall Daedalus's "remigium alarum" (the rowing movement of his wings) in *Aeneid* 6.19. These are admittedly generic features of a stormy crossing. One feature is so strange, however, that it must have inspired Ulysses's sight of a "montagna, bruna / per la distanza, e parvemi alta tanto / quanto veduta non avëa alcuna" (a mountain dark in the distance . . . that seemed the highest I had even seen) (*Inf.* 26.133–5). Augustine provides us both with the mountain and its meaning:

> All who sail toward the land of happiness must be very careful to avoid at all cost that highest of mountains that rises up before the port, leaving a little room for those who would enter . . . what else would reason tell us that this mountain represents, to be feared by all who approach or enter, except proud vainglory? A mountain that is so hollow and empty, although apparently solid, that it will crack under those triumphant ones who tread on it, causing them to sink into the darkness below, depriving them of that beautiful homeland that they had just begun to discern.
>
> *De beata vita*, prologue

The contrast between the slope of the mountain and its infernal belly inevitably remind us of the equally oneiric juxtaposition of the cones of Purgatory and Hell, Dante's version of "mountain gloom, mountain glory." In his commentary on the Gospel of John, Augustine sums up the horror of the mariner's mountain: "If a mountain is not illuminated by the sun it remains in darkness; remember this, lest, mistaking the mountain for the light, you suffer shipwreck instead of finding help" (*In Johannis evangelium tractatus* 2.2.5).[21]

The clearest recall of *De beata vita* in the *Commedia* occurs in the longest and most moving exordium in the poem, in canto 2 of *Paradiso*, studied by Curtius, who was unaware of the Augustinian subtext. In his treatise, Augustine began by distinguishing three types of mariners: the timid, the adventurous, and the foolhardy. So in the last *cantica*, Dante addresses those "in piccioletta barca" (little barques), whom he tells to turn back, then those who have already had a taste of the bread of angels, whom he invites to follow in his wake. He identifies himself as the Jason of poetry, "L'acqua ch'io prendo già mai si corse" (the water which I take was never coursed before) (*Par.* 2.7).

The journey through *Paradiso* is a celestial navigation, with Beatrice as his guide. When she appears to him in Eden, to scold him, he describes her with the most startling simile in his catalogue of her praises: "Quasi ammiraglio che in poppa e in prora / viene a veder la gente che ministra / per li altri legni" (Like an admiral who goes to stern and bow to see the men that are serving on the other ships) (*Purg.* 30.58–60). She will lead him on his voyage through the celestial spheres. As the first mariner of the highest seas, returning with the golden fleece of the poem we read, he is the anti-type of Ulysses.

In his address to the reader, Dante compares himself to the captain of the Argonauts: "Que' glorïoso che passaro al Colco / non s'ammiraron come voi farete, / quando Iasón vider fatto bifolco" (those glorious ones who crossed the sea to Colchis, when they saw Jason turned plowman, were not as amazed as you will be) (*Par.* 2.16–18). Ovid tells the tale of Jason taming the bulls, but in this context, the word "solco" (14) means "wake," as well as "furrow." It is Dante's metaphor for the writing of poetry and following in his wake means reading it.

Much later in the *cantica*, as he circles with the constellation of the Gemini, there are two similes of Olympian detachment. The first is his truly epic glance down at the earth, which he calls "L'aiuola che ci fa tanto feroci" (the little threshing floor that makes us so ferocious) (*Par.* 22.151), with all its hills and streams. The second is intensely private, edgy, and a touch triumphalist, when he looks down at the blank page of the ocean, marked only by an allusion to his own text: the "varco / folle d'Ulisse" (the mad wake of Ulysses) (*Par.* 27.82–3). With those two glances, he removes himself from the upheaval of his times and, perhaps, from the philosophical arrogance that he once shared with his first friend.

Finally, at the end of the poem, Dante finds himself unable to recall his vision and compares his forgetfulness to the oblivion of history since the voyage of the Argonauts: "Un punto solo m'è maggior letargo / che venticinque secoli a la 'mpresa / che fé Nettuno *ammirar* l'ombra d'Argo" (one point is greater forgetfulness for me than have been the twenty-five centuries since Neptune wondered at the shadow of the Argo) (*Par.* 33.94–6).[22] Neptune's amazement is also ours, greater than that of the Argonauts (*s'ammirarono*), as we follow in Dante's wake. For us, the shadow of the Argo is the poem. At the outset of *Paradiso*, Dante prayed to Apollo to enable him to make manifest the shadow of Heaven in his memory (*Par.* 1.23). The poem is that manifestation, a shadow of a shadow. Our distance from the experience, twice removed, gives us the perspective of Neptune, who sees the navigation as an overhead flight. The shadow of the Argo is a momentary eclipse of the light, the negative evidence of an otherwise omnipresent, and therefore imperceptible, deity. It is a metaphor for the *via negativa* of mystic theology. What makes it coherent is the ambiguity of the single word "punto": the point in space, which is the vision of God, and the point in time, which is the *now* of the poem.

We recall that Ulysses referred to his navigation as a flight ("il folle volo"), but it ended, like that of Icarus, in disaster. Ulysses's words, "de' remi facemmo ali," echo the "remigium alarum" of Daedalus, but it is Dante who was the "fabulous artificer."

# The Portrait of Francesca: *Inferno* 5

As far as we know, there is no record of the love story of Francesca da Rimini before Dante's account in canto 5 of *Inferno*. His portrait of her emerges in astonishingly few verses and, in its passion and pathos, emulates and rivals Virgil's portrayal of Dido. Francesca tells us nothing of her life in the first part of her monologue, apart from her place of birth, which she identifies with elegant periphrasis. Instead, she sums up in retrospect the genesis, consummation, and fatal consequences of the love she shared with her inseparable companion in Hell, whom she does not name. Her celebrated apostrophe to love, the unforgettable anaphora on "Amore," is at once succinct and profound, a rhetorical representation in miniature of consciousness and interiority without precedent in the Middle Ages. We shall see that part of it is ultimately derived from Plato's *Phaedrus*, yet it anticipates the "subjectivity" we associate with the modern novel.

In three anaphoric *terzine*, Francesca describes love and its effects, not abstractly, as had other poets and especially Guido Cavalcanti in his abstruse *canzone*, "Donna me prega," but existentially, relating how she and her lover fell prey to that passion and so were led to their death. This first half of her meditation ends with a prophetic imprecation consigning their killer to the circle of Cain. The name of the original fratricide identifies the killer as her lover's brother. When the opening lines of the next canto refer to the couple as in-laws ("i due cognati," *Inf.* 6.2), we have all we need to know about Francesca's marriage, adultery, and death.

FIGURE 1. Frontispiece to *Opera nova del magnifico cavaliero Messer Antonio Phila-remo Fregoso intitulata Cerva biancha. Corretta novamente*, printed by Niccolò Zoppino, Venice, 1525. University of California, Los Angeles Library Special Collections, Ahmanson-Murphy Collection of Early Italian Printing. Photo: Danielle Callegari.

After a pause and the pilgrim's compassionate plea that she explain how she succumbed to her dubious desires, she resumes her monologue in a different key, narrative rather than analytic, to describe the "first root" of their love. They were reading together of Lancelot, seized by love. Here, too, she provides no external detail, describing only their solitude, their glances, and their embarrassment. She relates only one event: the notorious "kiss."[1] This second half of her monologue is of the same length as the first, but contradicts it in one important respect. In the first, love was described as spontaneous combustion, "kindled quickly in a gentle heart," which would mitigate the lovers' culpability. In the second part, she describes the occasion of their sin and the mediation of the book by which they were seduced. Like the first half, this part ends with a curse: "Galeotto fu il libro e chi lo scrisse" (A Gallehaut was the book and he who wrote it) (5.137). She first cursed the fratricide for their death and now the book for their damnation. The two parts of Francesca's monologue are like what came to be called *engaño* and *desengaño* in Spanish drama of the Golden Age, the juxtaposition of the illusion of love with the stark reality of its consequences.

Francesca was a historical personage, the aunt of Guido Novello, Dante's host in Ravenna. The details of her life were probably well known to the poet and his sympathetic portrait of her has often been taken as his tribute to the generosity of his friend. Nevertheless, he gives us few of those details. He does not say that she was duped into her marriage; nor does he suggest that her sin was a singular tragic encounter, rather than the habitual conduct that would merit damnation. When Francesca says that she and her lover were led by love to a single death, it is unlikely that this means the simultaneous death at the hands of love's assassin. The text alludes to her murder only obliquely— "'l modo ancor m'offende" (5.102)—and to its perpetrator never by name. We are familiar with what are supposed to be the exterior circumstances of her story, some of them wildly improbable, from glosses on the text written by Boccaccio, who forged them into a coherent plot in what might be called the medieval "romance" of Francesca.

We owe to the commentary of that master story-teller the exculpatory *mise-en-scène* of the affair: a fraudulent marriage, true lovers caught *in flagrante* by a predictably ugly and deformed husband, Paolo's attempted escape, and the swashbuckling climax in which the lovers are killed by a sword-thrust meant for Paolo but skewering the interposed Francesca instead. A second thrust then reaches its mark, killing her hapless lover. The next day they were buried together in the same tomb.

The account of a botched attack by Francesca's husband probably reflects Boccaccio's desperate attempt to translate Dante's verse literally: "Amor condusse noi ad *una* morte" (love led us to a single death) (5.106), which the commentator construes to mean that her husband first killed her by accident, since he truly loved her, and then his original target. With that, Boccaccio turns Dante's tremendous figure into lurid literality. We shall see, however, that all such fearsome loves, in pursuit of the absolute, result in a single death.

With Boccaccio's pop version of the tale, Francesca and Paolo attained their legendary status.[2] As Virgil transformed Dido, the founder and sober Queen of Carthage, into a tragic and lovesick heroine, so Dante gave to a historical personage the consciousness and voice of love's secular martyr. It remained for Boccaccio, however, to turn her into the heroine of medieval romance and, eventually, of nineteenth century melodrama. Boccaccio's story became something of a "penny-dreadful," the Victorian version of pulp fiction, having little to do with Dante's text. In illustrations of the critical moment, the jealousy-crazed husband was depicted as interrupting their first embrace, the open book lying face-down at Francesca's feet, like a grotesque parody of the Annunciation (see Figure 2).[3] The sword drawn as the couple embrace hints at double vendetta: not only to kill them, but to kill them before they have time to repent so as to send them directly to Hell. The scene is pruriently fascinating, but theologically absurd. In Dante's system, first-time offenders are sentenced to Purgatory. Hell is reserved for obdurate sinners, whose sin is grievous, habitual, and premeditated. Even then, as we learn from Buonconte da Montefeltro in Purgatory (5.88–108), pierced in the throat and uttering the name of "Maria," forgiveness is only a gasp away.

Robert Browning was more faithful than his Victorian contemporaries to Dante's style. His "dramatic monologue,"[4] "My Last Duchess," is reminiscent of Francesca's story, but told from the perspective of the Duke, the lady's husband. Showing a visitor a portrait of his late wife, he is terse, enigmatic, and a touch defensive. His description of her is ominously understated: "[she had] a heart—how shall I say?—too soon made glad." The circumstances under which the Duchess died are suspicious, but never revealed, and remain the subject of conjecture.

FIGURE 2. Fra Angelico, *The Annunciation*, 1425–1428. Museo del Prado, Madrid, Spain. Photo: Erich Lessing / Art Resource, New York.

Dante's text, in its stunning originality, is no hackneyed romance. It represents Francesca's meditation, a pithy anatomy of love's progress. It lacks the exculpatory detail, social context and sentimental clichés of Boccaccio's narrative and relates only one action. Paradoxically, it is in fact a proleptic critique of the genre into which Boccaccio tried to transform it. When the pilgrim asks the question perennially posed to the guilty by the presumptively innocent—"how could you?"—she turns away from the illusions of romance and acknowledges that, like actors, they were reading themselves into an all too familiar script.

What she imagined to be a unique and spontaneous passion turns out to have begun as the mimicry of someone else's story. Reading about Lancelot and Guinevere was the first root of their love and their kiss was its first incarnation.

The phenomenon of mimetic desire is at the center of the work of René Girard, one of the most powerful theorists of culture of our time. Perhaps because his early work on the novel has been overshadowed by his profound influence in anthropology, social studies, and comparative religion, few students of Dante seem to know his essay of fifty years ago, dedicated to the canto of Francesca. In the briefest of terms, his point was that the desiring subject imagines, as does Francesca, that desire springs spontaneously from within, while the truth that is revealed by Dante and the greatest of novelists, is that desire is always triangular, "mediated" by the desires of the other—in this case, as in the case of Don Quixote, by a book. In a few mordent pages, Girard debunked the romantic reading of Francesca's story, showing that it was simply a repetition of her own initial mystification. When Girard wrote, the best-selling love story of the time was entitled *By Love Possessed*; Girard's title was polemic, summing up the delusion propagated by all such "romance" stories: "By Literature Possessed." His point was that desire is essentially imitative, searching for a model, and that literature provides it with an imaginary map. Dante's text was not complicit in "romantic" deception. On the contrary, Francesca's last words exposed the *roman* as a panderer and seducer, leading the lovers to their destruction. Her story anticipated those of Chaucer, Shakespeare, and Cervantes in the genre of the *"anti-roman."*[5]

Nevertheless, Boccaccio's "romance" of Francesca had its effect on learned as well as popular speculation about her character. So real did she appear to Dante's readers that even serious critics debated her moral qualities, her relative guilt or innocence, as though she were a "personality," rather than simply a character in the infernal drama. The debates have been so vigorous that a distinguished scholar, in his survey of the bibliography, classified the critics as "hawks" or "doves," according to whether they disputed her human weakness or the justice of her condemnation.[6] Yet her guilt is undeniable; it is axiomatic in Dante's moral system. To dispute that would be to call all of Hell into question.

Leaving aside the naïveté of some of the commentaries, however, the situational irony of Hell fosters the illusion of what György Lukács called "real personality" in Dante's poem, distinguishing it from earlier literature and foreshadowing the rise of the modern novel.[7] Only in Hell do we find a clash between the worldly outlook of the characters and the mute otherworldly reality to which they are unwillingly subject. For Lukács, such discord is absent in the epic, where heroes may fight mightily against monsters and gods, but nevertheless inhabit the same homogenous reality, observing the same rules of the game. In contrast, the novel, Lukács's principal concern, recounts an interior adventure, in which the protagonist is alienated from a fragmented world, separated from all others by an unbridgeable gap. The novel is the "epic of a world from which God has departed." In Dante's poem, which might be thought of as an epic of transcendence, *Inferno* is an autonomous realm, a "doloroso regno" totally separate from God. It corresponds exactly to Lukács's definition of "novelistic reality." For this reason, he thought of it as the transition from ancient epic to the modern novel.

In Hell, the sinners are alone even when they are together, individual and separated from the Church and the communion of saints. They are banished from the kingdom of heaven, where God is King ("il re dell'universo," *Inf.* 5.91). The illusory "personality" of Francesca and of all of the dramatic figures in Hell who have occasioned debates between "hawks" and "doves" is a function of their respective "singularity." They are surd elements in a hegemonic otherworld. There is no such singularity in the happy family of the blessed and therefore no possible debate among critics about their moral character. No one has ever questioned the heroism of Manfred or the virtue of Piccarda.

The stories recounted by the sinners are inevitably self-serving. Like the testimony of convicts, the truth of their stories can often be impugned. If they have been "framed" in this blind prison (*Inf.* 10.58–9), it is not by false accusation, as in crime stories, but literally, in a thematic sense, by the author, who frames his characters within the larger context of his fiction. Hell is the *cornice* for their stories, an infernal decameron, in which the surroundings cast doubt over the inmates' tales. The contrast between their defensiveness and the self-evident judgment against them casts shadows of doubt in the open mind of a reader who is neither "hawk" nor "dove" and further enhances the illusion of "real personality."

The stories within Dante's story invite ironic interpretation and critical debate, as do the tales told by prisoners protesting their conviction. But in Dante's autobiographical story, he is at once the prosecution and the defense. There are two Dantes, just as there are two Augustines in the *Confessions*. Italian editors of the latter work take pains to distinguish "Agostino narrato" from "Agostino narratore" in their commentaries. In Dante studies, the distinction between the pilgrim and the poet serves the same purpose. In a conversion narrative, the distinction creates the temporal illusion of an experience retrospectively recounted. The relevance of this for the portrait of Francesca is that its moral ambiguity arises from the clash between the secular and human perspective of the damned, once shared by the pilgrim and now by most readers, and implacable Justice, which is the perspective assumed by the poet. The compassionate pilgrim "narrato" is en route to becoming the stern "narratore," who, paradoxically, has been with us from the beginning.

When the accretions of oral history and romance have been removed, Dante's text reveals itself to be at once the origin and the refutation of its own midrashic tradition. Like the barnacles and shells scraped away from the body of Glaucus to restore the sea-god's form (*Republic* 10.611), the sentimental "romance" of Francesca has often served to obscure Dante's pristine conciseness, nuance, and intellectual rigor. When it is cleared away, there emerges the simulacrum of a "real personality," the more poignant for having been condemned by its creator.

The following pages survey the dominant themes of the canto: the analysis of desire, reciprocity in love, the adumbration of subjectivity, and the mediation of the book. It will become apparent that Dante owes many of these themes to Augustine, who has been called the discoverer of the "inner self."

## The Wings of Desire

Dante's Hell is an autonomous region, totally separate from deity, where the sinners are sorted according to the coils of a monster's tail. Minos, the judge of Virgil's underworld, is transformed into a Kafkaesque bureaucrat, impersonally and implacably meting out punishment as though the sinners' guilt were a weight seeking its appropriate place in the abyss, according to its specific gravity. The "weight of love" (*pondus amoris*) is a structural principle in the *Commedia,* derived from the Augustinian formula, "pondus meum, amor meus" (*Conf.* 13.9.10). It determines the placement of the sinners, the massiveness of Satan and the spontaneous ascent of the pilgrim through the heavenly spheres. It suggests that one *is* metaphorically what one loves and that sin is therefore its own punishment. Justice is immanent in the sinners; among them, the carnal sinners are the least culpable. They are the best of the worst.

The Kingdom of Heaven, according to the Gospel of Matthew (13:31), is like a flourishing tree, where the birds of the air come to rest in its branches. In the kingdom of Hell, the avian imagery is chaotic. The subterranean sky is filled with sinners swept up in a maelstrom, like dense flocks of starlings in winter, impelled by shifting winds and driven in every direction. The paratactic verse, "di qua, di là, di giù, di sù li mena" (hither, thither, downward, upward, it drives them) (*Inf.* 5.43) mimics the staccato blasts and intermittent lulls in the infernal hurricane.

Out of the shifting swarm, there emerges in contrast a formation of souls, flying like cranes in single file, as though passing in review. The verse that introduces them is not only syntactically flowing, but rhythmic as well: "E come i gru van cantando lor lai, / faccendo in aere di sé lunga riga" (And as the cranes go chanting their lays, making a long line of themselves in the air) (*Inf.* 5. 46–47). The ending of the verse, "lunga riga," is spondaic, as though to extend the "line," in the image as well as the meter. Virgil, guiding Dante, then calls the roll of more than a thousand "donne antiche e' cavalieri," the ladies and knights of old, as they peel off from the nameless and innumerable horde.[8]

The avian similes are juxtaposed, but sharply contrasted. The flight of starlings is random, while cranes fly in linear order, "cantando lor lai." The word "lai" is usually understood as "lamentations," but one can scarcely avoid the association with its literal sense: the "lais" sung by the troubadors, or the Breton "lais" of Marie de France, in which the theme is love. Given that nuance, the literary overtones of the verse are reinforced by the ancient belief that the patterns traced by cranes flying in consort were signs, portents, or even letters of the alphabet. Such formations were the closest thing to sky-writing the world had ever seen before the invention of the airplane.[9] If cranes may be said to "chant their lays," then starlings merely make noise. The thematic importance of these emblems of disorder and order at the beginning of the infernal descent is clear: to distinguish the notorious and aristocratic lovers catalogued by Virgil from the swarms of common and anonymous carnal sinners. So, nothing is further said of the generically lustful crowd. The ancient ladies and their knights, however, constitute a pantheon of the literature of love.

Avian imagery permeates the work of the poet who claimed to have flown from the highest perch of Tuscan poetry (*Purg.* 11.99) to the nest of Leda in the starry heaven (*Par.* 27.98) and whose surname suggests "a bearer of wings" (Latin *aliger*). In a masterful essay on the ancient theme of the wings of love, Leo Spitzer traced its variations, including the Dantesque, from Plato to the *Vol de nuit* of Saint-Exupéry.[10] Here in canto 5, the imagery serves a narrative purpose. Starlings connote the chaos of lust, while the flight of cranes suggest the channeling of passion into the formulae of the literature (or even the courtly religion) of love. They are apt emblems of popular literature, flying unswervingly in an aerial "follow-the-leader," corresponding to the tradition of what Girard calls the "mensonge romantique": "imitators imitating imitators in the name of spontaneity."[11]

From the flock of Dido, "la schiera ov'è Dido," there emerge a pair of doves, marking at the same time the emergence of Dante from his literary forebears and his contemporaries. In a lull in the blasts of the infernal wind, Francesca and Paolo respond to the pilgrim's affectionate cry:

> Quali colombe dal disio chiamate
> con l'ali alzate e ferme al dolce nido
> vegnon per l'aere, dal voler portate;
> cotali uscir da la schiera ov'è Dido
> a noi venendo per l'aere maligno,
> sì forte fu l'affettüoso grido.

> *Inf.* 5.82–8

> As doves called by desire, with wings raised and steady, come through the air, borne by their will to their sweet nest, so did these issue from the troop where Dido is, coming to us through the malignant air, such force had my compassionate cry.

The simile is a reminiscence from the fifth book of the *Aeneid*: "As a wild dove when startled into flight / Beats her affrighted way over the fields / . . . But soon in quiet air goes floating on / with wings extended motionless . . ." (5.273–9). Dante's verses are close enough to Virgil's to make the difference between them all the more salient. Virgil's comparison describes the gliding of a boat after furious strokes of its oars. Dante's doves are impelled by thoroughly human emotions: the doves are called forth by desire and moved by will. The metaphorical wings of Paolo and Francesca, who yearn for peace, echo Virgil's words, but are more reminiscent in sentiment to the poignant verses of Psalm 54: "Who will give me the wings of the dove [*pennas colombae*] so that I might fly away and be at rest?" (54:7). In his commentary on this Psalm, Augustine suggests that the psalmist in these words longs in vain for the peace of death (*Enarrationes in* Psalmos, ad loc. Ps. 54v). That longing is Francesca's *leit-motif.*

Like cranes, the doves too are emblems of love, but they bear Dante's inimitable theological mark. As they descend from their flock, so Dante parts company from his literary predecessors. Doves appear elsewhere in the poem: in *Purgatorio* (2.120) in a penitential setting, as Casella "sings" a *canzone* from the *Convivio.* In *Paradiso*, Saints James and Peter lavish their affection on each other, murmuring like doves, but this time, the literary allusion is to the Gospels.

The wings of the dove in *Inferno* are called by desire and moved by will. The words "desire" and "will" may at first seem redundant, but Dante is, as always, precise: They are called from without by [the object of] desire and impelled from within by the will. They seek the sweet nest, as all do, the peace and quiet that doves may reach, but that human lovers will never find. At best, they hover, during a pause in the infernal storm.

The insatiability of human desire is a major theme in *Inferno.* Its specific emblem is the insuperable she-wolf of the prologue scene, "la bestia sanza pace" (1.57), but its sway goes beyond the sensitive appetite and infects the mind and heart as well. Francesca yearns for "pace," deliverance from desire, but even death provided no escape for her. As Virgil says of souls in Limbo, "sanza speme vivemo in disio" (4.42). The peace for which Christians pray, as the lovers would, were they God's friend (4.90–1), is the peace of the Lord, the *quies* that "passes understanding" (*Philippians* 4:7). From this, as from death, the souls of the damned are eternally excluded. Francesca is the exemplary victim in Hell of an "unquiet heart."

Augustine's *Confessions* begins and ends with this theme. In the first paragraph of what has been called his "pilgrimage of the soul" he says, "fecisti nos ad te et inquietum est cor nostrum donec requiescat in te" (you made us for yourself and our heart is unquiet until it rests in you) (*Conf.* 1.1). He returns to the theme in the final paragraph of his work: "nos requieturos in tua grandi sanctificatione speramus" (we hope that we shall have found rest when you admit us to the great holiness of your presence) (12.38). In our day, Jacques Lacan was perhaps thinking of this passage when he said that the tense of desire is always in the future perfect.[12]

This desire is a metaphysical hunger that cannot be satisfied except by the beatific vision. Appetites, human or animal, are readily, if only temporarily sated, but yearning always exceeds its putative object, seeking the absolute. The first books of the *Confessions* trace metonymically the trajectory of desire throughout Augustine's stages of development: The breast in his infancy, human love in his youth, fame and glory as an adult, but none of these can bring *quies* to the soul. Even what he takes to be the truth of the faith, after his conversion, cannot diminish the heart's yearning.

The wings of human desire, unlike those of doves, will never find rest. Hannah Arendt, who wrote a remarkable thesis on Augustine under the tutelage of Karl Jaspers, does not mention Dante, but virtually paraphrases the meaning of his simile: ". . . the very act of desiring presupposes the distinction of an 'inner' act (*volere*) and its 'external' object (*disio*), so that desiring, by definition, can never attain its object, unless the object, too, is within man, and so within his power."[13]

Twenty years after writing his simile of the doves, Dante returned to the distinction between desire and will at the ending of *Paradiso* and resolved the paradox of desire in a supernatural dimension, exactly as Arendt said was its the only possible resolution. The last lines of the poem describe the experience of beatific vision: "già volgeva il mio disio e 'l *velle*, / sì come rota ch'igualmente è mossa, / l'amor che move il sole e l'altre stelle" (my desire and *will* were moved, as a wheel is evenly moved, by the love that moves the sun and the other stars) (*Par.* 33.143–5). The otherwise perpetually exterior object of desire is internalized in the beatific vision and the descent of desire is arrested and transformed into what the theologians call fruition, the love of God within the soul. What Arendt does not say, but Dante must, is that this interiorization is not in man's power, but is a gift of grace.

All wheels on earth move in two directions at the same time, since they rotate around their own center, and, at the same time, move forward, thanks to their tangency with the ground. So the *motus rotabundus* of beatitude is a simultaneous movement in two directions: an *inner* rotation of the soul around God, now at its center, but also a forward revolution thanks to its integration with the universe, around God, center of the cosmos. In the last sentence of the poem,

Love moves desire and will together, along with the sun and the other stars.

The downward course of desire is implicit in its etymology. Etymologists generally agree that the word "desiderare" shares its root with the word "considerare": the noun *sidus, sideris,* meaning "star." However, there seems to be no agreement about the significance of that common origin. In an essay written many years ago, discussing the circular dance of the theologians in the heaven of the sun, I suggested that the word "considerare" was an evocation of the Platonic analogy between the circular movement of the heavens and the circular movement of mind, eternally thinking the same thoughts.[14] This would account for both the etymology and the meaning of the word "consideration." The theory usually advanced, that the etymon might have to do with augury or astrology, seems to be excluded by the prefix "con," meaning "with," and by a suffix derived from a verb of action. The etymology I proposed, "to move with the stars," seemed more probable. Essentially, "consideration" is like "contemplation," except that its locus is the heavens rather than a temple. The same hypothetical root, *\*siderare*, with the prefix of "de" instead of "con," yields an equally ancient significance for "desiderare": "to fall from the stars."

The myth of such a fall was widespread in Neoplatonic spiritualism and in the religion of the Gnostics. A passage in the commentary of Macrobius on the "Dream of Scipio" serves to illustrate the mythic theme in a widely diffused text that echoes Plotinus and that Dante probably knew: "the blessed souls, free from all bodily contamination, possess the heavens; but the soul that from its lofty pinnacle of perpetual radiance disdains to grasp after a body . . . yet allows a secret yearning for it to creep into its thoughts [*desiderio latenti cogitaverit*] and gradually slips down to the lower realms because of the very weight of its earthy thoughts."[15] This yearning for the body was said to be the cause of the fall from the stars of several mythic angels and souls in the religion of the Gnostics. In some versions, an angel named Sophia gazed lovingly at the earth, like Narcissus at the pool, and fell from the stars to become Helen, the companion of Simon Magus, whom Dante apostrophizes at the opening of canto 19. Etymologically, as well as mythically, the circularity of "consideranza" and the linear plunge of "disio" are as far apart as Heaven and Hell.

Francesca's lament is a death wish, to still her "unquiet heart." Human desire is insatiable because it is a thirst for the absolute. If God is excluded in the search, the only other absolute within reach would seem to be annihilation. The descent of the doves in canto 5 are reminiscent of the doves of Venus, but they do not alight. Their descent is a "desiderare," an eternal dying fall in search of peace.

## The Po Descends to the Sea

Courtly love is sometimes referred to as the religion of love; often it has little to do with sexual appetite. It demands the total devotion of the lover, with no claim to reward except for the gracious condescension of his lady. In Augustinian terms, it is quintessentially idolatrous, indifferent or hostile toward marriage and social values. Andreas Capellanus is famous for having written an etiquette book called "The Art of Courtly Love," setting forth the rules of conduct for courtly ladies and their faithful knights. Before Dante's time, the legends of Tristan and Iseult and of Lancelot and Guinevere were adapted into lais and romances embodying the courtly code. With some difficulty, the literature struggled to find some contrivance to reconcile courtly love with the code of knightly chivalry. When all else failed, there was always the love potion to mask the incompatibility.

Tristan was a dedicated knight of King Mark, yet he loved Iseult, who was betrothed to the King. Lancelot was a knight of the roundtable, who nevertheless slept with Guinevere, King Arthur's Queen. The lovers are portrayed as not being responsible for falling in love, since in both cases there were extenuating circumstances: Tristan and Iseult unwittingly drank a love potion, and Lancelot and Guinevere were seduced by the blandishments of Gallehaut. Nevertheless, their respective cases ended in death or dishonor, not to mention the end of Camelot. Death was the choice for lovers like Tristan and Isolde, the eponymous lovers of Wagner's revival of the story, which ended in a "liebestod." Although Francesca and Paolo were murdered by her husband, their love too bore within it the seeds of its own destruction.

Francesca speaks as a lady in a romance, to mitigate her culpability. She refers to God, from whose sight she is banished, with courtly circumlocution, "il Re dell'universo" (the King of the universe) and, of course, to her seduction by Gallehaut. The lines she uses to tell about her birthplace, Ravenna, contain a hint of a courtly motif: "Siede la terra ove nata fui / su la marina dove 'l Po discende / per aver pace co' seguaci sui." Singleton translates this: "The place where I was born lies on the shore where the river Po descends to be at peace with its followers" (1.1.53), but the English misses an exquisite nuance, without which it would be difficult to account for the memorability of the topographic detail. If the Po descends to seek peace (like the dove of Psalm 54), a dispersion into the sea, it must be that it is *pursued*, rather than merely followed, by its tributaries—we might say "hounded," until its dissolution. The striking assonance, "seguaci sui," invites an association with the phonetically and semantically related word, "segugi," meaning "hounds," hinting that the tributaries are like hunting dogs, yapping at the heels of a delicate prey. The faint allusion is to the motif of the erotic hunt, the "caccia amorosa."

In antiquity, the most famous example of such a hunt is the death of Acteon, in Book 3 of Ovid's *Metamorphoses*, who was punished by Diana for gazing at her as she was bathing naked in the forest. In indignation, she splashed him, transforming him into a stag, to be pursued and then killed by his own hounds. The Ovidian tale was widely read, elaborated, and embellished in the Middle Ages, but perhaps the most famous variation was the lai of Marie de France entitled *Guigemar*. There is no evidence that Dante knew it, but several of its motifs re-emerge in Francesca's story: A knight, who seemed immune to love, hunts and wounds a white hind, strangely transgendered with the antlers of a hart. He is himself wounded by the ricochet of one of his arrows and is swept away down a river in a magic boat, which eventually carries him out to sea. He comes to a castle, where he falls madly in love with the Queen (who has been burning a copy of Ovid's *Remedia amoris*!) and has a passionate and adulterous relationship with her. Her husband discovers them, they escape separately, but after many vicissitudes, are ultimately reunited.

The dream-like fantasy of Marie in the twelfth century, with the ricochet arrows of Cupid and the irresistible flow of the river in a magic boat, is brutally de-mystified two centuries later with Boccaccio's nightmare version of the "caccia amorosa." In the fifth book of the *Decameron*, Nastagio degli Onesti has an infernal vision of a naked woman hunted by her spurned knight and ripped apart by his dogs, only to be resurrected the following week, when the chase is resumed. The moral of this recurrent nightmare is the lover's wish-fulfillment: a lady should not spurn the advances of her suitor. The cautionary tale from the dark side of courtly love was made socially acceptable, barely, when it was portrayed in four exquisite panels by Botticelli, the last of which was a happy wedding banquet.

The amorous hunt and its history from antiquity through Petrarch to the Renaissance were exhaustively studied by D. C. Allen in an essay on Marvell's "Nymph's Complaint on the Death of her Fawn."[16] He missed one author, however, who provides us with a gloss on Dante's text. In 1502, Antonio Fragoso, a mediocre poet from Genova, wrote an allegorical poem about the pursuit of virtue called the *Cerva Bianca.* Dante may or may not have known *Guigemar,* but Fragosa certainly did. His "white hind" is also transgendered, as it has the antlers of a hart. The hermaphroditism is the emblem of heterosexual love, as it is in Guido Guinizelli's words in *Purgatorio* 26.82: "il nostro peccato fu ermafrodito" (our sin was hermaphrodite). The mythical animal is clearly neither male nor female, but a *surrogatus amoris,* Love itself.

There is little of romance in Fragoso's earnest allegory, except for the landscape. What is most interesting for us are the names of his hounds: they are called "desio" and "pensier," and are so labeled in the frontispiece (Figure 1). These are the words used by the pilgrim in canto 5 when he breaks into Francesca's monologue to express his compassion: "Oh lasso, / quanti dolci *pensier,* quanto *disio* / menò costoro al doloroso passo!" (Alas, How many sweet thoughts, what great desire, drove them to the woeful pass!) (*Inf.* 5.112–14). With the echo of these verses, the hounds pursuing the "cerva bianca" are interiorized as the inner struggle of love, the *erotomachia,* implicit in the story of Acteon and allusive in the descent of the Po, sweeping away Francesca to her doom.

### Eros and Anteros

The verses that follow have become familiar throughout the centuries to virtually every literate Italian. They confirm the role of Francesca as at once the heroine and the victim of love, from its inception to its death. It is a rhetorical tour de force:

> Amor, ch'al cor gentil ratto s'apprende,
> > prese costui della bella persona
> > che mi fu tolta; e 'l modo ancor m'offende.
> Amor, ch'a nullo amato amar perdona,
> > mi prese del costui piacer sì forte,

> che, come vedi, ancor non m'abbandona.
> Amor condusse noi ad una morte.

*Inf.* 5.100–6

> Love, which is quickly kindled in a gentle heart, seized this one for the beautiful body that was taken from me in a way that still offends me. Love, which absolves no one loved from loving, seized me so strongly with his pleasure that, as you see, it still has not left me. Love led us to one death.

In a famous essay, Renato Poggioli doubted that Dante intended with the first verse of this anaphora to allude to his own famous sonnet in the *Vita nuova*, *Amor e cor gentil son una cosa* (love and the gentle heart are one), and to the "school" of like-minded poets.[17] The easy rejoinder to Poggioli's doubt is that, if he is correct, then Dante was running the risk of being badly misunderstood. It is true that his early sonnet specifically credits Guido Guinizelli with that definition of love, but it is equally true that it came to be universally associated with Dante, if not from the little book, certainly from *Inferno*. In the *Knight's Tale*, Geoffrey Chaucer writes, "pitee renneth soone in gentil herte" (479), which unmistakably echoes Francesca's "pietà" and suggests that by Chaucer's time, Dante owned the allusion, even if he was not its sole proprietor. When Dante invokes the spirits to descend to the travelers (*Inf.* 5.80), it is not in the voice of the poet, but in the voice of the pilgrim, who is very much a character in this canto. We are not told what his affectionate cry ("affettuoso grido") is, but it is in a language that Francesca understands and to which she responds. He calls her in the name of the love that still drives the lovers ("per quello amor che i mena"), which can only be desire. Early in his career, in the "dolce stil novo," Dante spoke the same language.

The point is critical because it involves the dialectic of pilgrim and poet. If the allusion to the "gentle heart" is in whole or in part attributed to the young Dante, then it is clearly palinodic on the part of the mature poet, who would be rejecting his own theory as he rejects Francesca's. If this is the case, it would explain the celebrated fainting of the pilgrim at the end of the canto as a crisis of remorse for his naive acceptance of a then current poetic cliché. If, on the other hand, the allusion to the "gentle heart" is Dante's Olympian rejection of the theory of his erstwhile school, then the fainting spell at the end of the canto is merely an awkward transition to the next canto. That may be true, but it would certainly be uninteresting.

The second iteration of "Amor" is more complex: "Amor, ch'a nullo amato amar perdona." The observation that love should be requited is banal enough for critics to have adduced many potential sources for Dante's verse, from Scripture to Andreas Capellanus, without being particularly persuasive. What is distinctive about the verse is not the sentiment, but the word play. The proposition conveys the idea of reciprocity of love by repetition of its verbal root, just as Pier delle Vigne conveys the contagiousness of envy with variations on the word "infiammare": *infiammò—infiammati—infiammar* (*Inf.* 13.67–8). This sort of diction suggests the style of a rhetorician, rather than the biblical or medieval sources usually cited.

The early books of Augustine's *Confessions* are replete with virtuoso plays on the word "Amor," with the Silver Age rhetoric for which he is famous. He tells us that he loved most of all to love and to be loved (*amare et amari*), even when he had not yet loved (*nondum amabam, et amare amabam*). These were the loves that "Agostino narratore" deeply regrets. The closest analogue in his text to Dante's verses is one that stresses a moral imperative to reciprocate friendship, rather than physical love. In the fourth book of the *Confessions*, he explains what it is that is loved in friends: "Hoc est quod diligitur in amicis, et sic diligitur ut rea sibi sit humana conscientia si non amaverit redamantem aut si amantem non redamaverit" (this is what we love in friends. We love to the point that the human conscience feels guilty if we do not love the person who is loving us, and if that love is not returned) (4.9).

In his extraordinary book, *The Politics of Friendship*, Jacques Derrida gives Augustine's discussion great prominence in the ancient tradition of the literature of friendship from Plato, Aristotle and Cicero, subjecting it to an exhaustive and brilliant philosophical analysis. Of this passage in particular, he observes that its intricacies could be the object of "interminable meditation."[18] The similarity of the play on words to Francesca's suggests that it was so for Dante as well. Love in the physical sense ("two souls in one flesh") would appear to be antithetical to friendship ("one soul in bodies twain"); Francesca's play on the word "amare" elides the sharp distinction.

The question is whether body or soul constitutes the "oneness" of love. Francesca loved her lover with her body, so there is no hint in her words of the caveat that Augustine adds to his: "nihil quaerens ex eius corpore praeter indicia benevolentiae" (without demanding any physical response other than the marks of affectionate good will) (4.9). In the context of Augustine's remarks, a paean to the memory of his beloved friend, so fervent as to strike us as homoerotic, the admonition is critical. At stake is the clear line separating *caritas* from *cupiditas*, of love from lust. Proof that Dante knew Augustine's text is his version of the same caveat in *Purgatorio*, where he offers a restriction on the obligation to reciprocate a proffered love. When the poets meet Statius, Virgil explains why he responds to Statius's love: "Amore, *acceso di virtù*, sempre altro accese" (Love, kindled by virtue, has ever kindled other love) (*Purg.* 22.9–10). A love "kindled" by virtue is perforce chaste. Before Augustine's absolutism, the line between friendship and physical love was sometimes blurred.

Augustine's wordplay in turn precisely reveals his classical source. When he tells us that "the human conscience feels guilty if we do not love the person who is loving us, and if that love is not returned," not only does he invoke a moral imperative to which Francesca seems also to allude ("nullo amato amar *perdona*"), but he also indulges in "echolalia" more intricate than the poet's: "si non amaverit redamantem aut si amantem non redamaverit." The rare word "redamare" was coined by Cicero in *De amicitia.* Wishing to indicate the reciprocity necessary in friendship, the orator apologizes for the neologism he uses to describe a friend, who "vel amare, ut ita dicam, *redamare* possit" (is able to love or—if I may use the word—"re-love") (*De amicitia,* 14.49).[19] As the saying goes, "the Greeks had a word for it," even if Cicero did not. He knew Plato's work well enough to have translated some of the *Timaeus,* the only Platonic dialogue known in the Latin Middle Ages. It seems reasonable to assume that he invented the word "redamare" to render the word "anteros" from Plato's *Phaedrus* (255D), the *locus classicus* for the theme of erotic reciprocity.

The passage in Plato contains many of the themes we have been discussing. It is necessary to quote it at length:

> . . . as a breeze or an echo rebounds from the smooth rocks and returns whence it came, so does the stream of beauty, passing through the eyes which are the windows of the soul, come back to the beautiful one . . . filling the soul of the beloved also with love. And thus he loves, but he knows not what; he does not understand and cannot explain his own state; he appears to have caught the infection of blindness from another; the lover is his mirror in whom he is beholding himself, but he is not aware of this. When he is with the lover, both cease from their pain, but when he is away then he longs as he is longed for, and has love's image,

love for love lodging in his breast [*idolon erotos anterota echon*], which he calls and believes to be not love but friendship only, and his desire is as the desire of the other, but weaker; he wants to see him, touch him, kiss him, embrace him, and probably not long afterwards his desire is accomplished.

*Phaedrus* 50

The objective of the older lover in this difficult passage is to mask his seduction of the beloved by convincing him that whatever responses the boy may have are a product of his own god-like beauty rather than to the lover's importunate advances. A. W. Price paraphrases the sense of the passage: "desire overflows the eyes of the lover, and, like a sound echoing back to its source, re-enters the eyes of the boy . . . who in turn falls in love, but with what or whom he cannot tell. In a way, he is a Narcissus in love with his own reflection . . . Like Ganymede loving Zeus, who is a god, he loves the other as a god whom his own god-like beauty has attracted . . . his return of love (*anteros*) is a reflection of love (*eros*)."[20] The boy mistakes this love for friendship, but, inevitably, with day-to-day contact, in the gymnasium and elsewhere, and although his love is weaker than the fervor of the lover, the beloved succumbs to physical love.

According to Erwin Panofsky, "Plato's [metaphysical] theory of love has left no trace in Greek and Roman poetry."[21] The word "anteros" was sufficiently obscure, he tells us, that when it was revived in the Renaissance it was sometimes misinterpreted to refer to the rival brother of the profane and blindfolded Cupid—that is, "anti-eros," ultimately a symbol of sacred love. Yet this passage of the *Phaedrus* seems to have left some traces, not only in Latin prose, with Cicero and Augustine, but also, however faintly, in the poetry of Ovid.[22] Plato's paragraph reads as if it were the meditation of a still-mystified Narcissus, at once losing and finding himself in his image, an erotic *cogito*: "Iste ego sum!" (*Metamorphoses* 3.463). It begins with the streams of beauty reverberating like an echo. The exchange of glances, the lover as a mirror in which the beloved unknowingly beholds himself, create desire and the response to it, with desire, face to face. Only the endings of the two accounts are different. Plato seems tolerant of the slippage from friendship to physical love, but the myth ends in disaster, commemorated by the flower, marking the place where Narcissus died.

We should observe in retrospect that in Augustine's account of the death of his friend there is as well an erotic *cogito*, a wisp of potential narcissism in his love for his friend, a reminiscence of Ovid's "iste ego sum," but posthumous: "ille alter etiam." We assume that the premature conversion and death of his boyhood friend saved Augustine from experiencing any of the ulterior temptations of intense friendship such as those described in the *Phaedrus*. The echo of Ovid may very well be fortuitous, but the textual similarity of the two declarations underscores the potential narcissism of friendship when it is expressed as the identification, the *immedesimarsi*, of one with the other.

Plotinus was more severe than either Plato or Ovid, condemning any fall from the realm of ideal beauty to physical consummation. He used the myth of Narcissus as a caution to the lover to turn away from the physical embodiment of beauty to pursue instead the ideal. The descent of Narcissus in the following passage may have been the inspiration for Macrobius's cosmological version of the descent of desire, which we have discussed:

> . . . when a man sees "the beauty in bodies, he must not pursue them . . . they are images, traces and shadows . . . If a man runs to the image and wants to seize it as if it was [*sic*] a reality—like a beautiful reflection playing on the water, which some myth recounts that a man wanted to catch, only *to sink down into the stream and disappear* [cf. Macrobius: "paulatim in inferiora delabitur"]—then this man who clings to beautiful bodies and will not let them go, will be precipitated, not in body but in soul, like the man in the story, down into the dark depths of Hades."
>
> *Enneads* I.6.8

The narcissism described by Plotinus is not the vanity of self-sufficient autonomy, but the mistake of seeking a spiritual absolute in the corporeal beauty of the other. Plotinus's use of the plural ("beautiful bodies") suggests that the stunning allusion to the error of Narcissus in *Paradiso*, "l'error . . . ch'accese amor tra l'omo e 'l fonte" (the error . . . that kindled love between the man and the fountain) (3.17) evokes Plotinus more than Ovid. I have written elsewhere about that extraordinary simile; here I wish simply to point out that the pilgrim sees "più facce" (many faces) in the heaven of the Moon, rather than just his own.[23] This would seem to be a Neoplatonic, rather than an Ovidian, reading of the myth. In any case, on any reading, the love of Narcissus is clearly suicidal.

Given these fatal overtones, the last apostrophe to love, "Amor condusse noi ad una morte," seems impoverished by the literal interpretation it has usually been given, as though it were a stage direction for Ingres or other illustrators of the final scene. But the rhetorical efficacy of repetition, such as the anaphora of "Amore," depends upon its being a linear progression, without which it is merely boring, as Spitzer, in a different context, has observed.[24] Love's anaphora is precisely that: a causal linearity, moving from love's genesis, in a dependent clause, to the "entanglement" of reciprocity in a second dependent clause, to a direct dénouement in its definitive ending. The portentous finality of Francesca's words describes a personified Love so fearsome in its pursuit of the absolute that it annihilates its acolytes.

Thematically, the indefinite singular article, "una," reinforces the motif of the physical unity of the lovers, but it serves a rhetorical purpose as well, ensuring an echo of "amore" in the words "una morte" (unA-MORte). In the folk-etymology of Dante's poetic contemporaries, the lethal ending of such a passion was implicit in its name." The verse echoes the etymon "amor" with which it, like the passion, began. It suggests that the death wish of Love, the *Liebestod*, was merely assisted by a contemptible assassin, who is identified by Francesca only with a pronoun and dismissed with a curse.

The pseudo-etymological pun was used by Guittone d'Arezzo and was a commonplace, according to Gianfranco Contini, in the poetry of the time.[25] He cites Federigo dall'Ambra: "Amor, che tutte cose signoreggia, / Non fu chiamato amor senza cagione: / Amor dai savi quasi A MOR S'espone; / Guarda s'AMOR A MORte s'apareggia" (Love, which is Lord of all things, was not by chance called "Amor": by the learned it was defined as "A-MORte"; behold how "Amor" equals "A-MORte"). The verse is doggerel, but the sentiment is tremendous. It is this deadly power of love that led Guido Cavalcanti in his definition of love to describe it as "fero e si' altero" (fierce and haughty), which is itself a play on words.

There are logical, as well as thematic grounds for arguing that such a love was doomed to end in impasse. In her monologue, there are two Francescas: her consciousness and, in loving memory, her beautiful body ("la bella persona che mi fu tolta"). Of Paolo we can say nothing (as he says nothing), except that he weeps and he is *there*. Dante is at pains to portray in parallel verses the crossed symmetry of their erotic transaction: "prese costui / mi prese del costui," but all we know of Paolo is that his gaze, directed at her beautiful body, kindled his passion for her and in turn awakened in her a mirrored passion for her own body, valorized by his glance. Now that they are severed from their bodies, the grounds for their love is gone, and they are left as disembodied souls, alone together.

There is a touch of condescension in Francesca's "Amor, che nullo amato amar perdona," distinguishing her love from his. He loved her first and, so, presumably, more. Like the beloved in the *Phaedrus*, her desire is weaker, as if it were in part a moral obligation, as in friendship. But her loving memory of her own beauty and her enduring resentment for its loss ("'l modo ancor m'offende") suggest that her murder was a narcissistic wound that still festers. As she mourns her beauty in retrospect, she gives the impression of a consciousness whose physical charms, like those in a flirtation or a seduction, were instruments of foreign policy, serving as foils for her detached self-love. In abandoning her body to Paolo, she was paying homage to a virtual image of herself, projected into the eyes of the other and reflected in his ardor. Francesca's desire was *to be desired* and only then to reward her suitor.

This consideration sheds light on an ambiguous phrase in her words: "Amor, mi prese del costui piacer sì forte / che, come vedi, non m'abbandona" (5.104). It has been argued that, to complete the symmetry of the transaction, Paolo's "piacere" should be translated as the counterpart of Francesca's "persona": as he loved her body, so she loved his "piacere," a word that Dante uses in *Purgatorio* to indicate the physical manifestation of beauty, derived from Provencal "plazer," meaning charm. It is difficult, however, to understand how Paolo's body could continue to be so attractive to Francesca, now (in the present—*ancora*) that it is gone. It seems more likely that the word "piacere" is to be construed to mean "his *pleasure*," indicating her (narcissistic) satisfaction in the pleasure he took in the beauty of *her* body, now lost to both of them.

This construction would be consonant with the topos of the *Phaedrus*, *anteros* as a reflection of the *eros* emitted by the lover. Otherwise, her love would be a spontaneous and coincident replication of his *eros*, unmotivated by anything other than physical desire for his body. The compulsion that she felt (*a nullo amato amar perdona*) would then be inexplicable. Their coming together would be simply the physical transaction of beautiful and consenting adults, having nothing to do with the tremendous mystery of love.

An interior distance separates Francesca's consciousness from her "bella persona."[26] The transient physical contiguity of the lovers' bodies has had no effect on her inner self. The lovers persist as mutually isolated subjects, who objectified each other, and now, without bodies, are alone together. We have no idea of Paolo's consciousness. Because he is mute, he is simply a pawn in Francesca's analysis of her own love. For all we know, his love was a physical response to Francesca's beauty. Physical beauty can kindle lust as well as love, in hearts gentle or otherwise. In contrast to the law of reciprocity, the hallmark of friendship, consensual physical love tolerates dominance and acquiescence.

The fiction of Hell dramatizes in concrete terms the doubling of the self we experience when we withdraw within ourselves, conscious of an interior distance separating us from the reality in which we live, with our bodies as the front line between that inner self and the world. In *Inferno*, where the sinners are removed from both the body and the world, Hell is the front line; there is no return from that inner state, which is their sole mode of existence. The great figures in Hell look back with resentment, delusion or bitter regret, fixed and isolated in their respective memories. This permanently "subjective" state, their singularity in conflict with the established order, endows them with that novelistic "personality" that was, in its time, uniquely Dantesque.

Although Dante seems to have had no antecedents in western literature for the portrayal of self-reflexive consciousness, such a doubling of the self was of course implicit, in antiquity as well as Christianity, in what came to be called the "examination of conscience," the moral evaluation one makes of one's own actions in the world. It should be mentioned that Latin and the major European languages do not have separate words for "conscience" and "consciousness." Both meanings are assigned to the word *conscientia* and its modern derivatives. We have already seen an example of the reduplication of consciousness, or conscience, in Augustine's meditation on friendship, quoted earlier. Augustine explained that "the human conscience feels guilty if does not love in return." The reflexive construction of the verb expresses the guilt of an inner self: "rea sibi sit humana conscientia."

This interior distance is the forerunner of modern phenomenological analyses of consciousness from Hegel to Heidegger and Sartre; its ancient roots are to be found in Augustinian meditations. According to

Phillip Cary, it was the spatialization of memory in Augustine's theory of time that led to what Cary calls "the invention" of the inner self, living in a "memory palace," with a ceiling open to heaven.[27] To know oneself, for Augustine, it was necessary to close the doors (*extra nos*), enter within (*intra nos*), and rise above ourselves (*supra nos*). The metaphor of the "house of the soul" survived, in a radically different version, until the enlightenment. John Locke described the self as an empty room, a "camera obscura," through which reality entered only through a pinhole in the wall.

In the prison house of the damned, there is access neither to the world nor to the stars. The inmates are pure subjectivities, with only memories of a "tempo felice." We might note in passing that the durative "tempo felice," which contributes to Francesca's "dolore," gives the lie to the idea that the lovers' love was consummated in one brief moment, before they were killed. If, as Jacques Lacan maintains, desire is always in the future perfect, it is also true that mortal sin is always in the imperfect: that is, premeditated and obdurate. "Tempo felice" undoubtedly refers to a protracted liaison.

## Love by the Book

Having shaken with her words one key myth of courtly love, the myth of reciprocity, Francesca now smashes one most sacred, not only to courtly lovers, but to poets of the "sweet new style" as well, including Dante himself. She refutes the theory of the spontaneous nature of love, in spite of its importance for disproving premeditation in their sin, by confessing that their love took root first of all in their reading. The lover of Plato saw his reflection in the mirror of the beloved, while Ovid's Narcissus saw his reflection in a drowning pool. Francesca saw herself in the equally fallacious mirror of the book: the *roman* of Lancelot:

> Noi leggiavamo un giorno per diletto
> di Lancialotto come Amor lo strinse;
> soli eravamo e sanza alcun sospetto.
> Per più fiate li occhi ci sospinse
> quella lettura, e scolorocci il viso;
> ma solo un punto fu quel che ci vinse.
> Quando leggemmo il disiato riso

essere basciato da cotanto amante,
questi, che mai da me non fia diviso,
la bocca mi basciò tutto tremante.
Galeotto fu 'l libro e chi lo scrisse:
quel giorno più non vi leggemmo avante.

*Inf.* 5.127–38

One day for pastime, we read about Lancelot, how love seized him; we were alone, suspecting nothing. Several times that reading urged our eyes to meet and took the color from our faces, but one moment alone it was that overcame us. When we read how the longed for smile was kissed by so great a lover, this one, who never shall be parted from me, kissed my mouth all trembling. A Gallehaut was the book and he who wrote it; in its pages that day we read no more.

In the *Phaedrus*, the lover is the mirror of the beloved, who then condescends to love in return, with a love that is somewhat weaker. In the context of Platonic dualism, the slippage from friendship to physical love compromises the aspiration to ideal beauty in an effort to achieve total identity, body and soul, between the lovers. The *homology* of friends in the texts we have examined determines that the physicality to which they sometimes "descend" must be correspondingly homologous, which is to say *homoerotic*, so that their bodies, as well as their souls, mirror each other. On the other hand, heterosexuality means *difference,* a complement, rather than a replication, of one's body, with no *necessary* claim to spiritual unity beyond compatibility and mutual consent. The illusion of "Amor," in Francesca's "romantic" definition, is that one can find a soul mate and model in one who is simultaneously a heterosexual partner.

If there is a mirror in heterosexuality, a reflection of the self, it cannot be in the opposite gender; it can only be in one's own. The pool of Narcissus is located in inner space. Francesca's mirror is the book, in which, if she can persuade herself that her poor lover is a Lancelot, she can be the "virtual" Queen of Camelot, the fairest of them all, with no "Snow White" to challenge her. The first root of their love was not a mysterious, irresistible passion, but a casting call for one more performance of *Lancelot du Lac*, in which she assigned herself the role of Guinevere, with Paolo as a colorless stand-in for the greatest lover of the realm.

The scene of reading as a scene of seduction had an historical precedent in the century before Dante. In Peter Abelard's *History of My*

*Calamities*, the renowned philosopher seduced the brilliant and beautiful Heloise, entrusted to him as a pupil by her uncle, the canon Fulbert. As punishment for their scandalous elopement, Fulbert sent his henchmen to capture Abelard, whom they surprised in his sleep and castrated, after which Heloise was forcibly cloistered. The lovers achieved canonical status in Francois Villon's *Ballade des dames du temps jadis*. In the popular imagination of the nineteenth century, they were historical counterparts of Francesca and Paolo. In exactly the same year of Ingres's famous painting of the murder of Francesca and Paolo, 1819 (see Figure 3), Jean Vignaud depicted the discovery of Heloise and Abelard in a scene almost identical to Ingres's painting (see Figure 4), except that it is

FIGURE 3. Jean Auguste Dominique Ingres, *Paolo and Francesca*, 1814. Musée Bonnat, Bayonne, France. Photo: Erich Lessing/ Art Resource, New York.

FIGURE 4. Jean Vignaud, *Abelard and Heloise Surprised by Abbot Fulbert*, 1819. Joslyn Art Museum, Omaha, Nebraska. Museum purchase, Collector's Choice, 1985.

the canon Fulbert, in clerical garb, instead of Gianciotto, who looks in on the lovers from the doorway of their room.

Peter Dronke called attention to the parallel between the distraction from the text of Abelard's lovers and that of Dante's, as well as verbal similarities in the description of their exchange of glances and their respective embarrassment.[28] The critical difference in the scenes is that the book is irrelevant for Abelard: "Our speech was more of love than of the books which lay open before us; our kisses far outnumbered our reasoned words. Our hands sought less the book than each other's bosoms—love drew our eyes together far more than the lesson drew them to the pages of our text . . . What followed? No degree in love's progress was left untried by our passion. . . ."[29] Abelard's passion, as he portrays it, was pure lust. Of Heloise's love, faithful to death, we know little except for her letters, authentic or not. One suspects that her story would have resembled the "romance of Francesca," even to the detail of the single tomb, now in the cemetery of Père Lachaise.[30]

In contrast, Francesca's reading of the book is critical in her story. The verses that set the stage for her performance ought to be (and in fact have often been!) read *crescendo* to help us understand the role she intended to assume: "quando leggemmo il disiato riso esser basciate da cotanto amante . . ." (when we read of the longed-for smile kissed by such a lover . . .). The culmination of her romantic illusion, the delicate circumlocution of "disiato riso" to indicate Guinevere's lips and the description of Francesca's now silent but weeping partner as a substitute for the greatest of lovers, bring us to the cusp separating romance and reality. The very next word shatters the illusion. The bare demonstrative pronoun "questi," indicating, perhaps with a perfunctory gesture, her companion in misery, is said, indelicately, to have kissed her mouth, rather than her lips, all trembling.

The gap separating the erotic fantasies of literature from their sometimes awkward re-enactment in real life was exploited for comic effect in antiquity by Terence (*Eunuchus* 3.5), but for Augustine, it was no laughing matter. In the first book of the *Confessions,* the most "logocentric" Father of the Church rails against the seduction of the young by literature and uses the play by Terence as an example. He inveighs against the mythological fables of Homer, whose stories of the adulteries of Jupiter, the "thunderer," encourage his followers to commit adultery, while claiming the authority to do so by mimicking false "thundering." Augustine quotes the words of the young man in the play, gazing at the picture of Jupiter, impregnating Danae in a shower of gold: "What a god he is! His mighty thunder rocks the sky from end to end. You may say that I am only a man and thundering is beyond my power. But I played the rest of the part well enough and willingly, too!"[31]

The imitation of a book is a moral precept in Christianity, the basis for the *imitatio Christi* and, in popular religion, for moral guidance in the *sortes biblicae*, the random consultation of the Bible for a sign. In the eighth book of the *Confessions*, the scene of conversion, Augustine is commanded, through the voices of children, to take up the book and read: "Tolle! Lege!" He obeys because he remembers Ponticianus's story of the conversion of two young men when they read the life of St. Antony, who was in turn converted by the words he heard in a sermon. I have written elsewhere that conversion is a textual as much as a spiritual event, effected by the Word of God *in bono*, or, *in malo*, by the words of books.[32] Girard has observed that Don Quixote, infected by his reading, follows the precepts of chivalric romance and imitates Amadis of Gaul with the fervor of a Christian imitating the life of Christ.[33] Instead of a god, he worships an idol. The efficacy of both the Word of God and the words of man, the permeability of the heart to words of antithetical provenance, helps to understand why the cult of romantic love should have reached its apogee precisely in the age of faith.

For Augustine, language is born in desire, even in the infant's paralanguage of gesticulation. The infant "breaks in its mouth" to the sounds of language in order to express desire, which is insatiable, always exceeding the infant's needs.[34] Nevertheless, the "heart" seeks to channel overflowing desire with various "objects" of desire, chosen from a world that adults have named. It will never find its rest, unless and until (*donec*) it rests in God. Meanwhile, the literature that Augustine bitterly condemns offers myriad surrogate and illusory objects of desire, culled from a world meant to be used (*uti*), rather than enjoyed (*frui*), as only God should be. To enjoy what should be used is to counterfeit love and substitute for it idolatry. Diverting the heart away from its goal requires a powerful enchanter.

The words "Galeotto fu il libro e chi lo scrisse" compare the writer's craft to the mediation (to use the polite word) of Prince Gallehaut, between Lancelot and Guinevere. The analogy became a topos almost immediately. In the context of Francesca's damnation, it has the ring of a curse, but Boccaccio's *Decameron* proudly bears the subtitle of "Prencipe Galeotto," as if to announce boldly the seductive intent of the book: to bring solace to idle ladies, disappointed in love. In Chaucer's *Troilus and Criseyde*, the lady's uncle, Pandarus, fulfills the role of Gallehaut and bequeaths his name to the English language in a less polite word for erotic mediation: "pandering." Chaucer's masterpiece is a deft denunciation of cheap romance. After dozens of verses in which Pandarus extols the beauty and virtues of Troilus to cajole his niece, she finally sees Troilus from her window and asks herself "who gave me drink?" meaning, of course, a love potion (*Troilus and Criseyde* 3.1555). When Pandarus finally succeeds in getting the lovers into bed, he tucks them in and retires to the fire to read his "old romance."

Francesca's last words, "quel giorno piu' non vi leggemmo avante" (in its pages that day we read no more), use what rhetoricians call "reticentia," a figure to express by pointed suppression a meaning that is obscene, horrible, or otherwise unspeakable. Francesca's words allude to meaning, which is clearly, almost vulgarly, obscene. Yet Dante's *reticentia* is never quite that obvious. In the canto of Ugolino, for example, an equally famous instance of reticence are Ugolino's last words: "poscia, più che 'l dolor potè il digiuno" (Then fasting did more than grief had done) (*Inf.* 33.75), the meaning of which was debated by critics as famous as Byron and Shelley, who respectively affirmed and denied the allusion to cannibalism in the verse.

At opposite poles of *Inferno,* what these two instances of reticence have in common is that they are both spoken in the dramatic monologues of characters in Dante's fiction. Those characters perforce disappear at the borderline, where literature meets the voiceless reality of flesh and blood. In Dante's parlance, flesh and blood are the realm of the sensitive soul—the pre-human animality of sex, in the case of the lovers, or the post-human noise of a dog, with a bone in his maw. The clinical insistence on the mouth in both episodes marks the transition from words to the flesh.

We have seen that Francesca is what Lukács called a "novelistic" personality, whom we might think of as a medieval *Madame Bovary.* Whatever Flaubert meant by his enigmatic identification with his heroine, "Madame Bovary, c'est moi," it would apply at face value to the character "Dante" in this canto. The words placed in Francesca's mouth sound very much like words used by the poet as a young man, the religion of the "gentle heart," the spontaneity of love, the dark eros of the *Rime Petrose.* Her retraction in the second part of her monologue is at the same time his palinode. The character "Dante" disappears with her, falling as a dead man falls, silenced, leaving behind the stern narrator to revive him for the next stage of his pilgrimage.

# Epitaph for Guido

Hellfire was thought of in the Middle Ages as fire without light, tormenting the damned without illuminating their surroundings. The terror it inspired was memorably described by James Joyce in *Portrait of the Artist as a Young Man*, when his young protagonist hears a sermon on Hell at a Jesuit retreat and undergoes a convulsive, if temporary, conversion. The sermon itself, at the center of the novel, is filled with lurid hyperbole, remorselessly delivered by Father Arnall. Predictably, the passage conjured up among Joyce's readers comparisons to Dante, the undisputed authority on infernal torment, whose work Joyce knew so well that his friends referred to him as "Dublin's Dante."

In his correspondence with Joyce, Ezra Pound praised the depiction of the sermon from *Portrait* and, with customary erudition, reported having read a twelfth-century Provençal version of a "hellfire sermon" (July 16, 1914; letter to Quinn, April 18, 1917). In another letter, he offers to send Joyce what he modestly calls his "bad translation" of Guido Cavalcanti's famous and recondite *canzone*, "Donna me prega," and asks for help in translating an abstruse phrase (September 12, 1915). Neither he nor Joyce mentions the uncanny convergence in Dante's text of their respective preoccupations: It is precisely in the context of hellfire, in the circle of the heretics, that Guido's name makes its only appearance in *Inferno*, along with an unmistakable allusion to the poem that Pound so painstakingly translated and later incorporated into his own cantos.

Canto 10 of *Inferno* is Dante's "hellfire sermon," the masterpiece of Dantesque drama, unrivaled in the poem for its conciseness and power.

Its synthesis of theatricality and psychological depth has been universally admired by readers throughout the centuries. Some of the modern essays devoted to it have themselves become classic, such as those of Francesco De Sanctis, Benedetto Croce, Antonio Gramsci, and Erich Auerbach.[1] All of these praised the magnanimity of Farinata degli Uberti and were moved by the grief of Cavalcante de' Cavalcanti, but few had much to say about the character "Dante," who is himself an actor in the play. He is by turns combative, bewildered, and ultimately contrite with his interlocutors. Nothing could be further from the Olympian detachment of Dante the dramatist, silently staging the episode and constructing the dialogues with cool calculation and consummate irony.

The distinction between the author and his persona is especially critical in this canto. The stark contrast between the confusion of the character "Dante" and the subtle manipulation of the poet reflects the ambivalence of the historical Dante toward Guido Cavalcanti, his sometime rival and erstwhile friend. Their early intimacy is clear from their poetry, but we have no written evidence of their ultimate estrangement, apart from what can be inferred here, when the pilgrim mentions Guido, attributing to him an unspecified "disdain." The meaning of the word "disdain" is itself as obscure as the cause of the poets' falling out; we shall see that its deliberate ambiguity is Dante's covert attempt to convey his final negative judgment of Guido, while masking its severity. Guido's "disdain" is Dante's last word on the life of his "first friend." The judgment could not have been more severe.

No critics discuss Guido, who appears in the canto by name only and who is supposed by the fiction to be still alive. Nevertheless, he is at the center of the text and of our attention. The passage in which his name appears describes the encounter between the pilgrim and Guido's father, Cavalcante, condemned as a heretic. After the intervention of a heavenly messenger, Virgil and Dante gain entrance to the city of Dis and find themselves in the vast cemetery of the heretics, on level ground between the upper and lower slopes of Hell. Here the sinners await the last judgment in tombs that are ajar, perhaps to identify the more notorious of their number, or to make room for more to come. As they enter, the travelers for the first time, and for no apparent reason, turn to the right, rather than to the left, wending their way along the inner wall of the city, encountering the glowing sepulchres of Farinata and of the elder Cavalcanti. They then turn to the left, resuming their original course toward the center of Hell. As the pilgrim and Virgil make their way in darkness among the fiery sepulchers, Cavalcante, condemned as a heretic, rises up on his knees from his tomb looking for his son, then tearfully asks why Guido is not accompanying the pilgrim. When the pilgrim answers in the past tense, the old man mistakenly takes this to mean that his son is dead and, collapsing with grief, he falls back into the tomb:

> . . . "Se per questo cieco
> carcere vai per altezza d'ingegno,
> mio figlio ov'è? perché non è teco?"
> E io a lui: "Da me stesso non vegno:
> colui ch'attende là, per qui mi mena,
> forse cui Guido vostro ebbe a disdegno."
> Le sue parole e 'l modo della pena
> m'avean di costui già letto il nome;
> però fu la risposta così piena.
> Di subito drizzato gridò: "Come
> dicesti 'elli ebbe?' Non viv'elli ancora?
> non fiere li occhi suoi il dolce lome?"
> Quando s'accorse d'alcuna dimora
> ch'io facea dinanzi alla risposta,
> supin ricadde e più non parve fora.

*Inf.* 10.58–72

"If you go through this blind prison by reason of high genius, where is my son, and why is he not with you?" And I to him, "I come not of myself. He who waits yonder, whom perhaps your Guido had in disdain, is leading me through here." Already his words and the manner of his punishment had read his name to me: hence was my answer so full. Suddenly straightening up, he cried, "How? Did you say 'he had'? Does he not still live? Does the sweet light not strike his eyes?" And when he perceived that I made some delay in answering, he fell supine again and showed himself no more.

The pilgrim's piercing remark, "forse cui Guido vostro ebbe a disdegno," has been so scrutinized and debated by philologists in the history of the poem that the meaning of every word of it has been disputed, except for Guido's name. Because in the fiction Guido is supposed to be still alive, able to change his ways, the mention of his name to his father in so ominous a context suggests that the allusion, whatever it means, is in some sense an admonition, intended for a sinner. The pilgrim seems to intimate that Guido risks the condemnation his father has already incurred. In fact, because Guido had been dead for almost a decade when Dante wrote these verses, the pilgrim's reproof or warning is the poet's final sentence, passed posthumously on his former friend. The episode takes the form of a subtle and learned morality play, intended for Guido. For the poet, however, and for us, the problematic verse is an epitaph, like those inscribed on the sepulchers of the heretics, whose names make their cameo appearance in the drama, but who, like Guido, have no role to play. Far from the trivial matter that some critics have taken it to be, Guido's "disdain" represents the abyss that divided the two friends.

## Parabasis

We owe to Gramsci the characterization of this episode as a play, with minimal narration, apart from the setting and "stage directions."[2] His meditations on the canto marked a turning point in the history of its interpretation. On one hand, he disputed Croce's distinction between "poesia" and "struttura," insisting that every detail of the structure was intrinsic to the poetry. On the other hand, he asserted that the heroic figure of Farinata was not the dominant element in the representation. The Ghibelline captain had become something of a political icon in the Risorgimento, so much so that canto 10 was referred to by De Sanctis as "il Canto di Farinata," a designation that thereafter became standard in scholastic texts. It took the critical acumen of Gramsci, notwithstanding his political passion, to recognize that Cavalcante, and not Farinata, was central to Dante's concern. The old man was not merely a cowering contrast to the imposing figure of Farinata, but a tragic figure, unique in *Inferno*, portraying in action, if not in words, the very moment in which he was overcome by his grief.

The drama that Gramsci had in mind in his reading of canto 10 is tragedy, ancient as well as Shakespearean, both of which he had studied intensely. Frank Rosengarten's exhaustive essay on Gramsci's reading of canto 10 not only analyzes all of Gramsci's writing on tragedy, including reviews, but also the prisoner's uncertain memories of tragic themes depicted in the frescoes of Pompeii.[3] Rosengarten underscores the terrible parallel between the suffering of Cavalcante in his "cieco carcere" and the situation of Gramsci, languishing in a Fascist prison, gradually losing his sight, but not his political faith. The technical vocabulary Gramsci used to describe the "catastrophe" at the end of *Hamlet*, or the "catharsis" at the end of canto 10, do not mask their applicability to his own lived experience.

Gramsci established that Cavalcante's desperate and devastating questions are central to the structure of canto 10. To extend and confirm his analysis, we might add that they are quite literally central, verses 67–69 of 136 verses: ". . . Come / dicesti 'elli ebbe?' Non viv' elli ancora? / non fiere li occhi suoi il dolce lome?" They correspond to the turning point of the tragedy. In the interstices of those tormented questions, the interim between the hesitation of the pilgrim and the despair of the old man, lies the unspoken crux, the *nodus* of the entire drama. After the collapse' of Cavalcante, the pilgrim entreats Farinata: "solvetemi quel nodo / che qui ha 'n viluppata mia sentenza" (I prayed him, "solve the knot which here entangled my judgment") (95–6). Farinata's response is not the inappropriate "doctrinal" speech that Croce imagined it to be, but is, on the contrary, the poetically necessary *catastrophe*, wherein the pilgrim is enlightened and, in turn, asks Farinata to tell his neighbor that Guido is still alive. By an uncanny coincidence, the phrase "solvetemi quel nodo" corresponds exactly to the word used three hundred years later, and used ever since, to render the technical word "*catastrophe*": the untying of the knot, or *dénouement*.[4]

The silence of Gramsci on this verse, as well as that of De Sanctis and Croce before him and of Auerbach after, left the field open to academic philologists, who set about disputing among themselves the meaning and placement of every single word of those verses, except for the presence of Virgil ("colui ch'attende là") and the name of Guido. Not surprisingly, they have reached no consensus, because they have concentrated on linguistic details, ignoring Gramsci's insight about the dramatic nature of the episode. In classical or Renaissance tragedy, the import of a text does not correspond to what the characters think they are saying, but rather to what the playwright means to imply, between the lines. Critics refer to this as "tragic irony." We associate such subtlety with Sophocles, Euripides or Shakespeare, but do not expect to find it in a culture, like that of the Middle Ages, in which tragedy had supposedly been supplanted by divine providence. Yet all of Dante's encounters in *Inferno* (as distinct from *Purgatorio* and *Paradiso*) are as tinged with irony as any tragedy, since the perspective of the damned, like the perspective of all tragic protagonists, clashes dramatically with the ideological framework from which they have been banished.

Nevertheless, this resolution of the drama leaves one of Cavalcante's three questions unanswered: "Come dicesti 'elli ebbe'?" The pilgrim has no time to disabuse the old man and the poet has no desire to explain to us that verse with its troublesome tense at the very center of the canto. Even Gramsci, overwhelmed with empathy for the old man and, doubtless, with unspoken grief for his own situation, was more concerned with the poignancy of the moment than with grammatical subtleties and so passed over in silence the question that should occur to a dispassionate reader: If Guido is not in fact dead, what did the pilgrim mean to imply by his sibylline remark, ". . . da me stesso non vegno: / colui ch'attende là per qui mi mena / *forse cui Guido vostro ebbe a disdegno?*" (61–3). The tragic but mistaken inference of the old man is crystal clear. To speak of a continual, repeated, or habitual attitude would ordinarily call for a present or an imperfect tense. The use of a simple past, however, what we would call a past perfect, would imply no connection at all to the present; that is, it would imply that the subject of such an attitude were dead. The unanswered question is, what else can the pilgrim have meant by the past absolute "ebbe"? The flaw in Gramsci's brilliant reading of canto 10 is that he does not explain what the pilgrim meant to say when he referred to the "disdegno" of Guido.

The confusion among the philologists can be dissipated only by bearing constantly in mind what should be most obvious: The exchange between the old man and the pilgrim is not a conversation but a *contretemps* in the most literal sense. The pilgrim does not as yet know that the damned do not know the present and the damned do not know that he does not know. Their mutual ignorance inevitably leads to an impasse. The significance of the exchange between the pilgrim and his interlocutors cannot be determined by the word-for-word analysis of the philologist, for that would produce no more than the transcript of a dialogue of the deaf. A glance at the voluminous bibliography of philological studies of this crux will confirm that their interpretations simply trope the difficulty they set out to resolve. The significance of the episode can be established only by what some psychologists call a "transactional analysis," a reconstruction of the conflicting viewpoints of the participants in order to contrast them with the viewpoint of the author, the default "reality" of this or any other narration.[5]

Canto 10 is for several reasons an anomaly in *Inferno*. For one thing, it begins with what is a *digression* in the literal, etymological sense: We are told pointedly that the travelers turn to the right to enter this "secreto calle," rather than to the left, as they have up to this point in their journey: "O virtù somma, che per li empi giri / mi volvi . . . com' a te piace" (O supreme virtue . . . who lead me round as you will) (*Inf.* 10.4–5). The burning sepulchers they come upon occupy a marginal position, like the tombs of an ancient city, within the portals of the city of Dis, but separated by rocky landslides from the souls of the damned below. The canto is furthermore conceptually anomalous because the sin punished here, heresy, unlike the other sins in Hell, was unrecognized in antiquity and is passed over in silence by Virgil in his infernal survey, to which the next canto is largely dedicated. He reviews all the sins they have seen and those they have yet to see, yet makes no mention of where they *are*, except to describe it as a stop along their way—the only such pause on the journey—to accustom them to the stench of lower Hell. The circle is, in this sense, the vestibule of the city of Dis and therefore, like the vestibule of Hell proper, within the gates, but outside the philosophical system. Just as it would be absurd to say that the "ignavi" are less culpable than Francesca and Paolo because they are higher up, so it would be impossible to say that the heretics are more culpable than Filippo Argenti because they are lower down. They cannot be classified, because their sin is neither appetitive nor malicious. Unlike all other sins, which reside in the will, heresy resides in the intellect, *sicut in subiecto*.[6]

In theory, there should be no place in Hell for heresy because Dante's infernal classifications are based largely on Aristotle and Cicero, for whom the idea of heresy would have been incomprehensible. Heresy cannot be classified with ancient ideas of morality because it has to do with faith, an alien theological element in Dante's entirely philosophical categories. Only a believer would recognize it as a sin, but Dante's *Inferno* is meant to be an ecumenical Hell. Like the landscape, heresy is marginal and undefined, from the "Epicurean" denial of the immortality of the soul, to the denial of Christ's divinity. It has in common with all other sins in Hell that it is an aversion of the will from God, but it is unique, inasmuch as it is an attack against the True rather than the Good. The underlying pride it evinces is the choice to adhere to one's own truth, rather than to the truth of faith. For this reason, Aquinas classified it as a sin residing primarily in the intellect, although its root cause is pride, the source of all sin, beginning with Lucifer's fall (*Summa Theologica* 2.2, q.10, q.11). The ancients could not have imagined a *sin* of the speculative intellect, as opposed to an error, any more than they could have imagined a privileged truth, like that of faith. When Thomas says that heresy is opposed to the truth of faith, he points out that this is not like opposing the truth of geometry. Considering that heretics were sometimes consigned to fire in the real world, this is tremendous understatement.

Like all of the punishments in Hell, the glowing sepulchers represent the *contrappasso* with ghastly wit. Heresy, like hellfire in the sepulchers, produces much heat and little light. The fact that the sin was considered to reside in the intellect is particularly important in a context that includes the presence of Guido's name. The first tombs that the travelers reach are reserved for the "Epicureans," who "l'anima col corpo morta fanno" (make the soul die with the body) (*Inf.* 10.15). Given that definition, the "seguaci" of Epicurus in Dante's day would count in their ranks the Averroists and radical Aristotelians, who denied personal immortality by maintaining the separateness of the possible intellect from the body. Guido was conspicuously among them.[7]

Canto 10 is anomalous, but it is exquisitely structured, reminiscent of a Shakespearean play within a play. It may be thought of as an interlude in the descent, a *parabasis* in the course of the *catabasis*, in which we might expect to find the irony inherent in all such self-reflexive digressions. What is unexpected, however, is its extraordinary symmetry. I have said that the exact center of the canto is the climax or turning point and that the conclusion is the *denouement*. In terms of the movement of the characters, in spite of their confinement, what is striking is the sharp contrast between the rising up of Farinata to begin the action (the unforgettable "da la cintola in su . . . s'ergea" [from his waist upwards . . . he rose] in lines 33–5) and the total collapse of the old man to end it. The episode thus consists of five *actions*, which happen to correspond to the traditional five acts of tragedy: exposition, rising, climax, fall, and *denouement*.

The words I have used to describe the moments of the episode are anachronistic and therefore entirely irrelevant to Dante's composition, except as an empirical description in modern terms of what happens in the canto. The terms may not be irrelevant for Gramsci. A generation before Gramsci, a German theorist, Gustav Freytag, in a book called *The Technique of the Drama*, a compendium of the many theories of tragedy circulating in the nineteenth century from Aristotle to his own times, used these words, which were then adapted into a schema for drama that is still popular today, known as "Freytag's pyramid."[8] Between the linear approach of the exposition and the linear departure of the conclusion, there arises the "mountain of plot," the rising of what some grammarians called the *protasis* and the descent of the fall, or *catastasis*. At the summit, the apex of the pyramid, is the climax—in this case, the central knot, to which we now return.

## Dialogue at Contretemps

Cavalcante de' Cavalcanti mistakenly infers from the pilgrim's use of the simple past "ebbe" that his son is dead. In Dante's Italian, before the development of the *passato prossimo*, the simple past was used to express any completed action in the past, as it is in Latin. On the other hand, to use a verb in the simple past to describe a durative attitude toward someone or some thing, would normally suggest that the subject of such an attitude is no longer living. Otherwise, the sentence would call for either the present or the imperfect. For confirmation, we need only recall the "disdegno" of Capaneus, who *"ebbe, e par ch'egli abbia / Dio in disdegno"* (*Inf.* 14.69–70). These verses would seem to be a textbook example of how death would interrupt (temporarily, for one who believes in an afterlife!) an otherwise durative *disdegno*. The past absolute marks the discontinuity, the death of Capaneus, exactly as it would in Cavalcante's interpretation of the traveler's remark. When the traveler hesitates before explaining what he meant by his use of the simple past, "ebbe," the old man's worst fears are confirmed and he is forced to conclude that his son is dead. Overcome with grief, he falls back into his tomb.

For centuries, readers and commentators have almost universally understood Guido's "disdain" as does his father, in spite of the fact that we know Guido to be still alive. Writing about these lines in his own "cieco carcere," Gramsci was understandably more concerned with the father's grief than with the poet's subtlety and glossed the obscurity of the text with a powerful analogy.[9] He recalls a passage from Lessing's *Laocoon*, in which the critic explains why Medea is represented in a Pompeian fresco with her face blindfolded at the moment when she kills her children. Had the artist attempted to represent her grimace of horror and her pain, says Lessing, he would have rendered her as simply grotesque. So, Gramsci argued, the moment pain is inadvertently inflicted upon Cavalcante, he disappears, his unspeakable pain veiled in silence.

If Dante's text is covered like the face of Medea, as Gramsci suggests, it is because it is shrouded in complexity. When detectives, anthropologists, or psychiatrists receive from their subjects intricate answers to simple questions, they suspect a cover-up of obvious but unsettling truths. So here, we are led to wonder whether the tangled exchange between Cavalcante and the pilgrim might not serve to mask a simple but highly charged question: Is Guido damned? Dante may have been conflicted about the choice between the temerity of accusing his former "first friend" and the timidity of silence and so chose innuendo, in a verse subtle enough to pass for a crux through centuries of interpretation, but in fact a seismic fault line. The intricate structure and the vast human panorama of the *Commedia* usually obscure the subjectivity of the poet, hidden behind the impermeable wall of *terza rima*. In the poem, Dante is an authorial institution, never the elusive "consciousness" that we have come to expect in modern literature. Perhaps this once, however, a fissure makes it possible to catch a glimpse of Dante's very human and not particularly Christian subjectivity, closer here to the surface than elsewhere in his text. We shall see that, without doubt, Dante intimates Guido's damnation.

The encounters of canto 10 are like dialogues of the deaf, in which the characters recite lines calculated by the poet to be deliberately, not to say insidiously, ambiguous. A univocal philological reading of each of those lines can only reproduce the impasse into which the characters themselves have fallen and so it has been in the history of the interpretation of this passage. The interpreters have through the centuries "troped" the difficulty they set out to resolve. To the old man, the words of the pilgrim are unimportant, except for the crucial information he thinks they provide about his son. For the pilgrim, the words could not be more important because, as we shall see, they imply Guido's rejection of Christianity. As heresy suggests (to a Christian intellectual) incoherence, critics were content to accept confusion among the participants in the drama as an emblem of their sin. On the contrary, however, the exchange between the pilgrim and Cavalcante is far from muddled. It is, in fact, a lucid and dispassionate *representation* of utter confusion. Just as the representation of the madness of Ophelia or of Orlando required the consummate skill of their respective authors, so this representation of linguistic impasse demanded of the poet an astonishing control of grammatical subtleties. To understand the passage we must follow the logic, not of the characters, the old man and the pilgrim, but of their creator.

The first words of Cavalcante's interruption, referring to a descent to the underworld by "altezza d'ingegno," identify both Guido and Dante as philosophers and poets. The sentence has often been misread, as though Cavalcante were simply an achievement-oriented parent, complaining that his son is not being equally honored with the prize of a free trip to Hell. In Dante's day, "ingegno" (Latin *ingenium*) meant "natural endowment," usually contrasted with "arte," meaning the mastery of a discipline. It is a faculty, not an achievement, as is obvious when Dante recalls the punishment of Ulysses and vows to rein in his "ingegno," lest it run unguided by virtue. Winthrop Wetherbee has shown that *ingenium* was often associated with the faculty of the imagination, particularly of poets, but it admitted of all degrees.[10] Apuleius's summary of Plato states that *ingenium* is a faculty "neither wholly good nor wholly bad, but readily tending in either direction." "Altezza" is comparative, meaning "high," the "ingegno" of a poet or a sage, rather than the "ingenium infimum" of a sensualist. So the first words of Guido's father suggest no more than that Guido is a philosophical poet, as is Dante. What they do not say is why Guido's father would expect to see him in Hell.

The answer lies in an unspoken but easily inferred premise of Cavalcante's question. He must assume that the pilgrim's journey is like the *descensus ad inferos* of the mythographic tradition, an allegory for the search for secular wisdom, of which Orpheus's descent was the prototype. Cavalcante cannot know anything about the theological meaning of Hell—he would be less likely to be there if he did—nor, if he had known anything about it, would he have wished his son to come share his fate. He would have known, however, about Aeneas's descent and his meeting with his father in the underworld. On those grounds alone, he might have hoped to see his son. If "alto ingegno" were enough to allow for such a descent, as tradition held that it was, not only for Aeneas, but also for Orpheus, Hercules, Theseus, and Ulysses—pagans all—and if now he sees the pilgrim before him, then his expectation is justified. According to medieval allegorical commentaries on the *Aeneid*, Aeneas's descent into the underworld to meet with his father represents the attainment of philosophical wisdom.

According to Bernardus Silvestris's twelfth-century commentary on the *Aeneid*, which Dante may have known, the *descensus ad inferos* may be allegorically understood in four different ways: the descent of the soul to the body at birth, the descent to things of the flesh, the descent by virtue of necromancy, and, finally, the descent of the virtuous man to learn of the things of this world in order to transcend them and acquire wisdom.[11] Orpheus and Eurydice exemplify two of the types of descent. Orpheus, with his wisdom and eloquence, is the virtuous man who returns after his experience of earthly things, while Eurydice, who also descends, remains enmeshed in *temporalia* and so cannot return. Cavalcante assumes the descent to be a secular intellectual adventure, in which his son, famous as an eloquent "natural philosopher" and poet in the tradition of Orpheus, might equally well participate. He is disabused by the pilgrim's answer, which is that he is being led by one, who (the reader knows) is heaven-sent.

The pilgrim's response, "da me stesso non vegno," alludes to the relay of grace recounted by Beatrice in the second canto of the poem, from Mary and Lucy through her to Virgil. By itself, this is not an obvious answer to Cavalcante's question. It is, however, a denial of the old man's assumption that this is a philosophical journey and so is an indirect explanation for Guido's absence. According to a long tradition going back at least to Plotinus, the journey of the sage to ultimate truth is to be accomplished on one's own.[12] "You have no need of a guide," Plotinus says in the first *Ennead* (1.6.9). Plotinus's sanguine advice is tested and rejected by Augustine in the seventh book of *Confessions*, the background text for understanding Dante's prologue scene. The pilgrim's answer amounts to an assertion that his journey is of a theological order, a "descent in humility," Singleton would say, the "altro viaggio" indicated by Virgil in the prologue as the only alternative to philosophical presumption.[13] It has for its goal the summit of happiness, which can be glimpsed from afar, but not reached by a "corto andare."

The phrase that follows this first misunderstanding between the pilgrim and Cavalcante is so involuted that philologists have strained Italian syntax to the limit in an effort to understand it. It is incoherent, not only because the interlocutors do not share the same premises, but because they do not share the same temporality, on which verbal communication depends. At the end of canto 10 we learn from Farinata that the damned have no knowledge of the present in the world above, although they remember the past and have a dim perception of the future. Their ignorance of the present torments them, so they besiege the pilgrim for news, which is invariably somber. In return, they repay him with dark oracles concerning his own future. These elements of the fiction generate a spectacular confusion, first with Farinata, the Ghibelline captain, who knows nothing about the recent definitive defeat of his party, then with Cavalcante, stricken with grief when he wrongly infers from what the pilgrim tells him that his son is dead. These conversations at cross-purpose are driven by ignorance. Mutual incomprehension leads them finally to silence, with Farinata momentarily stunned, Cavalcante overwhelmed, and the pilgrim bewildered, until he learns that although these souls have a shadowy vision of the future, they are blind to what is happening now.

## Time and Aeviternity

The cognition of the damned is essential to a full understanding of our crux. In the interim between their death and the extinction of their consciousness at the end of time, the souls of the damned can see the distant future as if at dusk, when a glimmer of sunset is left to them: "Noi veggiam, come quei ch'a mala luce, / le cose" disse, "che ne son lontano; / cotanto ancor ne splende il sommo duce" ("Like the one who has bad light, we see the things," he said, "which are remote from us: so much does the Supreme Ruler still shine on us") (*Inf.* 10.100–2). In Pauline terms (I Thess. 5:5), we may say that although they have lost the day, they have not yet been entirely consigned to the night. Their twilight understanding is reminiscent of the *cognitio vespertina* ascribed by Augustine to the angels, before the light was separated from the darkness (*De civitate Dei* 9.7; *De Genesi ad litteram* 4.22). He read into the "fiat lux" of the first chapter of Genesis all of angelic history. The angels were created with a twilight understanding. Those that turned to the light became eternal day, the others turned away and "facti sunt nox." The damnation of souls would seem to recapitulate in time the damnation of the angels, which took place in a few instants after their creation, but before time began. Not until time ends, however, will night fall definitively on the souls in Hell.

In contrast, the cognition of the blessed is an eternal present. In the episode of Cacciaguida in *Paradiso* we learn that they see all contingent things in the "now" of God: "mirando il punto / a cui tutti li tempi son presenti" (gazing upon the Point to which all times are present) (17.17–18). God is like the center of a circle, seeing all things, while the souls of the blessed see all things through him, by participation. The metaphor of God as a point in space/time was widely diffused in Neoplatonic circles and received authoritative status in Boethius's *Consolation of Philosophy*, which described God as *totum simul*. Aquinas's analysis of God's eternity in the *Summa Theologica* relies on Boethius and the *Liber de causis* and may have been Dante's source (1, q. 10). The problem that so occupied Augustine in the *Confessions*, however, was to understand what we mean by "the present," a task in which philosophers, scientists, and linguists are still engaged. The eleventh book of the *Confessions* is the first and probably most famous work on the phenomenology of time. Augustine observes that the past is no longer, the future is not yet, and the present is the dimensionless place where they meet. Only the present in fact exists, but it cannot be localized. We might say that it is the "interface" between two non-existing things, yet our identity, our continuity in time, depends upon its paradoxical reality.

The problem is apparently solved theologically or mystically by an appeal to the Archimedean "punto a cui tutti li tempi son presenti," which bestows its reality on the otherwise ephemeral categories of past, present and future. It is not so readily solved otherwise. Aristotle had defined time in the *Physics* (4.11.219b2–3) as "succession of movement [of the heavens] according to before and after," a definition that Dante quotes in the *Convivio* (4.2.6) and to which he alludes in *Paradiso*. That will not do for a description of earthly time, for several reasons. For one, it makes a beginning or end of time unthinkable because there cannot be a moment before the first nor after the last. In fact, Aristotle thought of the world as eternal. Further, it makes no distinction between "now" as the flowing present and "now" as punctual, a moment in time. This is to ignore the difference between "static" time, a cosmic succession of uniform instants, and human time, a dynamic coming-to-be and passing away.

According to Philip Turetzky, it was Iamblichus, a Neoplatonist of the end of the third century, who proposed a theory of two different kinds of time: the first, a higher time, in which past present and future have equal reality and are arranged sequentially according to "before" and "after" (see Figure 5).[14] This is the time of Being. The other, the time in which we live, is a constant flow in which the past no longer exists and the future does not yet exist. The present, in this lower kind of time,

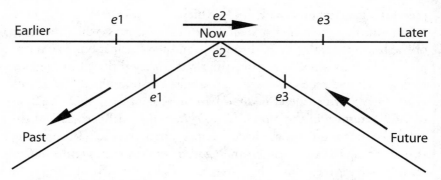

Figure 5. The intersection of present, past, and future according to pseudo-Archytas, from Philip Turetzky, *Time* (London: Routledge, 1998), 53.

must participate in higher time in order to achieve ontological reality. This happens when the two times meet at a point of tangency—"now"— in which intelligibility is conferred on our human and ephemeral time and physical reality is bestowed on purely intelligible succession. This is the present, the only time that can be directly perceived.[15]

The extraordinary importance of this theory of time for our inter- pretation is that it helps gloss the temporality of the pilgrim's infernal encounters. Farinata tells us that the souls in Hell know nothing of the present state of human affairs unless news is brought to them by others. We think of this as the poet's clever narratological device for providing dramatic tension, but the theory of the dual nature of time provides theoretical justification for this mode of cognition. The damned exist in a torpid state and spring to life to speak with the pilgrim, after which, like Ciacco, they wake no more until the resur- rection ("Più non si desta . . . ," *Inf.* 6.94). The present they know and that we read is only granted to them by the presence of the pilgrim, who brings them to "life" momentarily, when their static existence intersects his human time. This present vivifies shadowy omniscience and creates the "now" of every encounter of the pilgrim with the souls in Hell. It also provides a philosophical rationale for the mythology of descent in the epic tradition. The drink offered by Odysseus in Book 11 of the *Odyssey*, the potion that allows communication with the dead, brings them to life. It is the opposite of the waters of Lethe because it gives back to isolated instants of static memory the flow of time.

The poem does not provide enough information about the two-fold nature of time for us to trace its origin, but we can speculate about the genesis of the idea in terms familiar to the scholastics of the thirteenth century. Between the time that we know and the eternity of God was the time referred to as "aevum," the time of the angels and of spiritual substances. Time has a beginning and an end, eternity has neither, but between them is "aeviternity," a time with a beginning and no end. It is the time of the angels and the separated souls, who were created, but are immortal. It is very much like the time of the souls in Paradise, who see all contingent things in the light of eternity, although they are not themselves eternal. We might say that the "aevum" of the angels is like Iamblichus's time of being, a sequence of before and after times, omnipresent, but inferior to eternity, which is beyond time and beyond succession. The cognition of the damned is like the negative image of aeviternity, a twilight understanding of contingent things, which comes to life, momentarily, with the arrival of the pilgrim.

The bewildering misunderstandings that characterize the encounters in the circle of heresy derive from the fact that only the pilgrim is endowed with knowledge of the present. Unlike the pilgrim, who, like us, moves ahead, the souls must wait for future events to come toward them: "Quando [le cose] s'appressano, o son, tutto è vano / nostro intelletto . . ." (When they draw near, or are, our intelligence is wholly vain) (*Inf.* 10.103–4). When he first meets the souls of the heretics, the pilgrim has reason to believe that they are omniscient. In canto 6, Ciacco recognized him on the basis of their past acquaintance and also made veiled prophecies. He also said that there are two just men in the city ("giusti son due," 6.73), which might have been taken as contemporary knowledge, but is in fact a continuous condition of unspecified temporality, rather than an event. So, when Farinata learns that Dante's family were Guelfs and therefore his enemies, he boasts that he twice drove them out of the city, unaware of the fact that his party was by then totally defeated and in turn driven out, never to return. The pilgrim can scarcely believe that the Ghibelline captain would boast of past victory in the face of actual and definitive defeat and so answers with sarcasm: My party knew how to return, which your party never learned.

It is in the stunned silence of Farinata that the exchange between Cavalcante and the traveler takes place. Cavalcante wishes to know why his son is not there and interprets the word "ebbe" to mean his son is dead. This time it is the turn of the pilgrim to be stunned into silence. He delays his reply so long that the old man, taking the silence to be confirmation of his own fear, collapses into the tomb. I will now ana-lyze the pilgrim's confusion in order to understand what he was saying when his words were misconstrued.

In the conditional sentence that begins Cavalcante's interjection, we have seen that the old man takes the protasis, the "if" clause, for granted. The words "se per altezza d'ingegno" are concessive and might well be translated "*given* that you descend . . . ," for he knows about the descent of Aeneas in search of wisdom, the allegorical objective of the search for the father. He presumes that his son will be following in Aeneas's footsteps, hence the question of the apodosis: "*where* is my son?" The response of the pilgrim reverses the priorities of the old man's question. It takes for granted that Guido is alive and therefore takes the question of his whereabouts as purely incidental. He instead disputes the protasis, which must be corrected: "Da me stesso non vegno," which is to say that this is not the *descensus ad inferos* of the mythographic tradition, of a hero on his own, but is rather the descent in humility, like Christ's descent into Hell, the first stage of a journey guided by grace. Once it has been established that the descent is providential and not a function of "ingegno," then the question would seem to answer itself. It amounts to saying that this is a journey of faith, not philoso-phy. Guido's future presence or absence here should be left to him and the Divine Will.

The poet's task at this point was to construct a grammatically cor-rect response to a question whose import the pilgrim did not as yet grasp, while guaranteeing that the old man would mistakenly interpret the response as the answer to the question he *did* have in mind. In other words, the poet had to create a grammatically correct exchange that would be totally ambiguous and therefore incomprehensible to the interlocutors, yet completely susceptible to logical analysis by the reader. If we reflect on the subject matter, the fate of a once-beloved friend, and the suffering of his father, the poet's detachment seems almost clinical.

When the pilgrim uses the past definite tense ("ebbe a disdegno"), it is not to imply the death of the subject, as the father assumes, but rather to indicate the finality of one of Guido's actions in the past, no matter how long or how recently past. If the subject is alive, as the pil-grim knows him to be, then the verbal form with "ebbe" *must* be interpreted as an isolated event in the past. The language in Dante's time permitted no other choice. A modern grammarian would say that it is a past verb of perfect aspect. If this is so, then we are further compelled to understand "avere a disdegno" as punctual, rather than durative: an action, rather than an attitude. It cannot be "to hold in contempt," but must be rather "to refuse." The tense of the verb is determined not only by time (the past), but also by *aspect*: that is, for example, whether the meaning of the word is punctual or durative. Perhaps the most solemn example of the punctual use of "disdegnare" in a past perfect tense appears in the hymn to the Virgin in the last canto of the poem. The Virgin so ennobled human nature that its Creator "non disdegnò di farsi sua fattura" (*Par.* 33.6). In *Paradiso*, obviously, the Incarnation was the act of the still *living* God.

Giacomo Devoto was among the first philologists in Italy to study verbal aspect in Italian (1950), but grammarians contemporary with Dante, the *modistae*, had already begun to question Aristotle's definition of the verb in his *De interpretatione*: "a verb is that which, in addition to its proper meaning, carries with it the notion of time" (3.16b6).[16] According to Boethius of Dacia, however, time is not the essence of the verb, but is rather "an accidental mode of signification of the verb, temporal *per accidens*: "tempus accidit verbo."[17] In the Florentine of Dante's day, a past of perfect aspect was regularly expressed with a preterit, following Latin usage, what we now call a *passato remoto*, even if it was proximate in time. The *passato prossimo* is a later composite form, like the French *passé composé*.

Charles Singleton called our attention to Cavalcante's immediate response to the pilgrim: "Come *dicesti* 'elli ebbe?'"[18] The past absolute, "dicesti," designates a single completed action that is definitively passed, if only by microseconds. Cavalcante, the first "anti-allegorist," as Singleton dismissively refers to him, was pre-disposed to understand "disdegno" in the imperfect or durative sense, as contempt for "colui ch'attende là," which indicated to him just a man, not a guide, much less the great poet. A habitual state in the past should be indicated by an imperfect, save when the subject of such an attitude is dead, in which case, the past perfect is normative. If, on the other hand, one knows the subject to be alive, then the past perfect is determinative for the meaning of "disdegno." It cannot be durative, but must be punctual. If the pilgrim had had time to formulate an answer to the old man's question, "come dicesti 'elli ebbe?'" he might have answered something like, "I said 'ebbe' exactly as you just said 'dicesti,' and Guido is as alive as I am." It is difficult to believe that the appearance of the verb "dicesti" immediately after the verb "ebbe" is not a deliberate provocation.

As for the difference between durative and punctual aspect of the verb or verbal expression "disdegno," it may be indicated in our text. Antonino Pagliaro first noted that the verbal form used in our passage is unusual: It is "avere *a* disdegno" rather than *in* disdegno, as one might have expected an analogy with Farinata, who held all of *Inferno* "*in* dispitto," or Capaneus, who "ebbe Dio . . . *in* disdegno."[19] Aspect in Slavic languages is clearly marked by morphological differences in the verbs, whereas in European languages, various indicators, such as auxiliaries or prepositions, are used. In our text, from the examples we have seen, the preposition "*in*" in the phrase "ebbe in disdegno" marks a durative state, an attitude toward a person. We infer that "*a* disdegno" must indicate its aspectual opposite: punctual refusal. The sense of "refusal" is conveyed in Petrarch's great *canzone* (*Rime* 23, 6e) with the phrase "a sdegno": "mentre amor nel mio albergo a sdegno s'ebbe . . ." as Dante uses it.

In defense of Cavalcante's misinterpretation of the pilgrim's words, it should be noted that because he has no "present" time of his own, it is impossible for him to distinguish the finality of an action (Guido's refusal) from the finality of its subject (Guido's death). The finality of an action is necessarily measured from the present, as are all indicative tenses. A perfect verb is final with respect to the present, whether completed seconds or centuries ago. Where there is no present, as in the cognition of the damned (or in modern scientific time measurement) there are no tenses, but only events "before" or "after," the dead past or the ominous future. The sly presence of the preterit "dicesti" is the single exception to Cavalcante's defective perception of the tense system, as if placed there by the poet as evidence of how the pilgrim bestows life—that is, the present—on the souls of the damned. It remains to be explained what *action* "disdegno" implies.

## From Convivio *to* Commedia, *from Aristotle to Augustine*

The conflict of the contradictory premises of Cavalcante and of the pilgrim has implications far more extensive than the few verses that dramatize it. For one, the old man stands vicariously for his son, the natural philosopher, haughty and elitist, "altero" according to some of the commentators, "un po' snob," in Contini's memorable characterization. These less than admirable traits are what endeared him to Ezra Pound, centuries later. Maria Luisa Ardizzone shows Guido to have been radically contrarian in his philosophy and in his attitudes toward human love.[20] He was a fervent follower of Aristotle and his commentators, who conceived of an autonomous human nature, independent of its divine vocation, and of philosophy as a comprehensive doctrine of natural knowledge that could lead to the attainment of happiness in this life. His theory of love, in Ardizzone's reading of "Donna me prega," insisted on love's origin in the sensitive soul, as far as can be imagined from the spiritual inspiration for it claimed by Dante.

Dante's Aristotelianism was fervent, but not hostile to theological elaboration. The *Convivio*, the philosophical treatise he abandoned one-third of the way toward its projected length early in his period of exile, marks the transition in his writing from exuberant Aristotelianism to the great Christian synthesis of his poem. The third book is an almost lyrical celebration of the *Donna gentile*, the allegorical representation of a philosophical ideal, which Dante defines as the "amoroso uso di sapienza." So confident is Dante that the lady can help prepare the way for us to ascend to the "celestial Athens"—along with ancient philosophers, including "Epicureans"!—that he denies the existence of any natural desire for the beatific vision, thereby contradicting the opinion of almost all Christian theologians. The *canzone* that introduced Book 3, "Amor, che ne la mente mi ragiona," reappears as the song of Casella in *Purgatorio*, unceremoniously interrupted by Cato, to the embarrassment of both the pilgrim and his guide.[21] So in the *Convivio*, after an interruption of two years or so, Dante begins the fourth book with a change of subject, style, and tone because he perceives an unaccustomed hardness in his lady. Her change of mood was a harbinger of crisis in the poet's philosophical quest for happiness.

In the *Commedia*, we find the *Convivio*'s philosophical quest for knowledge, epitomized by Ulysses's "mad flight" and shipwreck, domesticated by the poet's Christian faith. The ancients who might have aspired to dwell in the celestial Athens find themselves instead on a greensward in a lugubrious Limbo, comforted not by the sun, as in Virgil's Elysium, but by artificial illumination. There they live in eternal yearning, without hope ("sanza speme vivemo in disio," *Inf.* 4.42). This malaise of the greatest of pagan philosophers was noted by Aquinas, who otherwise strained in every way to reconcile Aristotle and the faith (*Summa contra gentiles* 3.48).[22] In a moving passage of the *Summa contra gentiles*, he expresses sympathy for the *praeclara ingenia* of Aristotle and two of his commentators, Alexander of Aphrodisias and Averroes, all of whom lived in perpetual *angustia*, notwithstanding how close they may have come to human happiness, because they could not achieve the ultimate knowledge, of God in his essence. Between the *Convivio* and the *Commedia*, Dante discovered that the philosophical quest for happiness could approach its goal asymptotically, but never reach it without grace.

The God of Christians is hidden to them in this life and can be known only through the Son.[23] In the Acts of the Apostles (17:23), Paul, addressing precisely the Athenians, acknowledges their proverbial interest in everything religious, but singles out one of their altars dedicated to an unknown god, *deus absconditus*, whom he identifies with Jesus: "What you worship but do not know—this is what I now proclaim." However, the highest authority on the inability of human wisdom to know God are the words of Jesus, thought to be older than the Gospel in which they are contained:

> I thank Thee, Father, Lord of heaven and earth, for hiding these things
> from the learned and wise, and revealing them to the simple. No one
> knows the Son but the Father, and no one knows the Father but the
> Son and those to whom the Son may choose to reveal Him. Come to
> me, all whose work is hard, whose load is heavy, and I will give you
> relief. Bend your necks to my yoke and learn from me, for
> I am meek and humble of heart and your souls will find relief.
>
> Matthew 11:25–30

This exhortation to the humble is the key text for contrasting the presumption of the philosopher with the humility necessary for salvation.

Much of the subsequent history of Christian thought has been concerned with resolving this apparent contradiction: We learn from philosophy that God exists, as the final cause of all things, and that therefore all who desire to know, desire to know Him. Yet Scripture insists that God can be known in His essence only through a gift of grace. It follows that the desire to know God is natural, but that the satisfaction of that desire is beyond our power. This paradox is at the heart of the mystery of the supernatural, the goal of which is to go beyond the human ("trasumanare," *Par.* 1.70).[24] The mystery is prominently alluded to in the opening verses of canto 21 of *Purgatorio*, not fortuitously the canto of a poet's conversion: "La sete natural che mai non sazia / se non con l'acqua onde la femminetta / sammaritana dimandò la grazia" (The natural thirst which is never quenched, save with the water whereof the poor Samaritan woman asked the grace) (1–3), and it begins and ends the story of Augustine's conversion, with the metaphor of the unquiet heart: "you made us for yourself and our hearts are unquiet until they rest in you."

Allusions to Augustine abound in the *Commedia*, but they are not to be read as Dante's choice of one philosophical or theological school over others, as though Augustine were an authority in the same way as were Albertus, or Aquinas, or Bonaventure. He was the universal authority on the mystery of the supernatural and was recognized as such by the Church, by all of those theologians and by many more besides, to the present day. When the issue of philosophical pride arises in the poem, there are often recalls to his text. So, for example, the prologue scene of *Inferno* dramatizes the difference between a purely philosophical aspiration to the truth and the need for spiritual help to reach it. It bears a striking resemblance to texts in the seventh and eighth books of the *Confessions*, including the "piè fermo," echoing the "semi-saucium" will of the conversion scene. The episode of the "corda" to summon Geryon is unintelligible without reference to Jesus's dismissal of Peter at the end of the Gospel of John: "when you were young you fastened your girdle about you and walked wherever you chose, but when you are old . . . another will bind you and take you where you have no will to go" (21:18). In his commentary on this passage, Augustine identifies the girdle of youth as presumption, to be replaced in midlife by humility, represented in *Purgatorio* as the "umile pianta" (*In Johannis evangelium tractatus* 123; *Purg.* 1.35). A final example is the voyage of Ulysses, clearly the emblem of philosophical presumption, which Giorgio Padoan first suggested had as its source the prologue of Augustine's *De beata vita*.[25] That text recounts the principle elements of Augustine's spiritual odyssey not as a realistic account, but rather in terms of a sea voyage, complete with sirens and shipwreck. We should not be surprised that the disdain of Guido has as its context Book 7 of the *Confessions*, where it describes philosophical presumption.

Books 7 and 8 relate two climactic events in Augustine's life. In Book 7, Augustine discovers the books of the Platonists and in 8, reading Paul, he experiences a conversion under a fig tree in a garden of

Milan. The first event is sometimes referred to as his "conversion" to philosophy and the second his definitive conversion to Christianity. Toward the end of Book 7, he struggles to attain the truth on his own, as Plotinus had suggested, but although he catches a glimpse of the light, he is beaten back by it and *hears* the words of the light refusing his attempt to advance toward it. Dante may have had the passage in mind in the first canto, with a glance at the sun and the subsequent plunge into darkness, expressed with the same striking synesthesia ("là dove 'l sol tace," *Inf.* 1.60). To his amazement (and ours!), Augustine claims to have found in the Platonists passages that seem to coincide with the doctrine of the Word enunciated in the Prologue to the Gospel of John in all its particulars, except for one: "But that the Word was made flesh and dwelt among us I did not read." He contrasts the "puffed-up pride" of the philosophers with the humility of Jesus who assumed human flesh and asked us to emulate him. Four times he cites the saying of Jesus in Matthew 11:25–9 and concludes that the humility of the Incarnation is the difference between presumption and confession, between the truth sought by the philosophers and the truth found only in faith. At the very end of Book 7, he paraphrases Matthew 11:25–8, interpolating a single phrase that no attentive reader will forget:

> No one [in the Platonist books] hears him who calls "Come to me, you who labor (Matt. 11:28)." *They disdain to learn from him,* for "he is meek and humble of heart" "For you have concealed these things from the wise and prudent and have revealed them to babes (Matt. 11:25)."
>
> *Conf.* 8.21

The phrase "dedignantur ab eo discere, quoniam mitis est et humilis corde" describes the philosophers' refusal to learn from the Gospels. It is the turning point in Augustine's story, marking his rejection of philosophical pride and his embrace of Christianity. It corresponds exactly to the difference in Dante's story between the "philosophism" of Guido, which Dante in some sense shared in the *Convivio,* and the commitment to the supernatural quest of the *Commedia.*[26] It perfectly describes Guido's disdain. Any doubt that Dante took careful note of the interpolation is dispelled by the subsequent words, which end Book 7 and, figuratively speaking, inspire the beginning of Dante's prologue scene: "It is one thing from a wooded mountain top (*de silvestre cacum-*

*ine*) to see the land of peace and not to find the way there when one's path is beset by the lion and the dragon, and quite another to reach it through the way defended by the heavenly emperor."

The grammatical structure of the phrase "forse cui vostro ebbe a disdegno" is analogous in several ways to Augustine's interpolation into Christ's words. "Dedignantur discere" suggests an action, a refusal, rather than a mental state. The name of Christ is not mentioned by Augustine's phrase, out of pious reticence, but the context leaves little doubt who is intended by the ablative of agency, "ab eo." The phrase in the tenth canto also contains a pronoun in an oblique case unspecified by any preposition: "cui." It is, however, ambiguous, as it is understood by Cavalcante as an accusative, a direct object of a verb in the past indicating an emotional attitude toward a person ("colui ch'attende là . . . cui"), which would ordinarily be expressed in the past perfect if the subject of that emotion were dead. On the other hand, for the speaker, who knows Guido to be alive, "cui" is a relative pronoun, intended as an indirect object with a dependent infinitive (comparable to "discere" in Augustine's interpolation), not expressed, but clearly understood by any Christian who has read the Gospel of Matthew: Jesus called to the humble and weak, "Come to me!," and *Guido refused*.

Pagliaro was unaware of Augustine's text and of the relevance of Christ's *vocatio* in Matthew 11, but on syntactic grounds alone offered an analysis of the pilgrim's elliptical response that comes closest to the one I propose.[27] After demonstrating that the doubt expressed by "forse" must refer to the goal of the journey and that the word "cui" in Dante's time had wide semantic latitude, he paraphrased: "costui mi conduce per questi luoghi da chi Guido vostro [stimò cosa spregevole l'andare]." The phrase I have bracketed in Pagliaro's suggested integration of the ellipsis contributes a purely grammatical coherence to the enigmatic verse, but misses its meaning. Without an awareness of the allegorical dimension of Dante's journey and the context from which it is derived, Pagliaro could not have known that Dante was invited to Heaven ("da me stesso non vegno"), as is everyone in the parable of the King's wedding feast in the Gospel of Matthew (22:14), but that Guido *refused* to come. The ellipsis should be integrated as follows: "costui mi conduce per questi luoghi da chi Guido vostro si rifiutò [di venire]."

As Augustine referred to Jesus obliquely, so for the speaker, "cui" must refer obliquely, through a series of mediators, to the goal of all

Christians. Gianfranco Contini objected to the hypothesis of an unexpressed dependent infinitive, in spite of Pagliaro's assertion that it was common practice in the Italian of Dante's day. In fact, the infinitive *venire* would be simply repeating the finite form of the same verb in the main clause: "Da me stesso non *vegno*." When we reflect that the verb "to come" also appears in Jesus's call to the humble and is known to all Christians as the most solemn imperative of their faith, the contextual aptness of supplying the verb *venire* to the pilgrim's response is beyond question: "*Venite* ad me omnes qui laboratis et onerati estis et ego reficiam vos." Guido refused the invitation.

Finally, it should be pointed out that Augustine's interpolation also supplies an infinitive for a finite verb in the next sentence of Matthew 11:29: "Tollite iugum meum super vos et *discite* a me, quia mitis sum et humilis corde." Augustine's interpolation described the philosophers' refusal: "Dedignantur ab eo *discere*." One can assume that Dante had before him both the text of Matthew 11:25–9 and that of the *Confessions*. The omission of the infinitive *venire*, although grammatically permissible, was also a sly guarantee of the total ambiguity (especially to non-believers) of the "pregnant" exchange.

There is no doubt that pride, the root of all sin, is an element in all of the sins of *Inferno*, but because the system of Hell is Aristotelian rather than Christian, pride has no explicit place in it, as it does in canto 10 of *Purgatorio*, where the schema is biblical and homiletic. Nevertheless, pride dominates in the drama of *Inferno*. Commentaries make special note of the characterization of Farinata as "magnanimous" in the Aristotelian sense, which is close to what Christians would think of as pride, in spite of attempts by Thomas and the early Dante to subsume it under the virtue of fortitude. The wretchedness of Cavalcante would appear to be its opposite. But when the pilgrim turns to look at Farinata after the disappearance of the Guido's father, he refers to him as "quell'altro magnanimo." In spite of the sleight-of-hand of some editors, who manipulate anachronistic commas to force *magnanimo* into apposition ("quell'altro, magnanimo, a cui posta / restato m'era . . ."), the clear sense is that Cavalcante is "magnanimo," too, not withstanding his plangent tone and submissive posture. Maria Corti suggested that the heretics are "magnanimous" in a pejorative Christian sense, because of their "altitudo cordis," as opposed to Christ, who is "humilis corde."[28] Because pride resembles magnanimity so closely, Aristotle would not have recognized it as a sin, anymore than he would have recognized the sin of heresy. So the circle of heresy may be thought of as the circle of pride, even if does not bear that (or any) label, a "singularlity" in the infernal system. There is a thematic continuity between pride condemned in *Inferno* 10 and pride purged in *Purgatorio* 10. Canto 10 of *Paradiso*, on the other hand, celebrates not only Wisdom, but humility as well, in the light of the *Sol Sapientiae*.

## Friendship

Guido's "disdegno" is a refusal to await proffered grace, the most serious sin of pride, in that it resembles the sin of Lucifer, who "per non aspettar lume, cadde acerbo" (for not waiting on the light he fell unripe) (*Par.* 19.48). In the absence of any other, more obscure or suspect motive for condemning Guido, this would be reason enough. Both Aristotle in the *Ethics* (8) and, more extensively, Cicero, in *De amicitia*, reviewed the circumstances under which even ideal friendships might become compromised. Dante and Guido had their philosophical differences, which have been analyzed by Ardizzone, and of course their poetic differences, exhaustively studied by Contini and Teodolinda Barolini.[29] These would be grounds for estrangement, but scarcely for the threat of damnation. The clash between Dante and Guido was far more fundamental than these intellectual differences, because it involved the faith into which they were born. Ardizzone has suggested that when Boccaccio refers to Guido in the *Decameron* as having had a reputation as a "natural philosopher," he probably means that Guido was an atheist. In Christian terms, this would be the gravest of sins, although incomprehensible to the ancients. To find an analogous schism among former friends in the classical literature of friendship, we would be obliged to turn to Augustine, writing on the cusp between paganism and Christianity.

Just such a falling out is recounted in the fourth book of Augustine's *Confessions*, in a passionate and moving paean to friendship, but the roles are reversed. It is Augustine, the narrator, who is the nonbeliever and his unnamed best friend, who is the recent convert. We can be sure that Dante knew the text, for he follows it closely and even cites it, in canto 22 of *Purgatorio*. The meeting of Statius with Virgil is an idealized pendant piece in the *Commedia* for the stormy relationship of Guido and Dante—it is presumably what Dante thought the relationship of poets ought to be, especially given that it resulted in the conversion of Statius. The meditation on friendship in the *Confessions* is the subtext that relates the two episodes in the poem: the falling out of intimate friends on a question of faith and the subsequent eulogy of true friendship.[30]

I do not believe there is a more moving account in antiquity of bereavement than the pages that follow this passage of the *Confessions*. It has remained a classic in the literature of friendship even in modern times. The occasional circumstances, the end of a friendship in a quarrel concerning the faith, is peculiarly Christian and peculiarly reminiscent of the quarrel between Guido and Dante, but bereavement is significantly absent in Dante's text. On the contrary, unless we are misreading, there is sarcasm in the canto that seems to derive more from poetic rivalry than from fraternal correction.

The sun is the visible manifestation, "il sole sensibile," of the sun of the angels described in *Paradiso* 10.53. In the *Convivio* (3.12.7), Dante had said that nothing in the universe is more worthy than the sun of being a symbol of God. From the prologue scene we are told that it leads men straight by every path, an echo of the Prologue to the Gospel of John, "the true light that illuminates every man that comes into the world." This is the "sommo duce," whose afterglow provides whatever light is left to the souls in Hell (10.102). It is the light for which Lucifer refused to wait and so fell "unripe." All of these are variants of the Platonic dichotomy between the visible and the invisible light, the eye of the body opposed to the eye of the soul. In canto 10, the way out of the "cieco carcere" of Hell is illuminated by the sweet light of Beatrice, "il dolce raggio," whose beautiful eyes see all things in God (130).

Cavalcante's lament for his son is centered on the sweet sensible light that Guido will never see again, the light whose transcendent significance neither ever understood: "non fiere li occhi suoi il dolce lome?" In his essay, Erich Auerbach makes reference to these words at least twice, suggesting that they manifest the suffering of an autonomous individual and are free of all interpretative complexity. In fact, however, the "sweet light" is a *topos* of lamentation. First of all, it echoes Andromache's words when Aeneas comes upon her in the settlement known as "little Troy": "Vivisne? aut si lux alma recessit, Hector ubi est?" (Are you living, or if kindly light has fled, where is Hector?) (*Aen.* 3.311–12). It also echoes a passage from Ecclesiastes, warning against the frivolity of youth: "Surely the light is sweet and it is a delight for the eyes to behold the sun. But if a man live many years and enjoy them all, still let him be mindful of the days of darkness, for they shall be many.

All is vanity" (11:7–8). Most important of all is the recall to Guido's own verses in his father's lament. The most famous of Guido's poems defines love as an obscurity that comes from Mars and is established in the sensitive soul. It is therefore part of the corruptible body:

> In quella parte dove sta memora
>> Prende suo stato, sì formato, *come*
>> diaffan da *lome*, d'una scuritate
> la qual da Marte vène e fa *demora*.
>> Elli è creato ed ha sensato *nome,*
>> d'alma costume e di cor volontate.
>
> *Donna me prega*, 15–20

> Le sue parole e 'l modo della pena
>> m'avean di costui già letto il *nome*;
>> però fu la risposta così piena.
> Di subito drizzato gridò: "*Come?*
>> dicesti 'elli ebbe'? Non viv' elli ancora?
>> non fiere li occhi suoi lo dolce *lome?*"
> Quando s'accorse d'alcuna *dimora*
>> ch'io facëa dinanzi a la risposta,
>> supin ricadde e più non parve fora.
>
> *Inf.* 10.64–72

Barolini has discussed the antithetical theories of love represented by Guido's *canzone* and what we know to have been Dante's transcendent view, so that this echo of the crucial lines from "Donna me prega" in canto 10 must be taken as polemic.[31] The nature of "light" is a major difference between the two poets: for Guido, light compared to a physical influx of planetary influence; for Dante the "dolce raggio" mediated by Beatrice and ultimately of divine origin. The passage from *Inferno* contains the rhyme words, italicized above, of Guido's poem as well as the word "dimora," lest one think the parallel were coincidence. I have kept the original orthography of the crucial word "lome," rather than the corrected form, "lume." Philologists tell us that the "sicilian rhyme" of "lome" was "permissible" as a rhyme with "come" and "nome" in place of the Tuscan form for the word, "lume," and so, following Contini, they correct the spelling to "lume." Such a rhyme may be permissible, but no one ever claimed it was elegant, which is probably why Dante cited it. It is Guido's rhyme, not Dante's. Of all of the rhymes Dante could have chosen to represent the presence of Guido in the text, he chooses one that requires the erudition of philologists to defend its legitimacy. Dante uses "rime siciliane" sparingly in the *Commedia*, usually in pronouns or in verb forms. Here he uses "lome" as an immediately recognizable "Cavalcantism," in a crucial echo of the famous text. He does the same thing in the canto of Ulysses, where he gives Ulysses, surely a Cavalcantian figure, a Cavalcantian word: "fatti non foste a viver come bruti, ma per seguir virtute e *canoscenza*" (you were not made to live as brutes, but to pursue virtue and knowledge) (*Inf.* 26.119–20). Dante does not use the form "canoscenza" elsewhere in the *Commedia*, but Cavalcanti uses it often, most obviously in "Donna me prega." When used with the equally Cavalcantian word "virtute," in a clamorously pre-Christian sense, it also recalls the Orphic quest for secular wisdom in the natural world. The poetic barb is palpable in these echoes, a whiff of parody, the poet quoting a rival poet's "permissible" but anomalous ticks, from a difficult poem-manifesto intended to overthrow spiritualistic and disembodied theories of love, such as Dante's own. Curiously, Petrocchi, in his edition of Dante's text, changes "lome" to "lume," but does not alter "canoscenza" in canto 26, because there is strong manuscript support and because, as a philologist, he says that it doesn't really matter.[32]

The contrast between the sensible sun and the illumination of which it is the symbol has its psychological counterpart in the dialectic of the "eye of the body" opposed to the "eye of the soul." This opposition is of Platonic origin, immeasurably reinforced by the language of Paul regarding blindness and insight. The most familiar elaboration of the Pauline theme was that of Augustine, whose entire epistemology was constructed around the doctrine of illumination. Speaking of the sensible light, he says, "In this our earthly life, the light is a seasoning, tempting and sweet, but dangerous to those whose love for it is blind" (*Conf.* 10.34). On the other hand, just before his disquisition on the nature of time in the eleventh book, he invokes the sweet light of the eyes of his soul: "dulce lumen occultorum oculorum meorum." These two forms of light, the physically tempting "seasoning" and the "dolce raggio" of the soul, correspond more or less to the conflicting theories of the light of love.

### Fathers and Sons

To return once more to Cavalcante, I suggested at the outset that the father, perhaps remembering Aeneas' *descensus ad inferos* looked forward to a meeting in the other world with his son. Such a meeting was obligatory in the epic tradition, beginning with Homer, and was imitated by Dante in his meeting with his ancestor, Cacciaguida, in *Paradiso*. The significance of such meetings is at once historical and personal because they affirm the continuity of a lineage—the succession of military heroes as a figure for the survival of Rome, for example—and establish at the same time a personal identity within that lineage. In the same way, the succession of fathers and sons in the Bible corresponded to the course of history in the Old Testament, with the generations of patriarchs standing for the survival of Israel. The participants in this history, beginning with Abraham, are at once themselves and signs of a meaning to come. In Dante's terms, they are shadow-bearing prefaces of their own truth. We would call them figures in an allegory. In an extraordinary passage, Augustine translates the true inner light of soul into the history of faith:

> The true light is the light which Tobias saw when, though his eyes were blind, he taught his son the path he should follow in life and himself led the way . . . It is the light which Isaac saw when the sight of his eyes was dimmed and clouded with old age . . . and it was granted to him to bless his sons and to know them by blessing them . . . It was the light which Jacob saw when, though his eyes were blinded . . . he foresaw the tribes of Israel in his sons.
>
> *Conf.* 10.34

The dominant emblem of *Inferno* is neither Israel nor Rome, but Thebes, the city of Oedipus and his sons. If the succession of the patriarchs may be thought of as the movement of allegory, then by contrast the irreconcilable clash of generations may be said to dramatize ironic impasse. The time of allegory is the gradual unfolding of meaning in a present that recapitulates the past as it moves into the future. Irony has no time, but is rather the endless alternation of contradictory assertions, with no synthesis possible. The time of impasse, where the past of the father and the future of the son compete for the present, has been referred to by Gianni Vattimo as Oedipal time. It is the time thematized in *Inferno* by a succession of false fathers: Cavalcante, Brunetto, and Ugolino. Cavalcante's fate is perhaps supremely ironic. Having missed a rendezvous with his son, he is now a dead soul at a dead end, where his philosophy always expected him to be.

In the fiction, Guido is still alive, "co' vivi congiunto," but Oderisi tells us in *Purgatorio* that he has yielded the primacy in poetry to another: "Così ha tolto l'uno a l'altro Guido / la gloria de la lingua; e forse è nato / chi l'uno e l'altro caccerà del nido" (So has the one Guido taken from the other the glory of our tongue—and he perchance is born that shall chase the one and the other from the nest) (*Purg.* 11.99). There is little doubt that the character alludes to Dante and that the adverb "forse" is obligatory modesty. Nevertheless, the ironic allusions to "Donna me prega" and the many allusions to Guido's poetry in the Earthly Paradise suggest that although Guido was dead when Dante mentioned him, he was far from forgotten. There might even be a note of uneasiness in the poet's triumph. When we press the matter beyond the confines of the narrative to ask what Dante *really* thought, the text is mute. As Contini and Barolini have suggested, Dante, so dogmatically self-confident in his judgment in matters moral and esthetic, leaves it to the reader and to posterity to decide whether Guido, who himself did not believe in immortality, lives on in his verses.

# The Eternal Image of the Father

T he quest for the father was an obligatory theme in the epic tradition, from Homer to the *Somnium Scipionis*, for it served both to authenticate the hero's (usually noble) lineage and to provide him with an identity and a mission that transcended the purely mortal. In the *Commedia*, Dante's meeting with Cacciaguida is obviously patterned on that epic theme, specifically as it appears in the *Aeneid*, but the way is prepared for the meeting in canto 15 of *Paradiso* by an encounter with a very different father image. In canto 15 of *Inferno*, the pilgrim extols the "cara e buona imagine paterna" (dear, kind, paternal image) of Brunetto Latini (83). The infernal encounter is probably also inspired by a passage in the *Aeneid*, as we shall see, but the portrait of Brunetto that emerges is shaded by an irony that owes nothing to the Virgilian text to which it alludes. Such ironies at Virgil's expense usually reflect the inevitable clash between ancient values and mandatory Christian adjustment: in this instance, the clash between antiquity's conception of paternity and the claim to universality of God the Father.

For Christians, there was no doubt about who was the Father: "Et patrem nolite vocare vobis super terram: unus est enim Pater vester, qui in caelis est" (You must call no one on earth your father, since you have only one Father, and He is in heaven) (Matt. 23:9). Perhaps the most memorable dramatization of the conflict between ancient ideas of paternal authority and the divine command is embodied in the *Confessions* of Augustine, which might be thought of as Augustine's rejection of the "father of the flesh" in search of the true Father, through baptism and the mediation of Monica. The element in Augustine's narrative that is particularly significant for our purposes is that his quest for spiritual authority is of an intellectual rather than a civic or military order. Furthermore, in keeping with the confessional theme, Augustine records the errors in his search, revealing the paradox of providential logic, which retrospectively transforms every apparent deviation into a necessary step toward the truth. One of the surrogate fathers he chooses and ultimately rejects is Faustus the Manichean, a writer of encyclopedias and an astrologer to whom he had looked for the solution of his intellectual problems. Faustus reveals himself to be an ineffectual old man, with an engaging rhetorical gift but little else to offer the young man in his quest. Such disillusionment was to become a topos of confessional literature, the disappointing but ultimately salutary discovery of human flaws in a once-revered authority. In its most modern and comforting variant, the Wizard of Oz proves by his incompetence that one need not go farther than Kansas to find the truth.

The condescension of Augustine toward Faustus is far more tolerant than Dante's condemnation of the encyclopedist who was his contemporary: Brunetto Latini. This is in part due to the fiction of *Inferno*, which purports to describe the state of the souls after death and must therefore express a judgment on all of the figures from Dante's past. In part, however, the virulence of the condemnation and the extent to which the pilgrim is dissociated from it leads us to suppose that its target is not only Brunetto, but much of what Dante learned from him as well.

The meeting of father and son in the otherworld stands for a triumph over time, at once an acknowledgment of the hero's mortality, inasmuch as it confirms his kinship with the dead, and an affirmation of continuity, inasmuch as the dead continue to live through him. Generational difference is obliterated, and with it all distinction between past and future disappear in a prophetic present: This is the central point, "il punto/a cui tutti li tempi son presenti" (the Point to which all times are present) (*Par.* 17.17–18), from which Cacciaguida speaks to the pilgrim, as Anchises had spoken to Aeneas.

Given that the damned have no knowledge of the present, however, there is no common ground on which they can confront the living. In the absence of comprehension, which must be based on shared premises, there is only ironic impasse. The struggles between fathers and sons in *Inferno* dramatize this impasse. The past and the future contend with each other to occupy a middle ground that will admit no individual autonomy. In the case of Guido Cavalcanti and his father, it is as if the foreboding surrounding the figure of Guido, as well as the echoing of some of his most famous verses, obliterated the figure of the old man, whose only vital sign is his obsessive concern for his son. In the case of Ugolino, the survival of the father is literally at the expense of his children, upon whose flesh he feeds in a ghastly parody of the Eucharist, with perhaps a mythic allusion to Saturn's eating of his own children. Between these parodic father figures runs the scorched shade of Brunetto, Dante's own father image, who taught the poet how man makes himself eternal.

There can be little doubt that the episode of Cacciaguida, in canto 15 of *Paradiso*, was meant to be read in the light of canto 15 of *Inferno*, as several allusions make clear. Perhaps the most interesting is the ironic play on the title of Brunetto's book, a play that suggests the displacement of the father image by Cacciaguida. As the rhetorician is about to run off, he says to the pilgrim: "Sieti raccomandato il mio Tesoro / nel qual io vivo ancora, e più non cheggio" (Let my *Treasure*, in which I yet live, be commended to you, and I ask no more) (*Inf.* 15.19–20). In *Paradiso*, Dante refers to his ancestor as his "treasure": "la luce in che rideva il mio tesoro / ch'io trovai lì" (the light wherein was smiling the treasure I had found there) (*Par.* 17.121–2). That arch reference is not only the poet's claim to have superseded Brunetto's work with his own, but also a hint at the nature of their difference: Brunetto's text is reified, autochthonous, and eternal; Dante's text is in the making, a series of glosses on the "magno volume" of God's Book.

It is Virgil's text or, at least, the commentaries on that text that explain why the two encounters should be juxtaposed. Before he comes to the underworld, Aeneas has a dream in which his father appears to him and tells him to make the descent into Hades. In a commentary by Bernardus Silvestris, which Dante may well have read, the various stages of the quest for the father are outlined:

> Monetur imagine patris ad inferos descendere visurus patrem ibi i.e. cogitatione quadam imaginaria quam de creatore habet. Non enim perfectam potest habere, cum deus incircumscriptus sit cogitatione. In qua ille monetur, ut ad mundana per cognitionem descendat, ibique videbit patrem quia quamvis in creaturis non sit, cognitione tamen creaturarum cognoscitur. Ideoque iubetur apud inferos quaerere patrem licet celsa inhabitat.

By the image of the father Aeneas is instructed to descend to the lower world to see his father there. That is, Aeneas is instructed by a certain mental image that really comes from the Creator. . . . He is admonished thus: to descend to earthly things through thought and there he will see his father, because even though God really dwells on high, one can nevertheless have some knowledge of the Creator by comparing things of this world and recognizing their frailty. Thus, Aeneas is commanded to seek his father in the underworld even though his father dwells on high.

*Commentum* 27.25–28.1[1]

The interest of this passage, apart from its accounting for Dante's phrase "imagine paterna," is its suggestion that even a false image of the father, in all of its frailty, can convey a glimpse of God.

The salutary effect that Brunetto had on Dante's life, attested by the words of the pilgrim, is irrelevant to the moral judgment placed on the old man: This is the essence of the irony of his portrait in *Inferno*, an irony inherent throughout the *cantica*, where every secular, even humane, affirmation awaits retrospective correction from the perspective of conversion. The radical difference between the pilgrim's perspective and that of the poet is clear even in the landscape, which seems to conspire against the pilgrim's reverential demeanor. The height from which Dante looks down gives the lie to this deference: Brunetto must reach up to grasp the hem of the traveler's garment in order to attract his attention, for the traveler towers over him. The pilgrim's respectful use of "voi" and the title "ser" seem incongruous in such a situation, as does his attempt to show respect by walking with his head reverently bowed. The pilgrim's shock at finding Brunetto here—"Siete voi qui, ser Brunetto?" (Are you here, ser Brunetto?) (*Inf.* 15.30)—is matched by our own, each time we realize that it is the very same Dante who places him among the sodomites.

Apologists for Dante in the twentieth century have strained, without success, to find a shred of evidence from contemporary sources of Brunetto's vice, in the hope that notoriety would somehow exculpate Dante for this apparently gratuitous revelation of Brunetto's sin. Moreover, the text lends no support to the theory of Brunetto's notoriety as a sodomite, for if that were the case, it would be difficult to explain the astonishment expressed by the pilgrim: "Siete voi qui, ser Brunetto?"[2] The naive reader fares better, concluding that Dante came upon Brunetto there and had no choice but to report the results of his infernal survey. This simpleminded reading has the effect of heightening the mimetic fiction, for it is somehow easier to believe that the infernal order is God-given, rather than to believe that, for all of the respect and admiration shown by the pilgrim, Dante the poet would defile Brunetto's memory and his name. Yet, as difficult as it may be in human terms to imagine such perfidy, Dante does precisely that, and adds to the outrage by implying that the devastating portrait is repayment of a debt of gratitude toward his teacher: "Quant' io l'abbia in grado . . . / convien che ne la mia lingua si scerna" (How much I hold it in gratitude it behooves me, while I live, to declare in my speech) (*Inf.* 15.86–7). It would be difficult to imagine a more radical rejection of an erstwhile father surrogate than charging him with being a sodomite; the irony is too biting not to be intentional. This is disillusionment that borders on the vindictive. It requires explanation even from so uncompromising a moralist as Dante.

There is an even more serious source of interpretive malaise occasioned by this portrait of Brunetto: the company he keeps. He tells us that his companions "tutti fur cherci / e litterati grandi e di gran fama" (all were clerks, and great men of letters and of great fame) (15.106–7). There would seem to be more than a casual link between the literary vocation and the vice. For obvious reasons, the association has been largely evaded in Dante criticism, usually by separating Brunetto's humanism from his sin, but sometimes, as in a famous book by André Pézard, by redefining the sin to make it less reprehensible to a modern sensibility, without, however, changing Dante's judgment concerning its gravity. Yet the association between literary and sexual perversion was a commonplace by Dante's time, part of Nature's complaint against mankind in Alanus ab Insulis, repeated at length by Jean de Meun in the *Roman de la rose*. What is particularly unsettling about the condemnation of Brunetto is that there would seem to be no hint of an accusation against him of literary perversion; on the contrary, Dante seems to praise him for having taught "come l'uom s'etterna" (how man makes himself eternal) (15.85). That is virtually all we are told about Brunetto's life and teaching—that and the fact that he is condemned to the circle signed with the seal of Sodom. We have no choice but to conclude, irrespective of our modern preconceptions, that Brunetto's sin and his achievement are somehow related.

If this has not seemed obvious, it is probably because we have assumed anachronistically that the vague accusation of sodomy was tantamount to a much more specific accusation of homosexuality. On the one occasion that Dante refers indirectly to homosexuality, however, in canto 26 of *Purgatorio*, he seems to treat it as a technicality, simply a variant form of concupiscence—heterosexuals and homosexuals purging their lustful proclivities run in opposite directions. Here there would seem to be an important nuance in the condemnation of Brunetto and his colleagues. Sodomy would appear to be a transgression not only against society's rules concerning gender, but also against its rules—which are also Nature's rules—concerning age. Teachers and *grammatici* are often guilty of this sin, Cristoforo Landino tells us in his commentary on the *Commedia*, because they are surrounded by "copia di giovanetti" (many youngsters). Like the Athenian condemnation of Socrates, the charge against Brunetto would appear to be of corrupting the young. If those who are corrupted happen to be of the same sex as their teachers, this is more a result of the social makeup of medieval institutions than it is of sexual tastes. The conclusion is inescapable: One of the ways in which man makes himself eternal, or at least tries to do so, is by refusing to acknowledge his precise place on life's trajectory. The humanist and the pederast have in common the evasion of their own temporality in the pursuit of an eternal ideal.

This, too, is a recurrent motif in our literary tradition, beginning with Socrates and ending, perhaps, with Thomas Mann's parable about the decline of the West, *Death in Venice*. The temporal distance between us and Brunetto Latini has enabled Dante's readers to dismiss the accusation against him without too much discomfort, while Mann's story is too close, in every sense, to allow for snickers. Yet they tell much the same story, set in analogously artificial locales. The desert plain of *Inferno*, in fact, recalls not only the biblical Sodom, but Venice as well, inasmuch as it would seem to be art, or artifice, that makes it traversable by Dante and his guide, with bulwarks set against a hostile environment. Even the geographic simile—"quali Padoan lungo la Brenta" (as the Paduans do along the Brenta) (*Inf.* 15.7)—invites the comparison: Hell's oxymoric landscape of fiery rain and bloody water serves as a rhetorical emblem for its inhabitants, just as, in Mann's story, Venice's inversion of land and sea stands for the perversion of sexuality. Whether or not Mann had Brunetto in mind, in both stories the struggle against nature seems alternately heroic and pathetic, but doomed in any case by the absurdity of the ambition: to make oneself—the reflexive underscores the impossibility—eternal.

In the relative innocence of antiquity, or at least in the antiquity of Romantic scholarship, Socrates was the archetypal figure of the quest for immortality in its heroic phase, although just as Brunetto had his Dante, so he had his Aristophanes. The text that is the locus classicus for the analogy between sexuality and the pursuit of worldly fame is Plato's *Symposium*. According to Socrates's informant, Diotima, all men desire immortality. They achieve this either by begetting according to the soul, that is, by earning fame and glory for their virtue, or by begetting according to the body, by having children. As one would expect, begetting according to the soul is for Plato the higher form of immortality, for it guarantees immortality for the individual rather than just the species.

The paradox of having children is that while it guarantees a certain immortality for the species, it means that the individual must accept death. It was because of this collaboration with the body and, therefore, with death that some currents of thought in the early Christian era condemned marriage and chose virginity instead. Augustine was considerably less extreme, yet completely unsentimental about what reproduction implies for the individual:

> Num deinde nati sunt tibi filii in terra tecum victuri, an te potius exclusuri et successuri? . . . nati enim pueri tanquam hoc dicunt parentibus suis: Eia, cogitate ire hinc, agamus et nos mimum nostrum. Mimus est enim generis humani tota via tentationis.

> Are your children born to live always with you, or rather are they not born to push you aside and succeed you? . . . At the birth of children, it is as if they said to their parents, "Begone now, it is time for us to play our parts in the play." For all of our life of temptation is a play.
> *Ennarrationes* 127.i5

Sexuality is the guarantor of life for the species, but for the individual, it is indissolubly linked to death. To accept one's sexuality is to accept all of the limitations that mark one's place precisely on the trajectory of the life span: limitations of age, of gender, of relationship. The "stage" of life to which Augustine refers, echoing Plotinus and anticipating Shakespeare, is the battleground of generational conflict, an oedipal *space* that is the locus for the encounters of fathers and sons in *Inferno*. Seen in this light, sexual deviance such as is attributed to Brunetto might be thought of as death-defying, an effort to transcend mortal limitations.

In a Platonic context, one could win a certain individual immortality through fame or glory, but those purely secular values were the object of severe attack in the Christian era, notably by Boethius in the second book of the *Consolation of Philosophy*. Because ancient values predominate in Dante's *Inferno*, the celebration of fame and *gloria* seems to be accepted uncritically until the inevitable corrective is offered in *Purgatorio*.

For the reader who shares the perspective of the poet, however, a critique of ancient values is already implied in the ambivalence of some key words and phrases that appear in the pilgrim's dialogues with the damned—one thinks, for example, of the word "magnanimo," which, unlike its English cognate, has both good and bad connotations. Such words recur in Brunetto's language. He asks Dante, "Qual fortuna o destino / anzi l'ultimo dì qua giù ti mena?" (What chance or destiny brings you down here before your last day) (*Inf.* 15.46–7), when it is clear to any reader that neither fortune nor destiny has anything to do with his descent. The formulaic question, with its reference to purely secular categories, is reminiscent of the uncomprehending question asked by Cavalcante de' Cavalcanti—"Se per questo cieco / carcere vai per altezza d'ingegno . . ." (If you go through this blind prison by reason of high genius . . .) (10.58–9)—and it elicits the same kind of response, stressing the pilgrim's election, as personified by Virgil, rather than his innate gifts. Again, when Brunetto predicts, "Se tu segui tua stella, / non puoi fallire a glorïoso porto, / se ben m'accorsi ne la vita bella" (If you follow your star you cannot fail of a glorious port, if, in the fair life, I discerned aright) (*Inf.* 15.55–7), the allusion to a "glorious port" is richly ambivalent; in this of all voyages it is obvious that Paradise is the glorious port, while Brunetto, referring to Dante's talents ("tua stella"), clearly has earthly success in mind. When the old man adds the qualification ("se ben m'accorsi nel a vita bella"), it is virtually an invitation to ironic interpretation.

The pilgrim's acknowledgment of the lessons learned from Brunetto—"come l'uom s'etterna"—must also be read with the clash of antiquity and Christianity in mind. The pursuit of immortality may be perfectly laudable from a secular point of view, but the secular point of view is a luxury restricted to the living. It contrasts as sharply with the transcendent meaning of eternity, that is, salvation, as the pilgrim's filial piety contrasts with the degrading circumstances in which he finds his father image. Under the rain of fire, the reflexive *si* of verse 85 is more charged with the pathos of Thomas Mann than with humanistic optimism.

The seal of Sodom stands for the refusal to be bound by limitations of age or family or gender, but it also suggests sterility, mirrored in the desert plain of *Inferno*. If the foregoing analysis is correct, these are sinners who refused progeny of the body (without, however, refusing the body itself) and sought instead a purely individual immortality. In such a setting, the title of "father" would seem to be completely inappropriate. The isolation of Brunetto from his fellow sinners underscores his exile from the human family: "de l'umana natura posto in bando" (banished from human nature) (15.81).

The eternity that Brunetto has achieved is emblematized by the punishment of the sodomites, who run endlessly around the plain, in a race without a finish line, different, in that respect, from the race of life of which St. Paul speaks. Brunetto drops back from his group momentarily in order to talk to Dante. When their conversation is interrupted by the approach of a new group, he recommends his book, the *Trésor*, to the pilgrim and runs off to catch up with his set:

> "Gente vien con la quale esser non deggio.
>> Sieti raccomandato il mio Tesoro,
>> nel qual io vivo ancora, e più non cheggio."
> Poi si rivolse e parve di coloro
>> che corrono a Verona il drappo verde
>> per la campagna; e parve di costoro
> quelli che vince, non colui che perde.
>
> *Inf.* 15.118–24

"People are coming with whom I must not be. Let my *Treasure*, in which I yet live, be commended to you, and I ask no more." Then he turned back, and seemed like one of those who run for the green cloth in the field at Verona, and of them he seemed he who wins, not he who loses.

The extraordinary comparison that ends the canto is more admired in the history of Dante criticism than properly glossed, for it seems to capture within it all the play of irony in this canto. Brunetto is in hell, and therefore he is a loser; but in fact, because of his book, he lives forever, and therefore he is a winner—where does the reader place the emphasis, on winning or losing? The question is undecidable on the endless and circular track of irony, just as it is impossible to decide in our reading generally in *Inferno*, without a sense of the poem's ending, whether to ignore the noble words of the characters in hell or the infernal framework that undercuts them. Critics who argue about the moral quality of the characters in hell are swept up in the same ironic recursions, from which there is no escape within the confines of a *lectura dantis*. The one element that is indisputable is that Brunetto falls so far behind his own group that he seems to be leading the next. If the infernal race were thought of as analogous to the succession of generations, then Brunetto would be the man who attempts to pause in the race toward death and so, momentarily, seems to be out in front of the succeeding pack. It is an extraordinarily apt way of making the point that regression in an aging humanist can sometimes pass for leadership among the young.

Turning and movement would seem to be the leitmotiv of the episode; there are at least seven instances of verbs that convey that meaning: "Poi si rivolse" (Then he turned back) (15.121), "si volse in dietro" (turned around on his right) (98), "volsi le spalle" (I turned my back) (52), "rivolto mi fossi" (I turned to look back) (15), "ritorna 'n dietro" (turns back a little) (33), "tornand' ïo" (I was returning) (53), "reducemi" (leads me) (54). The rhetorician turns—*tropes*, in the etymological sense—endlessly, a dramatization, as it were, of the atemporal conflict of an irony that cannot be resolved in a circle, where there is no beginning or end. The linear course along the dike, however, moves toward a goal of which the pilgrim had once lost sight. He tells Brunetto that after being lost in a valley, he is homeward bound:

> Pur ier mattina le volsi le spalle:
> > questi m'apparve, tornando' ïo in quella,
> > e reducemi a ca per questo calle.

*Inf.* 15.52–4

Only yesterday morning I turned my back on it. He appeared to me, as I was returning into it, and by this path he leads me home.

*Volgere le spalle*, "turning one's back," is the movement of conversion. To continue the translation of these spatial terms into their spiritual equivalents (and it is clear from this passage as well as from many others that the whole poem is a form of *itinerarium mentis*), we might translate Brunetto's endless circling with a word that has both rhetorical and sexual connotations and contrasts sharply with *con*version: Brunetto's troping is *per*version.

The difference between those two movements, or tropes, may be taken as an emblem of the difference between infernal irony and the allegory of conversion. The difference is most obviously perceptible in the contrast between Brunetto's prophecy about Dante's future and the pilgrim's reaction to it. We are told that it will be interpreted later on, retrospectively from the perspective of paradise:

> Ciò che narrate di mio corso scrivo,
> > e serbolo a chiosar con altro testo
> a donna che saprà, s'a lei arrivo.
>
> *Inf.* 15.88–90

> That which you tell me of my course I write, and keep with a text to be glossed by a lady who will know how, if I reach her.

Allegorical interpretation in the Middle Ages meant reading a text not according to the intentionality of its human author (Virgil's intended meaning in the fourth *Eclogue*, for example, was irrelevant to its effect on Statius, as we learn in *Purgatorio*), but rather as a partial, provisional truth, to be fully and adequately glossed only eschatologically, from the ending, according to the paradigm set forth in the Bible. When Beatrice introduces Dante to St. James as the man who has come out of Egypt into Jerusalem in order to see, she effectively gives the gloss for all of the obscure sibylline prophecies that the pilgrim has collected on route through *Inferno*. The latter prophecies are like the oracles of antiquity: true, but in ways that are ironic and unforeseeable, like meteorological forecasts, which can be confirmed only when it is too late to do anything about them.

However, it is Cacciaguida, rather than Beatrice, who gives Dante the detailed gloss on the future, and, once more, it is Virgil's text to which we must appeal in order to understand. Marguerite Chiarenza has shown that if there is a difficulty here in the text it is Virgil's difficulty, not Dante's.[3] In the third book of the *Aeneid*, Helenus tells Aeneas that he will learn of the future from the Sibyl, whereas it is Anchises who tells him about the glorious future of Rome. Chiarenza suggests that this change, at least in Dante's reading, marks the shift from oracular destiny to concrete historicity, just as the shift from the vague "donna" in canto 15 receives its precise historical embodiment in Cacciaguida: At some level, Beatrice *is* Dante's enlightenment, as was promised at the end of canto 10:

Quando sarai dinanzi al dolce raggio
    di quella il cui bell' occhio tutto vede,
    da lei saprai di tua vita il vïaggio.

*Inf.* 10.130–2

When you are before her sweet radiance whose fair eyes see all, from her
you shall know of your life's journey.

Although it is Beatrice who ultimately provides enlightenment, it is
Cacciaguida who, "setting the woof across the warp" (*Par.* 17.101), ini-
tially fleshes out in precise historical detail the paradigm of Exodus. So
the mythic scene of Brunetto's prophecy, sorb-trees and sweet figs, the
Fiesolan goats, and the sacred seed of Rome, give way to prophecies
from within the walls of the city, when Florentine family names set out
in detail and Dante's future spelled out in "chiare parole e con pre-
ciso / latin" (in clear words and with precise discourse) (*Par.* 17.34–5).
This is not the only time in the course of the poem that the reader's
expectation is met with a gender reversal. In *Purgatorio*, when the
angels sing *"Benedictus qui venis"* (30.19), the gender of the verb and its
context lead us to expect a Christological event, when in fact it is
Beatrice who appears. The point seems to be that Beatrice, the sweet
light, is the essential mediatrix for both the pilgrim's enlightenment
and his salvation.

    I have said that the theme of the meeting with a father image in
*Inferno* is characterized by irony, while the meeting with Cacciaguida in
*Paradiso* seems to be the fulfillment of an allegorical referentiality, a
partial truth glossed repeatedly and painstakingly until it is finally
revealed at the ending of the poem. There is a sense in which the theme
of the clash between father and son, when neither will yield, is illustra-
tive of the clash of irony, where no resolution but death is possible
between two antithetical yet equally plausible assertions. We might say
that the oedipal struggle is the thematization of the atemporal and corrosive quality of ironic impasse. To introduce temporality into this
impasse, however, and to order the past to the future with the mediating
influenced of a third term in which both participate, like the covenant
in the story of Abraham and Isaac, is to transform irony into allegory,
and generational conflict into the unfolding of salvation history.

    In another context, Erich Auerbach has spoken about the mimetic
quality of *Inferno* and particularly of canto 10.[4] There is a primordial
mimesis, however, that is logically prior to and potentially far more dis-

ruptive than the representation of reality in a literary text: the rivalry of
the male child with the father, as the son seeks to find the ways in which
he is and is not like his parent. That these two forms of mimesis are not
unrelated is suggested by the fact that so many of Auerbach's chapters
that purport to be stylistic analyses of modes of representation have as
their unacknowledged subject matter the various permutations of a
child's relationship to its parent: Homer, Genesis, Dante, and Virginia
Woolf. What the two forms of mimesis have in common is the potentiality for irreducible conflict. In the mimesis of the child, the conflict is
oedipal struggle. In literary representation, the conflict is irony. Literary
mimesis always contains within it the potentiality for irony, inasmuch as
it simultaneously affirms and denies its identity with the reality it seeks
to represent—sameness insofar as it is an imitation, and difference insofar as it is, after all, a *text*. So too, the oedipal struggle in its exacerbated
form is an irreducibly ironic confrontation of the past and the future in
the battleground of a present moment, which has room enough only for
one. The brief survival of Ugolino requires the death of his sons, while
the equally brief life of Guido can resume only after his father is eternally
silenced. These might be thought of as thematizations of the corrosive
and ultimately destructive force of infernal irony. In the case of Brunetto,
the pilgrim's reference to the old rhetorician as "father" is belied by the
poet's condemnation of him as a sodomite, as far from paternity as any
sin can be. This dissociates the mature Dante from his former teacher,
but most of all it dissociates him from his former self.

The pilgrim tells Brunetto that he is homeward bound. The way
home inevitably evokes the figure of maternity, the promise of Beatrice,
no longer solely as lover but also as nurturer, as she is portrayed especially in canto 33 of *Paradiso*. The theme of fathers and sons in antiquity
is inseparable from the concept of *pietas*, the often somber duty that
binds son to father and both to Rome. Robert Ball has shown how
radically that word changed meaning in Christianity and especially in
Dante's text.[5] It is enough for us to think of what the word *pietà* suggests to a general audience—the figure of suffering maternity—to get
some idea of the gulf that separates the two concepts rendered by the
same word. As in Augustine's *Confessions*, so too in *De civitate Dei*, the
mediation of the mother, *Mater ecclesia*, is essential for the transformation of the sometimes bloody rites of male successions into the peaceful
transitions of salvation history. As far as our theme is concerned, the
mediation of a female principle—or, if one prefers, of the Church—is

accomplished by the journey to Beatrice. She is identified in both canto 10 and canto 15 as the "sweet light," the goal of allegorical referentiality. In hell, the best that one can hope for is to be led to her through the darkness by a blind father.

The *Confessions* defines the search for the truth precisely in these terms:

> O lux, quam videbat Tobis, cum clausis istis oculis filium docebat vitae viam, et ei praeibat pede caritatis nusquam errans; aut quam videbat Isaac praegravatis et opertis senectute carneis luminibus, cum filios non agnoscendo benedicere, sed benedicendo agnoscere meruit; aut quam videbat Iacob, cum et ipse prae grandi aetate captus oculis in filiis praesignata futuri populi genera luminoso corde radiavit . . . Ipsa est lux, una est et unum omnes, qui vident et amant eam.

> The true light is the light which Tobias saw when, though his eyes were blind, he taught his son the path he should follow in life and himself led the way, charity guiding his steps so that he did not stray. It is the light which Isaac saw when the sight of his eyes was dimmed and clouded by old age and it was granted to him, not to bless his sons in full knowledge as to which was which, but to know them by blessing them. It is the light which Jacob saw when, though his eyes were blinded by old age, a light shone in his heart and cast its beams over the tribes of Israel yet to come as he foresaw them in the persons of his sons . . . This is the true light. It is one alone and all who see and love it are one.

> *Conf.* 10.34[6]

This succession of fathers and sons requires the acceptance of old age and death. It is the linear movement of time (and, as we know from *terza rima*, any such movement requires a mediation between past and future) toward an unspecified goal, the ultimate truth promised by allegory. In *Inferno*, it is personified by Virgil, who provides a light that he himself does not possess. Statius says of him in *Purgatorio*:

> Facesti come quei che va di notte,
> che porta il lume dietro e sé non giova,
> ma dopo sé fa le persone dotte.

> *Purg.* 22.67–9

> You were like one who goes by night and carries the light behind him and profits not himself, but makes those wise who follow him.

Dante's Christian humanism—the adjective is important for marking the distance between himself and his teacher—transforms Virgil's text into the status of Old Testament history. Virgil, like Tobias, Isaac, and Jacob, prepared the way for a fulfillment that he could not foresee.

# Allegory and Autobiography

A mong the last words spoken by Jesus in the Gospel of John are those directed to Peter, predicting the disciple's martyrdom:

> Verily, verily, I say unto you that when you were young you girt yourself and walked wherever you wished; but when you are old you will stretch out your hands and another shall gird you and lead you where you would not go.
>
> John 21:18

In his commentary, Augustine explains that these verses mark the passage in Peter's life from youthful self-reliance to humility, from the sin of presumption to confession and contrition. In middle age (for Peter is neither young nor old), he is called upon to demonstrate his love by caring for the Lord's sheep and by being willing to accept crucifixion (*In Ioannis evangelium tractatus* 123).[1]

The conversion from presumption to humility is also the theme of Dante's descent into Hell, which likewise takes place in middle age: "nel mezzo del cammin di nostra vita." The landscape of the prologue scene borrows several details from Book 7 of Augustine's *Confessions*, where philosophical presumption is distinguished from confession: "it is one thing, from a wooded mountain top, to see the land of peace and quite another to reach it, when one's way is beset by the lion and the dragon" (7.21). It is likely that casting off the rope girdle halfway through *Inferno* signifies a surrender of self-reliance analogous to Peter's, while the rush with which the pilgrim is girt at the beginning of *Purgatorio* is a traditional emblem of humility (*umile pianta*).

If one attempts to read these episodes simply as autobiographical anecdotes, they are bound to seem enigmatic, raising more questions about Dante's life than they answer. So, for example, some early commentators felt compelled to gloss them with biographical details invented for the occasion, identifying the rope girdle as part of the Franciscan habit and suggesting that Dante may once have wanted to become a Franciscan. Such inventions are unnecessary, however, once we recognize that, whatever the events in Dante's life to which such episodes supposedly allude, they have been represented in the text in terms of a biblical figure of conversion. The passage from the Gospel of John authorizes us to read Dante's verses, "io avea una corda intorno cinta" (I had a cord girt round me) (*Inf.* 16.106), not as a description of his dress, but rather as an emblem of his spiritual state: He was guilty of the same presumption of which Christ accused Peter and of which Augustine accused himself. Unlike modern biographies, which seek to establish above all the uniqueness of their subject, Christian biographies stress conformity to a biblical pattern, even at the expense of originality. When it comes to plot, such biographies, like Tolstoy's happy families, are all alike.

Casting off the rope is meant to attract Geryon, "the filthy image of fraud." This image seems to have no direct biblical precedent, but is reminiscent, if only by contrast, of ancient allegories of transcendence represented in terms of flight. Its spiral path is clear indication that the monster is a celestial derivation, since the planets, sun, and moon all move in a spiral. Several studies have suggested that ancient allegories of flight, extending back to Plato, underlie the voyage of Ulysses as Dante recounts it.[2] The same may perhaps be said of the voyage on Geryon. In any case, along with biblical themes, ancient philosophical allegories of the ascent of the soul constitute another source for the figures or paradigms that the poet uses to represent the events of his life in general terms. Autobiography is represented schematically in Dante's poem by this synthesis of Platonic allegory with traditional biblical motifs, just as it was in Augustine's *Confessions*.

For all of its originality, Geryon's meaning in terms of the poet's biography is not difficult to decipher. Although the monster is fearsome, it is strangely docile, grudgingly responsive to Virgil's commands. This apparent inconsistency illustrates a familiar paradox of confessional literature: Adversity and evil turn out retrospectively to have been of spiritual help even when they seemed most threatening. Dante's reaction to his exile embodies this paradox. In the *Convivio*, he bitterly complains of the injustice done to him, while in the *Commedia* he seems to regard his exile as having been necessary for his salvation, irrespective of the culpability of those who condemned him. The contrast between the slow, spiral descent of Geryon and its almost instantaneous departure after its mission is accomplished, suggests a momentary, providential constraint of the forces of evil for the benefit of the pilgrim. Like Antaeus bending gently with the voyagers in his hand and then snapping back into place, Geryon participates in a "command performance" to speed the pilgrim on his way.

This providential intervention is a response to the submissiveness of the pilgrim, who will now be "led where he would not go." On this voyage, he is to be simply a passenger, rather than a Ulysses, and Virgil is there to sustain him. The self-reliance of Ulysses was interpreted by Dante (and by Augustine before him) as a form of presumption of which the young Dante—especially the Dante of the *Convivio*—might himself have been guilty. The voyage on Geryon functions as an ironic parody of the Homeric journey, a critique of the presumption of youth from the perspective of middle age.

Whatever the moral intent, Geryon is exquisitely literary; its various motifs form a patchwork whose seams Dante scarcely bothers to conceal. Elements of the monster's composition are drawn from the Apocalypse, or perhaps from the lunar dragon of the astrologers (from which the dragon of the Apocalypse probably derives). Scholars have suggested various classical sources for the image as well, notably from Virgil and Solinus. Apart from its thematic function, however, its literally central position in *Inferno*, and the elaborate address to the reader introducing it, suggest that it was also meant to stand for the poet's own prodigious imagination. Throughout the story, the progress of the pilgrim is, at the same time, the progress of the poem. Here, too, perhaps, Geryon is both theme and, like Ariosto's "hippogryph," a self-conscious emblem of the poet's creative act. Ariosto's fantastic steed is obviously a descendant of Pegasus, said to have sprung from Medusa's blood. That chthonic origin would qualify Pegasus as an ancestor of Geryon as well.[3]

The flight on Geryon seems to call forth as its antithesis the ship of Ulysses, a "navicella dell'ingegno" sailing to disaster. Both Geryon and Ulysses are recalled in the course of the poem: Ulysses is referred to twice in *Purgatorio* and once in *Paradiso*, while Virgil refers back to this flight as his claim to the pilgrim's continued faith in his guidance, even through purgatorial fire. His reminder to Dante, "Did I not guide you safely on the back of Geryon?" in *Purgatorio* 27 recalls Exodus 19:4: "you saw how I bore you up on eagle's wings."

The flight of Geryon is described with navigational imagery, while the navigation of Ulysses is described, with a memorable phrase, in terms of flight: "il folle volo" (the mad flight). This symmetrical opposition is reinforced by antitypes. The successful flight of Geryon evokes allusions to Icarus and Phaeton, while Ulysses is introduced by a comparison to the successful flight of Elijah. This parallelism suggests that the two journeys exist on the same level of signification, as dramatic representations of opposing attempts to reach the absolute. Because the voyage is also a figure for the writing of the poem (as is clear from the invocations to the second and last canticles, as well as from the narrative logic that makes of the journey's end the poem's beginning), the contrast between Ulysses and Geryon is also a contrast between literary genres.

The Homeric story had been interpreted since antiquity as an allegory of the soul's education. The disastrous conclusion of the story, in Dante's revised version, amounts to a Christian critique of philosophical presumption: specifically, of the claim that anyone could accomplish such a journey without a guide. The flight on Geryon, on the other hand, is providentially guided, like God's eagle in Exodus. It is a descent that precedes an ascent, in keeping with the Augustinian admonition, "Descend, so that you may ascend." Moreover, it takes place in the inner space of Hell, which may be said to stand for the interior distance of a descent within the self. Once more, Augustine comes to mind: "Noli foras ire; in te ipsum redi" (Do not go outside; enter within yourself).[4] This inner dimension is totally lacking in Ulysses's account of his journey. He may be thought of as the archetypal explorer in outer space, describing his feat with the same understatement, *litotes*, used by American astronauts when they landed on the moon ("one small step for man . . ."). This voyage, and all other such voyages, are the stuff of epic. In contrast, Dante's journey on the Geryon of his own experience is a descent into himself. Such a turning inward is distinctly confessional.

The bizarre vehicle of Dante's descent into Malebolge is neither ship nor chariot in the tradition of Neoplatonic allegory, although it bears a grotesque resemblance to those flights of the soul; the surly beast might be compared to the horse veering to the left in the allegory of the *Phaedrus*, while the navigational imagery in Geryon's flight, like the flight imagery in Ulysses's navigation, is reminiscent of allusions to flights of the soul in Plotinus, Ambrose, or Augustine, where the means of escape from this world are compared to horses, chariots, ships, and wings.[5] However, it is Providence, rather than a charioteer, who reigns in Geryon, and it is fraud, rather than passions, that must be dominated. This flight does not take place in an interior void, but rather in the course of Dante's life, reinterpreted from the perspective of Hell. Geryon adds to the Neoplatonic tradition a political dimension of meaning. One is enjoined not simply to escape the hypocrisy and fraud of human society, as Plotinus had urged, but to understand it from within and so transcend it. This is the social significance of Virgil's warning: "A te convien tenere altro viaggio" (It behooves you to go by another way) (*Inf.* 1.91).

Understanding in *Inferno* is a process that might be characterized as hyperbolic doubt systematically applied to the values of contemporary society. Each encounter in Hell amounts to the ironic undercutting of the values enunciated by the separate characters. Even when those values seem perfectly defensible from a human point of view, as is the case, for example, with the humanistic aspirations expressed by Brunetto Latini in canto 15, the values are undermined by the fact of being championed by the damned. An incidental phrase meant as polite qualification, Brunetto's "se ben m'accorsi nella vita bella" becomes charged with irony as the infernal context exposes it to the obvious and therefore cruel rejoinder: If his discernment were acute, why would he be *here*—"siete voi qui, Ser Brunetto?" (*Inf.* 15.30).

This corrosive irony gives *Inferno* its negative quality; not only is this canticle devoid of redemptive possibilities, it seems devoid of all affirmation as well. The goal of the descent is to reach the zero-point from which the climb of *Purgatorio* can begin. In order to do this, it is necessary first to strip away all the illusory values with which we ordinarily comfort ourselves. In Plato's myth, the star-soul had to shed all its layers of materiality in order to return to its celestial home; in the Christian myth, it is sin, rather than matter, that weighs down the soul. Before any ascent can begin, it is necessary to go through Hell simply to reach the cave (*natural burella*), which Plato assumed to be the point of departure. Christian ascent begins, not from a point zero, but rather from a point minus one. In the poem, that point is described in the prologue scene: The landscape is derived from what Augustine called "the region of unlikeness" (*Conf.* 6.10.6).[6]

The primary destruction that must take place in this mythic representation of biography is the destruction of the poet's former self. If Plato's myth of education is the account of *morphosis*, the formation of the soul, then the story of a conversion is a *meta*-morphosis, in which an illusory self must be destroyed before a new soul can take its place. One of the ways in which this destruction takes place in the poem is through a series of ironic autocitations, in which Dante undercuts his own previous work. The most obvious of these is his citation of his own earlier love poetry, placed in the mouth of Francesca da Rimini, who was ill-served by the theory of "love and the gentle heart." But it is perhaps the canto of Ulysses that constitutes Dante's most important and most critical autocitation.

According to a hypothesis first advanced by Bruno Nardi, there is a certain parallelism between the attempt of Ulysses to reach the absolute and Dante's attempt, in the *Convivio*, to outline a guide to happiness through the pursuit of secular philosophy.[7] Both attempts were doomed to failure. The parallel between this failure and the experience of Augustine was first pointed out by Giorgio Padoan,[8] who showed how Augustine, in the *De beata vita*, outlined the disastrous course of his life, including his search for happiness through secular philosophy, in terms of a tedious allegory based on the voyage of Ulysses. He suggested that the episode of Ulysses in *Inferno* is biographical in the same way that Augustine's prologue to the *De beata vita* was biographical: that is, an allegorical outline of an experience of which the literal elements are suppressed. The voyage of the *Divina Commedia* begins where the shipwreck of Ulysses ends, with the survival of a metaphoric shipwreck (*Inf.* 1.23). The survival, "come altrui piacque," marks the difference between Dante's own epic presumption and his novelistic conversion.

We can only speculate about the details of Dante's experience, for the text provides us only with figures such as these. In a sense, no experience can be conveyed except by a figure, since, according to a medieval maxim, what is individual is ineffable. Allegory and other figures serve to generalize experience so that it can be communicated, as Dante says with the simile of Glaucus in *Paradiso*: "Trasumanar significar *per verba* / non si poria; però l'essemplo basti / a cui esperienza grazia serba" (The passing beyond humanity may not be set forth *in words*: therefore let the example suffice any for whom grace reserves that experience) (*Par.* 1.70–2).

One would expect heavenly vision to be ineffable, of course, but there are good institutional reasons for expressing even penitential sentiments in general terms. Confession requires the translation of individual experience into general terms in order to affirm the equality of all sinners in the sight of God, no matter how imaginative their transgressions. Thus Augustine, in his *Confessions*, chooses to illustrate the nature of sin by confessing that as a boy he stole some pears from a neighbor's orchard. Had he been writing "confessions" in the modern sense, he might have dwelt upon any number of actions in his life that even today strike us as reprehensible. He might have gone into greater detail, for instance, about how, because of his mother's fear of scandal, he rejected his mistress, taking their son from her and sending her back to Africa. That gesture tells us more about Augustine as a young man, more perhaps than we might want to know, than it does about the humdrum sinfulness of Everyman.

The theft of forbidden fruit in Augustine's text was obviously meant to recall the sin of Adam and Eve. At the level of anecdote, any of his readers might have been guilty of such a sin; in an allegorical sense, they in fact were, through the sin of the first parents. At the other pole of the drama of salvation stands the fig tree of the conversion in Book 8 of the *Confessions*. It would also appear to be the recounting of a historical event—Augustine weeping under the fig tree and the voices of children singing "tolle, lege"—yet the scene recalls the calling out of Nathanael from under the fig tree in the first chapter of the Gospel of John. Whether or not Augustine actually ever wept under a fig tree, the episode is an allusion to the call for the conversion of the Jews at the beginning of the Gospel. For all of its apparent historicity, Augustine's conversion is a re-enactment of the paradigm for all conversion.

There is no symbolic theft involved in Dante's confession. Unlike Augustine's, his drama of self-appropriation is accomplished without transgression or parental interdiction. It takes place in the Earthly Paradise, when Virgil dismisses him with a secular blessing and Beatrice calls him by name. Whatever the nature of his guilt, it is represented here in erotic terms, but inscribed within a penitential context—Beatrice was once the occasion of his sin and is now its judge—as if to suggest that Eros is here redeemed rather than condemned. The return of Beatrice, in contrast with the banishment of Augustine's mistress or of Rousseau's Marianne,[9] marks the return of an Eros now domesticated and transformed into that amalgam of Christian and cosmic love that is distinctively Dantesque. This insistence on the recuperability of his erotic past distinguishes Dante's confession from virtually all others in the Christian tradition.

The confession itself is completely generic, with schematic allusions to the drama of salvation. There is a tree whose fruit must not be eaten, and a tree, perhaps even a fig tree, under which repentance takes place. These are elements of an elaborately stylized dumb show, revealing almost nothing of the concrete details of Dante's life. On the other hand, because of her previous appearance in the *Vita nuova*, Beatrice seems to be more than simply an allegorical figure. Her literary existence outside the confines of *Purgatorio* confers a certain reality upon her, just as reality is conferred upon Virgil. In both cases, intertextuality counterfeits a history, about which we would otherwise know nothing.

To return to the general outline of the autobiographical allegory in *Inferno*, it may be said that the descent itself—and particularly the figure of Geryon, which epitomizes it—is an allegorical motif claiming no existence outside the text. They structure elements of Dante's experience in such a way that an account of his life has at the same time a moral significance for "nostra vita." The protagonist of the story is at once Dante Alighieri and, as Charles Singleton pointed out, "whichever man," meaning not the abstract "everyman" of morality plays, but rather a historical individual, elected by grace.[10] If we were to ask about the "truth" of such an account, in the everyday, biographical sense, the answer would certainly not be found in these allegorical motifs—rope, dragon, abyss—but rather in the existential realities underlying them.

We have said that Geryon introduces a social dimension into the tradition of Neoplatonic allegories, inasmuch as it suggests that the corruption of society can serve as a vehicle for plumbing the depths and then transcending them. Similarly, the central cantos of *Inferno* embody a social and political critique unlike anything in Augustine's *Confessions*. Specific details of Dante's personal life elude us, as Augustine's do not, because they are represented—sometimes, perhaps, masked—by allegorical figures. Dante's public battles, however, are more readily accessible to interpretation.

The "veil" of allegory seems most transparent in the central cantos of *Inferno*. Luigi Pirandello once suggested that the so-called "comedy of the devils" in the circle of barratry should be understood autobiographically, as Dante's grotesque indictment of the political corruption of his day, especially of the Black Guelfs, and also as his defense against a trumped-up charge of barratry brought against him during his absence.[11] This, for Pirandello, is the significance of the episode in which the pilgrim is nearly "tarred with the same brush" as the barrators. In these cantos, Dante uses the weapon of farce, rather than moral indignation, to refute the charges brought against him by his enemies.

Pirandello's observations may be adapted to apply to the flight on Geryon and other mysterious and apparently irreducible autobiographical details. The description of the crowds in Rome during the Jubilee year suggests perhaps an association between Dante's flight and his embassy to Rome to avert the entry of Charles of Valois into Florence. The duplicity of the pope might aptly be represented by a duplicitous Geryon, while the imagery of Antichrist that is used to describe the monster in consistent with traditional descriptions of a corrupt papacy.[12] Finally, Dante's defense for the smashing of the baptismal font, in his letter to the Italian cardinals, would seem to be a New Testament version of the defense of having laid hands on the Ark: that is, for having interfered in ecclesiastical matters as a layman, as did Uzzah, who was struck dead for his pains (*Epistola* 32.9). The meaning of such a clearly symbolic action—to smash the font, literally, would have been impossible without a wrecking crew—and of others like it can be derived from reading the events of Dante's public career in the biblical figures and patterns by which he has represented them.

As for the rest, the personal details that we would expect in autobiography, the text is mute. Dante's realism, his ability to endow traditional allegorical motifs with realistic substance (as did Augustine before him, with similar protestations about the historicity of his account), should not obscure for us the extent to which the particulars of Dante's life escape us.

Dante's journey is neither a poetic fiction nor a historical account; it is exemplary and allegorical. Like Augustine's life, it was meant to be both autobiographical and emblematic, a synthesis of the particular circumstances of an individual's life with paradigms of salvation history drawn from the Bible. It is what A. C. Charity has called "applied typology,"[13] meaning the manifestation in Dante's life of the redemptive pattern of biblical history. In the following pages, we attempt to discuss the sense in which Dante's narrative may be thought of as theological allegory, and the degree to which its theological quality may be acknowledged even in a purely secular reading.

### Allegory of Poets, Allegory of Theologians

Just before Geryon appears, the narrator anticipates the reader's incredulity by insisting that he is telling the truth, even if it would seem to be a lie—"quell ver c'ha faccia di menzogna" (that truth which seems a lie) (*Inf.* 16.124). This remark amounts to distinguishing a fiction from a fraud: His story is the truth with the face of a lie, while fraud, Geryon, has the face of truth ("la faccia d'uom giusto"), hiding a lie, or at least the tail of a scorpion.

The contrast between a fraudulent lie and a fiction, a lie *secundum quid*, is reminiscent of Augustine's defense of poetic fiction in his *Contra mendacium*, where he remarks that "fictive narrations with true significations" are to be found in the Bible as well as in secular literature (13.28).[14] The episode of Geryon is just such a poetic fiction.[15] The narrator swears to the truth of his account by "le note / di questa comedìa" (the notes of this Comedy) (16.127–8), which is perhaps an arch way of attributing a purely verbal reality to the monster. If this central part of the journey can be characterized as a fiction, then we may be justified in thinking of the whole journey in that way. The *Epistle to Can Grande* gives us some encouragement because it uses the adverb "fictive" in order to describe the poem's *forma tractandi*. In spite of some complications, which will be discussed shortly, the poem could then be said to conform to the definition of the "allegory of poets" given in the *Convivio*: "truth hidden under a beautiful lie."[16]

We shall see that the "allegory of poets" may be interpreted broadly to mean all of the figures and tropes a poet must employ in order to express his intended meaning. Because the meaning is intended, theologians sometimes referred to this kind of allegory as "allegory of the letter." Like the fictive narrations mentioned by Augustine, it is to be found in the Bible as well as in secular literature. Beyond this kind of allegory, however, there is another kind, not in the writer's control, called the "allegory of theologians," which appears only in the Bible and was thought to be divinely inspired. From a modern, naturalistic point of view, it might be said that the allegory of theologians was sometimes a way of interpreting a text in spite of the author's intended meaning, as a way of superimposing a Christian significance anachronistically on an Old Testament text. The significance might also be referred to as the "allegory of the spirit," or, simply, the spiritual sense.

Obviously, the fact that both poets and theologians used the word "allegory" has led to considerable confusion, especially among Dante's interpreters. Most of the confusion has to do with the meaning of the word "literal." For poets, "literal" means what the words say, even if what they say is clearly a fable or a fiction. "Allegory" is what such fables or fictions mean: hence Dante's definition of allegory as truth hidden beneath a beautiful lie. For theologians, on the other hand, concerned with the historical authority of the Bible, the "letter" is thought of as the history of the Jews: the people, facts, and events of the Old Testament, rather than the mode in which the words convey that history. "Littera *gesta* docet," according to the mnemonic jingle of the Schools, "the letter teaches us *what happened.*" This is why the literal level is always true: No matter how poetically recounted, the events of the Old Testament did in fact take place. Such an assertion has nothing whatsoever to do with whether the words conveying those events are figurative or realistic.

An example will help to make this clear. Because the Bible is written in human language, it may be subjected to the same analysis as the writings of a human author. Thus, in a purely poetic analysis of Exodus 19:4, "You saw how I bore you up on eagle's wings," what the poets would call the letter is the figurative language, having to do with eagles and wings, while the allegorical sense has to do with what is signified by that figure, the events of Exodus. For the theologian, on the other hand, the letter lies beyond the words, in the historical fact: God leading the Jews out of Egypt into the desert. The metaphoric or figurative language conveying this literal meaning (wings and the eagle in the present instance) is simply rhetoric, what Thomas Aquinas calls "allegory of the letter."[17] Any meaning clearly intended by a human author is from a theological standpoint necessarily a *literal* meaning, even if conveyed by a most elaborate allegory of poets. No human author living in the time of Moses, however, could have foreseen what theological allegory would make of Exodus: for the theologian, the events of Exodus signify our redemption, wrought by Christ. The allegory of theologians is therefore an allegory *in factis*, not *in verbis*; it is not a way of writing at all, since the literal events were thought to exist quite apart from the words that commemorated them. It was, rather, the retrospective interpretation of the events of Jewish history in order to read in (or *into*) them the coming of Christ.

Theological allegory may be thought of as *meta*-allegory, in which the reality signified by the words of the text—say, Moses, or the river Jordan—is in turn taken as a sign to be further allegorized—Moses "means" John the Baptist, and Jordan "means" baptism—without any compromise of historicity. Taken together, all the persons and events of the Old Testament signify the coming of Christ. Put most simply, allegory in this sense is the relationship of the Old Testament to the New.

Only in a text of which God is the author can things both *mean* and *be*. From such a perspective, Joshua, for example, would not only *be* the man who led the Jews across the Jordan; he would also *mean* Jesus, whose name is the same as Joshua in Aramaic. Joshua existed, which is what is meant by the truth of the literal level, but he also functions as a figure for Christ. For this reason, he may be said to be a "shadow-bearing preface" of his own truth (*Par.* 30.78).

The Old Testament is not the only repository for such signs; theological allegory looks at all reality as though it were so many signs written into a book, of which God is the author. This is what Augustine meant when he said that men use signs to point to things, but only God can use things to point to other things. It is as though there were no "thing-in-itself," but only signs in the "book" of the universe. Dante makes this point in the heaven of Jupiter, where presumably historical individuals, some mentioned only in secular texts, function as signs, semiotic sparks spelling out a biblical text. This suggests that the Bible could be considered the divinely inspired translation of God's anterior "book," historical *gesta*, into human language.

Moses and the Jews really existed and the events of Exodus took place, irrespective of whether the history was recounted in descriptive prose or allegorical poetry. The literal level of the Book of Exodus is the same as the literal level of Psalm 113 (114), "In Exitu Israel de Aegypto," in spite of the fact that the words of the psalm could scarcely be more figurative, with the sea and the river personified and the mountains and hills compared to rams and sheep. The author of the *Epistle to Can Grande* certainly speaks as a theologian rather than a poet when he ignores the lyrical prosopopaeia, the "bella menzogna" of Psalm 113 (114), telling us simply that "the letter [of the first verse] presents us with the departure of the children of Israel from Egypt in the time of Moses." The truth-value of the psalm and that of the Book of Exodus are exactly the same, for it is the truth of history, not of words. "Realism" and "lyricism" are part of the poet's craft; to a theologian defending the truth of the literal level, they are irrelevant.

The theological meaning allegorically signified by the verses beginning "In Exitu Israel de Aegypto" is, according to the epistle, "our redemption, wrought by Christ." Here, too, it is clear that the author speaks as a theologian, since the meaning he ascribes to the verse is recoverable only by accepting on faith the authoritative interpretation given to the Exodus by St. Paul: "we were all with Moses, under the cloud and in the sea."[18] This significance, not discernible in the words of the text or even in the events they signify, could be read into those verses only by a Christian. In fact, theological allegory was virtually synonymous with the Christ-event: "quid *credas* allegoria." The New Testament was thought to be not so much a separate revelation, as the definitive ending of the revelation begun with the Old Testament, the fulfillment of its promise. If the letter of biblical allegory is the history of the Jews, then the spirit, the allegorical sense, is the coming of Christ.

The coming of Christ was believed to have been an event in time that transcended time, a *kairotic* moment that could be repeated in the soul of every Christian until the end of time. Thus, the advent of Christ was believed to be threefold: once, in the past, when He appeared among us in human form; again, in the present, in the soul of the convert or regenerate sinner; finally, at the end of time, in the Second Coming. It follows that the spiritual or allegorical sense, which is essentially the coming of Christ, is also threefold: the historical or allegorical sense as it is recounted in the New Testament; the moral or tropological sense (*quid agas*), meaning the applicability of those events to us now; and the anagogic sense (*quo tendas*), referring to the Second Coming and the end of time. The four levels of biblical allegory are more easily remembered as one plus three, meaning the history of the Old Testament interpreted by the threefold revelation, past, present, and future, of the New.

The word "historical" means *literal* when it applies to the history of the Jews, but it is also used to describe the first of the spiritual senses, meaning the historical coming of Christ. The ambiguity can be the source of some confusion, but it can also serve as a reminder that theological allegory is essentially the juxtaposition of two sets of events, two histories, rather than a rhetorical figure. As for the word "allegory," in its theological acceptance, it too can give rise to some confusion, as the epistle points out. "Allegory" in the strict sense means the second of the four levels of meaning, the historical coming of Christ. But "allegory" broadly speaking, in the theological sense, is synonymous with "spiritual" or "mystical," meaning all of the theological senses put together, the past, present, and future allegorical interpretations of the Old Testament.

Theological allegory may be said to be a reading of the Old Testament as if its plot were the Incarnation. However, there are other interpretive contexts in which the same allegorical principles have been applied. "Old Testament typology," for example, is the relationship of providential events in the history of the Jews to subsequent moments of their history, without reference to the coming of the Messiah. The same principles have also been invoked to establish connections between separate moments in the New Testament, without reference to the Old. Finally, just as the principles of poetic allegory were often applied to the interpretation of biblical texts, so theological principles have from time to time been applied to the interpretation of secular literature. Because of both its subject matter and its allegorical mode, the *Divina Commedia* in particular has been subjected to methods of interpretation that seem more appropriate to the Bible than to a literary work. What is more, many of the bitter disputes about literal truth in Scripture, fundamentalists against latitudinarians, have been recapitulated in the history of Dante criticism, often without the participants being aware of it.

If some interpreters have granted a quasi-biblical status to Dante's work, it is because the text seems to demand it by claiming to be prophetic and divinely inspired. The most obvious way to deal with such a claim is to accept it uncritically, and to attribute the poem's genesis to a vision, or to delusion. No critic has been so "fundamentalist" as to maintain that the entire text, complete with Virgilian echoes and autocitations, was dictated in *terza rima* to the poet/scribe. What has been suggested is that the vision of Beatrice that Dante claimed to have had at the end of the *Vita nuova* was somehow the inspiration for this very different literary text.[19]

The appeal to divine revelation (or hallucination) in the interpretation of a text has a way of ending all discussion. Source hunting is greatly simplified, and one need no longer be puzzled about whom Dante put where and why if he did so on such unimpeachable authority. The theory breaks down, however, when we try to determine which parts of the poem should be considered intrinsic to his vision, and which are simply literary elaboration. Few critics have difficulty accepting Dante's claim that he saw God, for example, but it is evident that not even the poet expects us to believe in Geryon. If, on the other hand, we suppose that Dante's vision is not localized in the text, then it is no more relevant to this poem than Paul's vision is to his letters: Such experiences may enhance the prophetic authority of the visionary among believers, but if they are not in the text, they have little to do with literary interpretation.

A more sophisticated way of dealing with the theological claim is to consider it a literary device, an attempt to imitate Scripture rather than to provide an account of a religious experience. Leo Spitzer perhaps anticipated this formalist approach to the poem when he attempted to understand Dante's impassioned addresses to the reader not as a claim to prophetic witness, as Erich Auerbach had argued, but rather esthetically, as a way for the poem to create its own audience.[20] By far the most influential formalist interpretation of the poem, however, is the work of Charles Singleton, for whom Dante's realism seemed to imitate, perhaps even rival, "God's way of writing."[21]

According to Singleton, Dante must have intended his allegory to be biblical given that he presented the poem's literal level as true, rather than as a "bella menzogna," and only the Bible could make such a claim. Singleton associated the extraordinary realism of Dante's poem with Scripture's claim to truth, construing the allegory of theologians to be, among other things, a superlative way of writing. The elegance of Singleton's argument masked its essential flaw: It blurred the distinction between what *seems* real and what really happened, between poetry and history, as distinguished by Aristotle in the *Poetics*. Singleton's tone was ironic and deliberately provocative, intended to challenge *dantisti* who were diffident about using theology or biblical exegesis to interpret Dante's text. Nevertheless, his argument soon became canonical and led to a certain confusion about the meaning of theological allegory and its applicability to the poem.

The dramatic and mimetic power of Dante's story made it seem too *real* to Singleton for it to be classified as one more poetic allegory "of this for that," in which the literal level is a lie, so he associated it with biblical allegory, in which the letter is supposed to be true. This, said Singleton, is the allegory of "this *and* that." What made this shift possible was the ambiguity of the word "literal." In poetry, the literal level is the fiction, while in theology, it is the historical event. Thus, to say that Dante's fiction is theological allegory is to say that it is not fiction, but fact. Singleton attempted to avoid the obvious contradiction by suggesting that Dante was only *pretending* to be describing historical events: "[the] fiction is that the fiction is not a fiction." This is true, but trivial; such irony might be used to describe any fiction whatever.

The mimetic power of Dante's verses tells us nothing about their historicity, nor would historical truth, if it could be ascertained, make the text more profound or even more interesting. On the contrary, according to Aristotle, poetry is more philosophical and more significant than history because it deals with universals, which may be merely possible, rather than particulars, however true. History makes particular statements that are subject to external criteria of truth or falsity, whereas poetry expresses universals and is judged by its coherence, or by what Northrop Frye called the "centripetal aspect of verbal structure."[22] Never was there a verbal structure more centripetal than Dante's poem, as Singleton, more than anyone else, has helped us understand. Its apparent substantiality does not imply historic truth, however, any more than figurality, in the psalm of exodus, precludes it.

No human author could possibly write theological allegory and still have any idea of its significance. It was precisely the point of theological allegory to take meaning out of the hands of an author and place it under the control of an exegetical tradition. So, for example, the Song of Songs was said to be about the relation of Christ to His Church, and Virgil's fourth *Eclogue* was about the coming of the Messiah, no matter *what* the words seemed to say. For theologians, the measure of all meaning, even in ancient literature, was the Bible, as interpreted by the New Testament. Whether the words of the Old Testament relate a fiction, such as the Song of Songs, or the realities of Jewish history, such as the Exodus, only God could make those elements *mean* the coming of Christ.

There remains the question of whether a human author can *imitate* theological allegory as Singleton suggests, by imitating reality. In fact, mimesis has the opposite effect, short-circuiting allegory and transforming it into irony. Instead of reaching out for meaning allegorically, realism turns significance back on itself by repeatedly affirming and then denying its own status as fiction. In Dante's terms, we might say that realism is alternately truth with the face of a lie, and a fraud that looks like the truth. Mimetic representation reaches ironic impasse rather than significance; it is a Geryon incapable of flight, a chimera with its tail in its mouth.

By its very nature, mimetic representation constantly affirms and simultaneously denies its identity with the original it seeks to reproduce. No matter how closely it resembles its model, we remain aware that it is merely a copy. Dante alludes to its inherent instability when he describes the reliefs on the terrace of pride in *Purgatorio*. They are so lifelike that they defy interpretation by the pilgrim's two senses ("Faceva dir l'un 'No,' l'altro 'Sì, canta,'" *Purg.* 10.60), leaving him unable to decide whether he is perceiving reality or its representation. The continual oscillation between the affirmation and denial of presence ("No . . . Sì, canta") is the same irony that we find expressed in Singleton's repetitive formula ("[the] fiction is that the fiction is not a fiction"). In spite of its mimetic virtuosity, "visibile parlare" remains difficult to interpret. It perplexes precisely because it is so lifelike, more like cinema than iconography.

It may be remarked in passing that if mimesis can provoke the uneasiness we associate with irony, it is also true that our failure to perceive irony may lead us to mistake it for mimesis. Thus Auerbach, in his famous essay on mimesis in *Inferno* 10, unwittingly revealed himself to be a victim of infernal irony when he perceived in the dazzlingly cerebral verses spoken by Cavalcante only "a direct experience of life which overwhelms everything else."[23] Praise for Dante's realism in this encounter masked Auerbach's impatience with the theological import of the father's lament. Far from indicating the biblical nature of the allegory, "mimesis" here indicates that even the most learned of Dante's critics reached an interpretive dead end.

Because he was anxious to account for the poem's extraordinary realism, Singleton associated it with the allegory of the Bible, and sought to distinguish both from the purely literary allegory of poetry. We have, however, seen that what distinguishes the allegory of theologians from the allegory of poets is not verisimilitude, but the fact that it is expressed in things and events, rather than words. Beyond the words of the Bible, there was said to be another allegorical significance, inherent in things signified by the written text, a "deep structure" of meaning independent of any scribal intention. This significance was thought to be part of God's plan for the entire cosmos, the text imagined by Augustine as inscribed on "the parchment of the heavens," without letters and without words (*Conf.* 13.15).

In reality, of course, this ideal allegory was nothing other than the church's interpretation of the Bible, particularly of the Old Testament, hypostatized as though it had an autonomous existence and were the source of the written text, rather than its spectral projection. Its "deep structure" was simply the virtual image of surface structure, a reduplication that created the illusion of origin: Derrida would describe it as a form of "archiécriture."[24] It is in the nature of allegory that it can make no claim to literal truth and that its significance is open to conflicting interpretations. For the believer, however, the illusion that the Bible derived from God's book, when in fact it was its source, had the effect of conferring ontological reality with significance. In such a perfectly intelligible universe, where things are as meaningful as words, the promise of allegory is already fulfilled by the presence of its Maker.

In *Paradiso*, the end term of both the journey and the poem are represented by the vision of the Trinity in the form of a book, made up not of words, but of things: "sustanze e accidenti e lor costume" (*Par.* 33.88). This divine text obviously belongs in the same tradition as Augustine's cosmic parchment, and has been studied in that way, most prominently by E. R. Curtius.[25] Nevertheless, Dante's representation of God's book is distinctively his own. Just as the inscription on the gates of Hell is written in *terza rima*, as though there were no distinction between what he saw and what we read, so the vision of God as a book corresponds to the closure of the text we hold in our hands, despite the protestations of its fragility and dispersion. Dante asserts that God's book is his transcendent source, that he is merely God's humble scribe. It might equally well be said that God's book is the idealized reflection of Dante's own text, serving to justify his prophetic (not to say Promethean) claim. He imitated the Bible by aspiring to its authority, not by copying its style.

## Theology and Literary Structure

We have seen that the allegory of theologians is analogous to poetic allegory, except that it was believed to be inherent in things, rather than merely expressed in words. The same might be said of the general relationship of theology to poetry. The two systems are analogous, except that theology claims to reflect spiritual reality rather than create it. From a modern point of view, theology would seem to be a form of collective poetry that attempts to bestow existence on the perfection to which it aspires, much as St. Anselm's ontological argument tried to confer substantiality on a syllogism. The doctrine of the Incarnation would seem the ultimate sanction for granting reality to verbal structures as it was itself described in the Gospel of John as the *Word* made flesh.

Once theology is recognized as a verbal system, rather than a religion, its affinity to poetry becomes clear. Both use what Kenneth Burke calls the "logic of perfection" to reach totality and closure.[26] Because of this affinity, theologians often used linguistic analogies to describe the spiritual world. According to Burke, it is possible to reverse the process—that is, to reduce theology to "logology" in order to show how theological principles were in fact derived from verbal systems. The interchangeability of theological and poetic coherence is particularly apparent in the works of Augustine, for whom the mystery of time, the relationship of signs to significance in the Eucharist, the creation of the universe, and the inner life of the Trinity, were all to be understood according to verbal and poetic models. Divine justice was like a poem with variable meter, death was like phonemic silence, even God's relationship to the world was thought of as the embodiment of a speech act, the incarnation of a proffered word. The fact that this verbal system was "made flesh" seemed to Augustine to distinguish it from platonism, which he thought of as an equally logocentric system.

A form of logological analysis will help us to understand the theological claim of Dante's poem in terms of narrative principles. Only a believer could accept the truth of theological allegory, since it entails a belief in the possibility of death and resurrection. Yet an analogous act of faith is required to take seriously the claim that autobiographical narrative is a faithful and definitive portrait of an author's former self. The apparent absurdity of theological allegory is much like the narrative absurdity, which we accept each time we are presented with a story that purports to be the true and final portrait of a protagonist who has become narrator and judge of his own story. Spiritual death and resurrection constitute not only the theme of such a narrative, but also the logical condition for its existence, since it cannot begin without a separation of the protagonist from the author, nor end without a return. Singleton is correct to say that Dante's allegory is biblical, but it is not the poem's mimetic power that so qualifies it. It is, rather, its narrative structure, identical to the narrative structure of the Old Testament in the Christian reading, or of any retrospective reading of one's own history, thematically represented as a conversion.[27]

Our discussion of theological allegory has stressed its diachronicity as the juxtaposition of two sets of historical events, rather than a trope. This corresponds exactly to the diachronicity of narrative structure, the "then" of experience reinterpreted in the "now" of the story. It might be argued that narrative diachronicity stands for the "conversion" of the Old Testament into the New, or for the experience of personal conversion. It might equally well be argued, however, that narrative diachronicity creates the illusion of retrospective reinterpretation, that there is no conversion unless and until the story is told. Whether the diachronism of conversion corresponds to an experience or is an illusion created by the narrative, it is the source of the irony that is pervasive in *Inferno*. Infernal irony is a dramatization of the conflict inherent in autobiography, the clash between the naive perspective of a former self, and the retrospective correction superimposed upon it from the ending of the story.

To some exegetes, it seemed that the first words of the Gospel of John referred back to the first words of Genesis. Universal history might be understood as the unfolding of God's word back to its own origin, from the Creation to the Incarnation. It was like a sentence, beginning with the intention of a speaker whose word is gradually unfolded until it has been completely uttered and "made flesh." An analogous circularity exists in the unfolding of autobiography. Beginning with what Burke would call a narrative tautology ("I am I"), a negative is introduced ("I was not always so") in order to be refined away ("therefore I am I").[28] Reconciling the diachronic linearity of the story with this circular return to the beginning is the narrative equivalent of squaring the circle.

The Incarnation is not only the final theme of *Paradiso*, but also the moment that, from the standpoint of narrative logic, makes the poem possible. The transformation of the omniscient, disembodied voice of the narrator into the voice of the pilgrim, speaking in the present tense—"cotal son io"—may be thought of as a novelistic incarnation, the coming together of an intelligible "word" with the "flesh" of individual experience. The geometrical paradox to which Dante alludes corresponds to a narrative paradox: the closing of a narrative circle, which is at the same time squared by the linear temporality of the journey.

# In the Wake of the Argo on a Boundless Sea

In the climactic scene of Joyce's *Portrait of the Artist as a Young Man*, the rowdy companions of the hero, Stephen Dedalus, pause in their seaside horseplay to taunt him by repeatedly chanting his funny name in their schoolboy Greek, as they had done before: "Stephanos Dedalos! Bous Stephanoumenos! Bous Stephaneforos!" This time, however, he is mildly pleased by their raillery, because for the first time his strange name seems to him prophetic: "stephanos" means "a crown," "stephaneforos" is one who wears a crown, and Daedalus, this time spelled with an "ae," is the fabulous artificer of ancient mythology. He interprets the words of his playmates, which they themselves do not understand, to be a prophecy of his future coronation as a sovereign artist.

It is characteristic of Joyce's ironic portrait of his hero that he stages Stephen's vocation as though it were a religious conversion. The voices of children, or in this case, of adolescents, recall the oracular voices of the children in the eighth book of Augustine's *Confessions*, chanting words as they play that Augustine cannot recognize from any childhood games he can remember: "Tolle, lege, tolle, lege!" Finally, he comes to understand that the unfamiliar words are a command directed at him to open the book of Paul's Epistles he carries with him and to read the first passage that strikes his eyes: "Take up and read!" the children seem to be saying. When he reads, he comes upon a passage that leads to his conversion.

Stephen's literary vocation is similarly structured, but the books that inspire him are the words of men, not of God, and, like all father figures for young men, their authors are at once models and rivals. They are identified only by faint allusion, as though their names were sacred. The first refers to "the ghost of the ancient kingdom of the Danes," an unmistakable evocation of Shakespeare. The second, the vision of a hawk-like man soaring to Heaven, can only be Dante. Young Dedalus foresees himself in the company of the greatest of writers, as did Dante when he visited Limbo and found himself to be the sixth "tra contanto senno." In young Stephen's pantheon, however, there are only two father figures. As T. S. Eliot put it, "Shakespeare and Dante divide the world between them; there is no third."

At the name of Daedalus, Stephen seems "to hear the noise of dim waves and to see a winged form flying above the waves and slowly climbing the air. What did it mean? Was it a quaint device opening a page of some medieval book of prophecies and symbols, a hawk-like man flying sunward above the sea, a prophecy of the end [Stephen] had been born to serve and had been following through the mists of childhood and boyhood, a symbol of the artist forging anew in his workshop out of the sluggish matter of the earth a new soaring impalpable imperishable being?" Joyce's purple prose conveys his callow hero's intoxication at the thought of supplanting those great literary ancestors. Had Stephen needed encouragement, Dante's text would have provided him with a precedent for his soaring ambition. In *Purgatorio*, Dante implies that he will wrest away "la gloria della lingua" from the two Guido's, his illustrious predecessors, and claims for himself the highest perch: "forse è nato / chi l'uno e l'altro caccerà del nido" (and he perchance is born that shall chase the one and the other from the nest) (*Purg.* 11.99). There is a hint of the birdman in this imagery; Dante is destined to rule the roost.

The Daedalus of mythology was literally an artificer, the craftsman who constructed his own wings. He was not a man of books, much less of prophecies and symbols. But Dante used the word "fabbro" metaphorically, as Joyce used the word "artificer," to mean a "wordsmith." In *Purgatorio*, Dante refers to Arnaut Daniel as the man who was in his time "il miglior fabbro" of the mother tongue. Eliot used those words when he dedicated "The Wasteland" to his contemporary, Ezra Pound. The assonance of the words "fabulous" and "fabbro" reveals the genesis of the mythic title Joyce gave to Daedalus, which Stephen claimed for himself: "the fabulous artificer."

Stephen's insistence on the medieval provenance of this image of a hawk-like man and the arcane contents of the book surely point to

Dante, who was an exile, like Daedalus before him and Joyce after. Mary Reynolds has shown how pervasive Dante's presence is in Joyce's work and, more recently, Jennifer Fraser has suggested that Joyce's Daedalus in the passage I have quoted even looks like Dante.[1] I would add to Fraser's hypothesis here that the winged form Stephen sees is referred to as "a hawk-like man," not because of his plumage, but because of his raptor physiognomy: the 1564 Venice edition of the poem bears a frontispiece with a portrait of Dante in a profile so startling that bibliophiles have bestowed on the volume an affectionate nickname: "Il Nasone." The frontispiece qualifies as what Joyce calls the "quaint device opening a page of some medieval book." The aquiline nose was in general much admired by physiognomists; the Renaissance polymath Giambattista Della Porta took "il naso adunco" as a sure sign of magnanimity.[2]

Whatever the value of the conflation of Daedalus and Dante to the study of Joyce—and one suspects that it is minor, given the work already done by Reynolds and the vast expanse of sometimes impenetrable Joycean texts still open to research and conjecture—its implications for our interpretation of the *Commedia*, especially of *Paradiso*, are potentially important. Joyce was a passionate Dantista: His friends jocularly referred to him as "Dublin's Dante." Mary Reynolds maintained that just as Dante knew the *Aeneid* by heart, so Joyce knew the *Divina commedia*. She tells us that he used the 1904 edition of the poem by Eugenio Camerini merely for its notes and commentary. Stephen Dedalus was Joyce's surrogate in both *Portrait* and *Ulysses*, an ironic portrait of himself as a younger man. Dante is more kind toward his former self, treating him with condescension rather than irony. When the greatest novelist of modernism suggests an affinity between Daedalus and Dante, he ought to be taken seriously. Joyce's text is an invitation to consider the flight of Daedalus as a prologue to Dante's ascent.

As the undisputed master of word-play, Joyce was unlikely to have missed the pun that Hugh Shankland pointed out to the rest of us some forty years ago: Dante's surname, Alighieri, is reminiscent of the Latin word "aliger," used by Virgil to mean "bearing wings."[3] Another pun, this time in Italian, helps to transform the Greek artificer into an Italian poet. The word "penna," like English "quill," means both "feather" and "pen." The ambiguity is often exploited in the *Commedia*, especially when the context involves both poetry and love. One of the most important instances occurs in canto 24 of *Purgatorio* in the exchange with Bonagiunta da Lucca concerning the "dolce stil novo," a passage that subsequently became canonical in Italian literary history. After Dante's famous definition, "I' mi son un che, quando / Amor mi spira, noto, e a quel modo / ch'è ditta dentro vo significando" (I am one who, when Love inspires me, takes note, and goes setting it forth after the fashion which he dictates within me) (52–4), Bonagiunta comes to understand and replies, "Io veggio ben come le vostre penne / di retro al dittator sen vanno strette" (Clearly I see how your pens follow close after him who dictates) (58–9) where the primary meaning of "penna" is the writing instrument for taking dictation. Immediately following Bonagiunta's words, however, there follows a simile that will echo in the memory of any attentive reader: "Come li augei che vernan lungo 'l Nilo, alcuna volta in aere fanno schiera, / poi volan più a fretta e vanno in filo" (As the bird that winter along the Nile sometimes make a flock in the air, then fly in greater haste and go in file) (64–6). The flight of the birds first "in schiera" and then in formation, calls to mind the fifth canto of *Inferno*, where the souls of the adulterers fly first like starlings, "a schiera larga e piena," then like cranes: "come i gru van cantando lor lai," where the verb "cantare" and its object, "lor lai," seem more appropriate to poets than to cranes.

The flight of doves recurs throughout the poem, most famously with Francesca and Paolo. Francesca's lamentation and her yearning for "pace" echo the Psalms: "Who will give me the wings of the dove [*pennas colombae*] so that I might fly away and be at peace?" (Ps. 54:7). The doves reappear in *Purgatorio*, as the souls listening to Casella's song from the *Convivio* are suddenly scattered like frightened doves by Cato. Finally, in canto 25 of *Paradiso*, Saints James and Peter lavish their affection on each other like doves murmuring and turning about. The wings of the dove in Dante, as in Henry James, are clearly the wings of desire, spanning the progression of the erotic theme established by Plato in the *Phaedrus*. In Dante, the theme of his love is inseparable from his poetry.

The images of the doves seem deliberately placed in the poem to survey Dante's literary career: the gentle heart of the *Vita nuova*, the "amoroso uso di sapienza" with Casella's song in the *Purgatorio* and finally the "caritas synthesis" of *Paradiso*, with the Gospel of John. At the beginning of *Paradiso* 23, when the pilgrim in metaphor is "posato al nido" with Beatrice as the mother bird, awaiting the dawn so that she may feed her fledgling, we may take that nest to be the nest of Leda, who gave birth to the Gemini, under which sign the poet was born. In mythology, the twins were sired by Jupiter, the father of gods and men, in the guise of a swan. For Dante, pagan myth was the collective dream of humanity, awaiting revelation for its truth to be revealed. In this new light, Beatrice is the mother who in this canto shows Dante the triumph of Christ and of all the blessed in an upside-down snow storm of glory. His return to the nest, a spiritual homecoming to the sign of his birth, is his poetic triumph.

It was the ingenuity and art of Daedalus that led young Stephen to choose the mythic hero as his spiritual godfather. In Ovid's beautiful story of Daedalus in Book 8 of the *Metamorphoses*, the fabrication of the wings is described in loving detail, explaining how the feathers were arranged, glued and tied, and shaped to resemble real wings. One delicate touch even suggests a melody of flight: The feathers are arranged in unequal lengths, like the rustic pipes of Pan. One might think of Stephen's aspirations as equally pagan as there is no hint of the supernatural in Stephen's literary vocation. His calling is so clearly a rejection of faith that he chooses the words of Lucifer to announce it: "Non serviam."

The hawk-like man of Stephen's vision flies only sunward—we do not know how far—and Ovid's Daedalus follows a moderate course, neither so close to the sun as to melt the wax from his wings, nor so close to the sea as to become water-logged. As for the price of his daring, he loses his son. Icarus is a brash and mischievous boy in Ovid's story, a daredevil with borrowed wings, as was Phaeton with his father's chariot. Dante mentions them both during his terrorizing descent on Geryon. Joyce scholars have attempted to read Icarus as the failed alter ego of Stephen's story, but in the myth, Icarus seems to be not much more than the powerful icon of a father's grief. The world's indifference to his death is portrayed indelibly in Pieter Bruegel's famous landscape called the *Fall of Icarus*, in which it takes the viewer a few minutes to find in the sea the disappearing legs of the boy, in the lower-right corner of a canvas filled with Bruegel's familiar peasants: a fisherman, a shepherd and his flock, a ploughman in a field, and a ship coming in to a tranquil port, their placid routine completely undisturbed.

Dante went far beyond the sun in his flight to the absolute, but so did Daedalus in the Neoplatonic allegories of the early Christian era. Pierre Courcelle has traced the flight of Daedalus not only among learned Neoplatonists, but also in popular culture reflected in numerous funerary inscriptions and monuments. In spite of the accounts of Ovid and Virgil, this Daedalus makes it to the stars and even beyond. In Boethius's thoroughly Christian version of the story, it is Lady Philosophy who affixes wings to the mind of the poet: "so that you may safely return home by my guidance, following the path I will show you, carrying you there."

The first meter of the fourth book of the *Consolation of Philosophy* is virtually an epitome of Dante's journey through Paradise, propelled by the "pennas volucres" through each of the spheres, one by one, to the furthest point of the fixed stars in the aether. Most astonishing, at journey's end, he will tread the outer convex "dorsum" of the universe, what Dante would describe as the "empireo," and behold the awesome light and the King of Kings. The traveler will say in memory, "Haec dices, memini, patria est mihi, hinc ortus, hic sistam gradum" (This is my home, hence was I derived, here I end my journey). There is no text that Dante knew better than the sixth century *Consolation*. He cites it as a source for his first person narrative in the *Convivio*, along with the *Confessions* of Augustine. Boethius is placed among the "spiriti sapienti" in *Paradiso*; we are told his body rests in "Cieldauro." It is in fact in the crypt of the church of S. Pietro in Cielo d'Oro in Pavia, directly below the tomb of Augustine in the upper church.

There is no room for Icarus in this meter, just as there seems to be little room for him in the funerary inscriptions collected by Courcelle, where the emphasis is on the return of Daedalus. Nevertheless, the interpreters of Joyce are probably correct in assuming that every Daedalus must have its Icarus, but one wonders if the mythological history of Icarus were not too slender a reed for such formidable opposition. Dante's celestial navigation does have its anti-type, however, whose death by drowning is much more dramatic than the fall of "Icaro misero." His presence is implicit in a rhetorical tradition based on Virgil's account of Daedalus in the sixth book of the *Aeneid*, told from the perspective of the ending.

At Cumae, Daedalus returned to earth and, heart-sick, dedicated his wings (*remigium alarum*) to Apollo. He then built a temple and on its walls portrayed his adventures in Athens and Crete, including Minos and the minotaur, Pasiphae, Ariadne, and the labyrinth. He was about to depict the fall of Icarus at the end of his life's story, but grief overcame him and twice his hands fell to his side.

The jewel-like passage, cut off in the narrative just as Daedalus is cut off in his depiction of Icarus, is fraught with meaning. Michael Putnam has pointed out that, inasmuch as the *Aeneid* itself is truncated, with the impious slaughter of Turnus by *pius Aeneas*, the story constitutes Virgil's grieving reflection on his own unfinished career.[4] For our purposes, the dedication to Apollo of the *remigium alarum*— variously translated as "steerage of his wings," "winged oarage," or "twin sweep of his wings," is the cue for the introduction of Dante's anti-Daedalus. The metaphor of the "remigium alarum" is mentioned by virtually all etymologists from Isidore of Seville in the seventh century to Uguccione da Pisa, Dante's near contemporary, who in his *Magnae Derivationes* begins his entry on the word "metaphora" with this figure. Isidore calls it a "reciprocal" metaphor because it can mean "wings like oars" or "oars like wings." It gives us *in nuce* the navigation both of Daedalus/Dante and of his anti-type, Ulysses, who says of his journey "dei remi facemmo ali al folle volo." Anyone who doubts the association of Ulysses with the fabled Icarus would have to explain why else Dante's last view from the starry heaven would be of a vast and empty sea and "il varco folle d'Ulisse."

As abrupt as Dante's transition from Daedalus to Ulysses may seem to us, it is entirely coherent in terms of Neoplatonic allegorization of the myths since both navigations were thought to represent the flight of the soul to the absolute. In fact, Courcelle's work on funerary inscriptions is entitled "Quelques symboles funeraire du neo-platonisme latin: Le vol de Dédale; Ulysse et les Sirènes."[5] In most allegorized versions of the Ulysses myth, the sea represents the evils of this world and in some the sirens are even a help rather than a hindrance.

Odysseus was shipwrecked off the island of the Phaecians in Book 5 of the *Odyssey*, but survived to meet Nausicaa and her father. In canto 26 of *Inferno*, however, Ulysses's shipwreck is definitive. One cannot help being intrigued by the reference to Dante as a castaway in the opening verses of the poem: "come quei che con lena affannata, / uscito fuor dal pelago alla riva" (as he who with laboring breath has escaped from the deep to shore) (*Inf.* 1.22–3). It recalls the swollen and heaving breath of Odysseus when he was washed ashore on his raft. That near-drowning became a topos in Neoplatonic allegorizations of the *Odyssey* and was probably available to Dante, by however circuitous a route. It speaks volumes about the poet's affinity with Ulysses. In the Christian exegesis of the Odyssey, Augustine identified the raft with the cross of Christ, saying that no one can survive the sea of life without the death and resurrection the cross implies. Dante probably alludes to that theme when he refers to the "pelago" as "lo passo che non lasciò già mai persona viva" (the pass that never left anyone alive) (1.26–7). I have argued that *Inferno* may be said to begin from the shipwreck of the *Convivio*, which has a flourishing navigational exordium but, for obvious reasons, no arrival in port. We might suggest that the pilgrim is in this sense a Ulysses who survived.

After ascending through all of the planetary heavens, the pilgrim reaches the starry Empyrean and looks back from the Gemini to survey in retrospect the spheres through which he has come. He smiles when his gaze reaches our humble globe, described in his *humilis* style: "l'aiuola che ci fa tanto feroci" (the threshing floor that makes us so ferocious) (*Par.* 22.151). This review of the heavens from the prospect of the stars has its source in "The Dream of Scipio," from Cicero's *De republica* (6.20.21–2), a text otherwise unknown to the Middle Ages, except for Macrobius's commentary on the dream, perhaps the most influential ancient literary text for medieval cosmological speculation. Boethius too alludes to the view from the heavens as a useful corrective for human vainglory (*Consolation* 2.7).

Since the vantage point is from his birth sign, we might expect the pilgrim to look back, not only in space to the humble earth, but also in time, over his own past. The first glance from the Gemini to the earth, with all of its hills and river mouths, is a spatial survey, with an implied public judgment addressed to all of us. Just before they leave the heaven of the fixed stars, however, Beatrice tells the pilgrim to look down at the earth once again, but this time the dimension is temporal and the reference is intensely personal. Commentators have traditionally interpreted this second look as a farewell to earth, much like the farewell of Glaucus, the fisherman who became a consort of the gods. At the opening of *Paradiso*, Dante had used Glaucus as an *exemplum* of his own ascent to the supernatural. Ovid's tale of the apotheosis relates the poignant farewell of the fisherman who transcended the human: "Repetenda . . . numquam terra, vale!" (nevermore to return, O Earth, farewell!) (*Metamorphoses* 13.947–8). The valediction of Glaucus might have been a suitable gloss of Dante's second gaze downward, had his farewell not been so definitive. However, the simple logic of autobiography, in which beginning and ending coincide, means that the pilgrim must return to earth as poet, to tell us all. The gaze must serve another purpose.

This second gaze earthward takes in no topographical detail at all, except precisely these waters, somewhere between Gibraltar and the shores of Purgatory. From this vantage point, the heaven of the fixed stars, Scipio in his dream had looked down at the whole Roman Empire, but the pilgrim's view is blocked by the sun beneath his feet: "E più mi fora discoverto il sito / di questa aiuola; ma 'l sol procedea / sotto i mie' piedi un segno e più partito" (more of the space of this little threshing floor would have been disclosed to me, but the sun was proceeding beneath my feet and was a sign and more away) (*Par.* 27.85–7). So, dazzled by the sun and unable to see anything of the inhabited world, Dante instead looks down and westward at a featureless ocean and thereby introduces something new into the epic tradition, never dreamt of by Cicero or Macrobius. It is a glance down at an interior sea, where the pilgrim sees what no else can, a retrospective glance down at his own history, staged in nautical terms.

Of all of the things that might have been seen on this downward gaze from the shore of Phoenicia to Cadiz and out to the ocean, Dante mentions only one, visible only to him and then only in his mind's eye: "io vedea di là da Gade il varco folle d'Ulisse" (beyond Cadiz I saw the mad wake of Ulysses) (27.82–3). The preternatural eclipse of part of the earth by the sun, erasing all of the Roman history conveyed by the ancient topos, seems sufficiently contrived to jolt us out of the public realm into the intensely subjective. I have translated "varco" as "wake" in order to give some concreteness to what is really an abstract noun, usually meaning a crossing or a passing—Singleton translates it as "track"—but neither his word nor mine helps us to visualize what Dante claims to have seen, since the wake of any ship is quickly effaced and can linger only in memory. The wake of Ulysses is a snapshot or a freeze frame from the past, a spectral line on an empty canvas or *page blanche*, timelessly heading toward disaster. It is a picture meant to be read, rather than seen. As he looks down from the heavens, Dante sees a line that can only be a line from his own text, "dei remi facemmo ali al folle volo" (we made of our oars wings for the mad flight) (*Inf.* 26.125), the words that Ulysses used to describe his disastrous course. Because whatever he sees is his own handiwork, the comparison with Daedalus is irresistible. As Icarus disappears in Ovid's story, Daedalus looks down at an empty sea at the flotsam of his wings and curses his own art: "pennas aspexit in undis / devovitque suas artes" (he saw the feathers on the waves, and cursed his arts) (*Metamorphoses* 8.233–4). It is the last thing the pilgrim sees before his beloved's face and his intense desire for her impel him upward toward the Primum Mobile.

The strangeness of this autocitation, highlighted on a blank background viewed from outer space, is compounded by our perplexity about the figure of Ulysses, who is undoubtedly the most important character in Hell and the least known, in spite of the enormous bibliography dedicated to him. He is the only major interlocutor among the sinners in Hell who is not a contemporary or near contemporary of the poet, but he is also the only sinner with an afterlife in the poem: He is mentioned once and alluded to twice in *Purgatorio* and named again here in the final cantica, in an episode of high relief. If the use of the pronoun "we" in the first, public, glance at the earth ("che *ci* fa tanto feroci") precluded condescension, that is not the case here, where the staging of the action tells us virtually nothing, except that the pilgrim looks down, if not with the grief of Daedalus, at least with elegiac regret, perhaps even for his former self. Ulysses may be thought of as Dante's own portrait of the artist as a young man. If James Joyce knew that, he deliberately reversed the chronology.

The figure of Ulysses, pervasive throughout the journey as is no other mythological person, hides his identity, like Odysseus in the cave of Cyclops, who says that his name is "nobody," hoping he will be believed. To say that Ulysses is only Ulysses, as we usually do, is to surrender interpretation in favor of the credulity of Polyphemus. The phantom wake of Ulysses in fact traces an essential line of Dante's life and work, at the end of which we might expect to find what Neil Hertz, in his book *The End of the Line*, described as "an edgy doubling of the author's consciousness," an alter ego, similar in every respect to himself, except for the intercession of Beatrice.[6]

Ulysses's exhortation to his crew in *Inferno* echoes Aristotle's words in the *Metaphysics* and the citation of them by Dante in the *Convivio*: "Considerate la vostra semenza: / fatti non foste a viver come bruti, / ma per seguir virtute e canoscenza" (Consider your origin: you were not made to live as brutes, but to pursue virtue and knowledge) (26.118–20). The words seem as noble to us as they did to Dante in his earlier work, when he dreamt of a celestial Athens, where the greatest of philosophers would meet to "philosophize." In the third book of the *Convivio*, Dante had gone so far as to deny any natural desire for the beatific vision, inasmuch as one could desire only what one knew, according to Aristotle, and no one could know God in his essence. Philosophy, enlightened by Theology, could lead the way to happiness through "conoscenza." By the time he wrote *Inferno*, the great philosophers dwelled in a castle surrounded by darkness and illuminated by firelight in Limbo, where happiness, as Virgil explains, is out of the question ("sanza speme vivemo in disio" [without hope, we live in desire]) (*Inf.* 4.42). In his poem, he returned to the fundamental paradox of Christianity, that the desire to know God is natural, but that knowledge is a supernatural gift. The wisest of human hearts is forever "unquiet" until, like the humble Samaritan woman or innocent children, it will have found rest: "nos requieturos in tua grandi sanctificatione speramus" (we hope that we shall have found rest when you admit us to the great holiness of your presence) (*Conf.* 12.38).

From the moment that Beatrice called Dante by name in canto 30 of *Purgatorio*, the novelistic dimension that distinguishes this epic from all others became explicit. The momentous and indescribably beautiful reunion with Beatrice ended with a scolding and a startling simile. As she takes stock of his past before the final part of his journey, she is like an admiral, "quasi ammiraglio," pacing between stern and bow, preparing to weigh anchor. The simile may have seemed less incongruous to Dante's contemporaries than it appears to us. The word "admiral" is of Arabic origin, but a widespread folk etymology in the Middle Ages confused it with Latin *admirari*, "to wonder at." This verb in turn had a technical theological significance. According to Thomas Aquinas, it describes the astonishment the soul will experience at the beatific vision (*Summa Theologica* 2, p.1, q.41, ad. 4; 2, p.1, q.32, ad. 8; etc.). With its derivatives it appears often in *Paradiso*, but pointedly, as we shall see, in connection with the Argonauts, at the beginning and at the end of Dante's ascent to Paradise. Using this otherwise incongruous simile to describe Beatrice identifies her as the commander of the pilgrim's celestial navigation. We might say that the late Ulysses is thereby commissioned as the new Jason.

The majestic and longest address to the reader that begins the second canto of *Paradiso* is a navigational metaphor that recapitulates the others we have been discussing and anticipates those that lie ahead. It derives from a somewhat tedious autobiographical allegory in the prologue of *De beata vita*, a text that is also essential for understanding the significance of Ulysses's voyage in *Inferno*. The prologue begins by distinguishing philosophically weak "mariners" from experts capable of sailing the open seas in order to arrive at the port of true happiness (*De beata vita* 1.2). In Dante's adaptation, Augustine's transparent allegory acquires historical depth and existential force from the allusions that prepared the way for it in the preceding *cantiche*. The voice belongs to someone who narrowly escaped the fate of Ulysses: "O voi che siete in piccioletta barca, / desiderosi d'ascoltar, seguiti / dietro al mio legno che cantando varca . . ." (O you that are in your little bark, eager to hear, following my ship that singing makes her way) (*Par.* 2.1–3). The poet warns those who are not prepared to follow him to turn back: "non vi mettete in pelago, ché, forse / perdendo me, rimarreste smarriti" (Do not commit yourselves to the open sea, or you might, if you lost me, remain astray) (2.5–6), recalling the "pelago" of the poet's own ship-wreck and his losing his way, "smarrita" in the dark wood. In this exhortation, the poet casts himself as the first successful mariner of the heavens.

He says of his poem/ship that it makes its way singing: "cantando varca." The word "varcare" is the verbal form of the noun we discussed in the phrase "il varco folle di Ulisse"; the context allows us to trans-late it as "to sail" and to extend that definition proleptically to the noun describing Ulysses's mad journey. By itself, this definition con-tributes no substantiality to the spectral line seen by the pilgrim in his last gaze at the earth, but when the address to the reader turns away from mariners in a fragile bark to those who have already converted to "the bread of angels," Dante encourages them to follow in the poet's *wake:* "mettere potete ben per l'alto sale / vostro navigio, servando mio solco / dinanzi a l'acqua che ritorna eguale" (you may indeed commit your vessel to the deep brine, holding to my furrow ahead of the water that returns smooth again) (2.14–15). So the lines of this address to the reader are to be followed as though they were the wake of the poet as he navigates through the spheres of Paradise, or the wake of Ulysses headed for disaster.

We, the readers, will be more astonished than were the glorious Argonauts when they saw Jason turned plowman: "non s'ammiraron come voi farete" (they were not as amazed as you shall be). The episode of Jason being forced to plow a field with fabulous bulls he had tamed is told in Book 7 of the *Metamorphoses* (100–58). The metaphoric asso-ciation with navigation is inevitable; a furrow is a wake on dry land. In Italian as well as in Latin, "solco" / "sulcus" has that double meaning.

But we have shown that the association with the writing of poetry is also inevitable in the terms set forth by this address to the reader. Readers of the poem will be more amazed in the wake of this poem than were the Argonauts by the lines traced by Jason's plough. The Argonauts are called "gloriosi," a word that exploits the contrary pagan and Christian valences of that adjective: Ancient heroes were valorous and sometimes even boastful (*gloriosi*), while their Christian counterparts aspire to beatitude, to dwell "in glory," like Beatrice, the "gloriosa donna" of the *Vita nuova*. "Ammirare," on the other hand, is unequivocally theological. It is a word that never appears in Hell and instead appears here and in the last canto of the poem, in the divine presence.

The word and the theme of the Argo appear at the ending of the poem, when the pilgrim sees God as a brilliant all-containing point of light: "Un punto solo m'è maggior letargo / che venticinque secoli a la 'mpresa / che fé Nettuno ammirar l'ombra d'Argo" (One moment makes for me greater oblivion than twenty-five centuries have wrought upon the enterprise that made Neptune wonder at the shadow of the Argo) (*Par.* 33.92). Georges Poulet discussed the significance of the daring double sense of the phrase "un punto solo" (one point alone). It is expressed in the present tense, and so the meaning of "punto" must be temporal—"now"—with respect to the narrative voice clearly established in the preceding verse: "dicendo questo, mi sento ch'io godo" (in telling this, I feel my joy increase). The forgetfulness is the poet's. In the experience of the pilgrim, however, he beheld the divine point in space, the infinitesimal, containing within itself all things, "conflati insieme" (fused together) and all that has happened since the voyage of the Argo. For the time that he beheld the light he participated in its synoptic view of all space and all time, *totum simul*, according to Boethius's description of God. Now, in the writing of the poem, nothing is left of the vision but "il dolce che nacque da essa" (the sweetness that was born of it) (33.63).[7]

In mythology, the Argo was translated to the stars after its successful voyage and became the largest constellation of the southern hemisphere. It does not, therefore, seem inappropriate that it should be the last extended figure in the poem. It is viewed at the end of the celestial navigation from the perspective of Neptune, looking up to its keel as it passes overhead. From the perspective of the King of the depths, it is a flight, an unprecedented eclipse of the light whose omnipresence had made it until that moment imperceptible. The story of the Argo as represented in antiquity might have prepared us to expect indignation on the part of Neptune for having discovered a trespasser in his realm, but Dante instead records the god's "ammirazione," the theologically charged word associated with Jason's feat at the beginning of the *cantica*. The stupendous figure is a dramatization of the principle of negative theology, according to which, like Neptune, we can perceive the divine light only by describing its absence, the shadow it casts over our understanding. It is extraordinarily apt for describing the poetry of *Paradiso* as well, the subject matter of which—"trasumanare"—is by definition out of reach. The divine light can be revealed only in shadows, like a pearl on a white forehead (*Par.* 3.14) or writing on a blank page.

Dante's reason for describing that momentary blocking of the light from the bottom of the sea is to suggest an analogy between Neptune's view of the Argo and our view of the cosmic poem. Only from the depths can a navigation be perceived as a flight. Neptune is wonderstruck by the Argo's shadow and we are wonderstruck by the shadow of Dante's celestial navigation. In the first canto of *Paradiso*, Dante prayed for Apollo's inspiration: "se mi presti / tanto che l'ombra del beato regno / segnata nel mio capo io manifesti" (lend yourself to me, that I may show forth the shadow of the blessed realm which is imprinted in my mind) (1.22–4). The poem is the answer to that prayer, the depiction of a shadow on the final page of the book of memory. This may be a reminiscence of a passage from a pseudo-hermetic anonymous book of aphorisms compiled in the twelfth century, *The Book of the Twenty-four Philosophers*. The twenty-first aphorism states that "Deus est tenebra in anima post omnem lucem relicta" (God is the shadow which remains in the soul after all light is gone).[8] If this is not a source for Dante's "ombra del beato regno" in his invocation to Apollo, it is nevertheless a superb gloss.

The shadow of the Argo brought together the themes of flight and of navigation, but these had already been adumbrated, appropriately enough, in *Inferno*, where the conflict between Dante and Ulysses, his anti-type, first became apparent. The midpoint of the pilgrim's descent into hell is a grotesque flight on the back of a patchwork monster, the image of fraud with an honest face and the sting of a scorpion, impressed against its will into the service of the descent into lower Hell. The monster docks on the edge of the abyss—"arriva" in the etymological sense—backwaters away, comes about and strokes the air. It is called a "navicella," of which Virgil is the pilot. The pilgrim is terrified by the flight and by the disastrous *exempla* he recalls of Phaeton and Icarus. In contrast, the daring voyage of Ulysses is defined by the hero himself as a mad flight, a "folle volo": "dei remi facemmo ali al folle volo," precisely the spectral line seen from the Gemini.

Canto 26 of *Inferno*, in which the reversible metaphor appears, is itself the canto of enemy brothers: The forked tongue of flame is compared with the forked flame rising from the funeral pyre of the Theban enemy brothers, Eteocles and Polynices. Dante's narrative voice takes the episode as a moral *exemplum*:

> Allor mi dolsi, e ora mi ridoglio
> quando drizzo la mente a ciò ch'io vidi,
> e più lo 'ngegno affreno ch'i' non soglio,
> perché non corra che virtù nol guidi
>
> *Inf.* 26.19–22

> I sorrowed then, and sorrow now again, when I turn my mind to what I saw; and I curb my genius more than is my wont, lest it run where virtue not guide it

Directing the *exemplum* to himself strongly suggests that he and Ulysses participated in a common endeavor. That power was memorably invoked in canto 10 of *Inferno*, comparing Dante's "altezza d'ingegno" to that of his "first friend," Guido Cavalcanti.

When the pilgrim reaches the Primum Mobile he moves from the material world to the spiritual and from memory to expectation. He is at last standing at the end of the universe, where Lucretius said no one could stand. In canto 28, he looks into the eyes of Beatrice, "quella che 'mparadisa la mia mente" (she who imparadises my mind) (3) and sees reflected in them the effulgent display to which he turns. He sees the divine point, a burning and dazzling light, closely surrounded by the whirling circle of fiery Seraphim and then encircled by the other angels of the hierarchy, in orbits which increase in circumference and decrease in speed in direct proportion to their distance from God. It is as if the universe were turned inside out. A wiseacre is said to have suggested that it is like someone thrusting his arm into the maw of a charging tiger, grabbing the root of its tail and yanking it toward himself, turning the beast inside out, so that it runs off in the opposite direction. For all of its irreverence, the anecdote exemplifies a thoroughly Dantesque reification of a figure of speech, like the punishments in Hell and Purgatory, literalizations of the various figures describing the transgressions. In this instance, the anonymous anecdote is a literalization of *hysteron proteron* ("the last put first"), which the poet uses to describe the ascent to Paradise: "forse in tanto in quanto un quadrel posa / e vola e da la noce si dischiava / giunto mi vidi . . ." (perhaps in that time that a bolt strikes, flies, and from the catch is released, I saw myself arrived) (*Par.* 2.23). The figure, of which there are other examples in the poem, became the leit-motif of Charles Singleton's essay, "The Vistas in Retrospect."[9]

In antiquity, the circular movement of the heavens was thought to be the distinctive mark of rationality. Aristotle believed that rest was the normal state of matter, so the uniform revolution of the planetary spheres had to be explained by the existence of motor "intelligences," which were later identified by Christians with the angels of Scripture. The angels are ranked according to the intensity of their love and their power, which is determined by their relative proximity to God, rather than by their magnitude, as are the planets in the material world. Here at the boundary, it is as if two inversely proportioned systems, one below and one above, were juxtaposed for the pilgrim's inspection: the real world and, in the phrase that is often used to explain the Platonic Ideas, the "*really* real."

The extraordinary implication of the pilgrim's gaze at the overwhelming brightness of the divine point is that the angelic hierarchy circling God geometrically resembles our own solar system. When the poet referred to God in the heaven of the sun as "il sole de li angeli" (the sun of the angels), he was using a traditional metaphor. A modern reader, more familiar with the order of our solar system than with the Ptolemaic system it replaced, might mistake the metaphor of the "sol angelorum" for a simple spatial analogy: The angels revolve around God as the planets revolve around the sun.

In the material world, God is outside of the system, enveloping the whole cosmos. Beatrice says of the primum mobile "non ha altro dove / che la mente divina" (no other place than the mind of God) (*Par.* 27.109–10). Yet He is the starting point upon which the heavens and all of nature depend: "parendo inchiuso da quel ch'elli nchiude" (seemingly enclosed by that which it encloses) (30.12). Alain de Lille used that metaphor to describe the womb of the Virgin, and Dante perhaps alludes to Alain's version, transforming it into an oxymoron of generation implicit in her title, Vergine Madre: "figlia del tuo figlio" (daughter of your son) (33.1). Although the mystic "infinite sphere" may be a metaphor as ancient as Parmenides, the earliest text we have is, once more, the *Book of the Twenty-four Philosophers* defines God: "Deus est sphaera infinita cuius centrum est ubique, circumferentia nusquam" (God is the infinite sphere for which the center is everywhere and the circumference nowhere). The history of the metaphor in literary consciousness was traced by Poulet in *Les Metamorphoses du cercle*.

Dante's use of the ancient metaphor is unique. Rather than leave it as a mystical paradox, he uses his geometrical imagination to make the theological mystery plausible. In the transition between Hell and Purgatory, for example, we were presented with two congruent shapes: the cone of Hell and the Mountain of Purgatory. We are explicitly told that they are of equal volume because the earth that filled the cone before time began rose up in fear when Satan fell, forming the mountain in the southern hemisphere. Hell and Purgatory together stand for the process of conversion. The theme is a butterfly dissection of a process that is logically two-fold but existentially one: the death of the former self and the birth of a new self. Although in real life the two processes take place at the same time, Dante's analysis represents them sequentially as the descent into Hell and the ascent of Purgatory. From a geometric standpoint, I have said that there is one ideal cone, within which the pilgrim and his guide descend, then turn upside down to retrace their path from the base of the cone, this time ascending on its surface. They move in the same absolute direction, but because of their inversion, they appear to be a winding to the right, instead of to the left.

In the last node of the poem, between matter and the Empyrean, the geometry is virtually impossible to visualize. In the linear narration of the story, the vision of the angelic hierarchy, the supernatural solar system, comes immediately after the account of ascent through the geocentric system of *Paradiso* and is juxtaposed to it as though the two systems were placed side by side, one after the other, before and after the text of canto 28. In fact, however, the two systems that the pilgrim sees in the middle ground between the physical world and the spiritual are one, as matter and spirit are one, although they can be intellectually distinguished. They cannot be visualized, however, any more than we can visualize a tiger running simultaneously in opposite directions, since this would require visualizing four dimensions: the three dimensions of any volume and a fourth dimension of space/time, connecting every point on the physical spheres with its inversely correspondent mover. God would be the circumference of the physical spheres, but the center of all of its movers, "parendo inchiuso da quel ch'egl'inchiude." The unimaginable result would be a hypersphere, boundless but finite, turning back on itself, to and from the God who is simultaneously its center and its circumference.

In a remarkable article, published in 1923, H. D. Austin confronted for the first time, as far as I know, the problem of Dante's representation of the immaterial reversal of all things in terms of hyperspace: "the concept . . . of the spiritual aspect of the cosmos as an inversely proportioned counterpart to its material ordering was a sublime inspiration of genius . . . that would nowadays be described as a rotation through the fourth dimension, in hyperspace—it must be turned inside out, [so that the pilgrim] will be able then to take cognizance of the world from the outside in."[10] Putting together the physical cosmos with its spiritual exemplar can be accomplished by topology, a branch of modern mathematics, but it is impossible to visualize more than three dimensions. The best that one can do is to draw analogies from our world and try to imagine what another dimension might be like. A passage in *Paradiso* describes two separate movements in time that we can try to imagine as if they were simultaneous.

The image is the last of the homespun images I will mention in Dante's poem. In canto 14, in a very different context, Dante says: "Dal centro al cerchio, e sì dal cerchio al centro,/movesi l'acqua in un ritondo vaso,/secondo ch'è percossa fuori o dentro" (from the center to the rim and so from the rim to the center, the water in a round vessel moves, according as it is struck from within or without) (*Par.* 14.1–3). If we could imagine God as the center of all of spirituality and as the rim of all of physical reality, and imagine Him striking from within and without at the same time, we would then be able to approximate the cosmological representation of the mystic aphorism. The difficulty is that if we imagine God striking from within and without at the same time, the rim and the center would have to coincide, as do the maximum circumference and the minimum point in the mystical geometry of Nicholas of Cusa. The "ritondo vaso" would have to become the boundless sea surrounded by its own center. It would be much like the mystery pervading Emily Dickinson's well: "A neighbor from another world/residing in a jar/whose limit none have ever seen/but just his lid of glass" (3–6).

Within the Empyrean, Dante manages to represent the simultaneity of the two divine "percosse," within and without, with an optical metaphor. After the pilgrim is himself transformed by bathing his eyes in a river of light, outside of the cosmos and in the divine realm, he sees God striking simultaneously with a ray of light both the angelic choirs and the spheres. The light is both refracted and reflected, down to the Primum Mobile and thence filtered in varying degrees throughout all of the heavenly spheres, but at the same time reflected back up from the surface of the last sphere, creating an amphitheater of light, which is the celestial rose, where all of the blessed are seated:

> E come clivo in acqua di suo imo
>     si specchia, quasi per vedersi adorno,
>         quando è nel verde e ne' fioretti opimo,
> sì soprastando al lume intorno intorno,
>     vidi specchiarsi in più di mille soglie
>         quanto di noi là su fatto ha ritorno
>
> *Par.* 30.109–14

As a hillside mirrors itself in water at its base, as if to look upon its own adornment when it is rich in grasses and in flowers, so above the light round and round about in more than a thousand tiers I saw all that of us have won return up there

The glorious image, essentially the cone of the angelic solar system, the "clivo," and its parabolic reflection from the surface of the Primum Mobile, might strike us as narcissistic, were it not for the basic premise, that all human beings have in fact been created in the image of God.

We know how the vision ends: in the single word "Amore," which sums up all of his life, his work, and his faith. Its emphatic position at the beginning of the last verse is the ecstatic culmination of the vision and would also be the end of the poem, but for the final dependent clause. Singleton, whose eye and ear for Dante's verse were unsurpassed, insisted on the importance of this clause because it shifts the perspective of the narrator from the Empyrean down to us, looking up with him to the sun and the other stars. I have been talking throughout this chapter about a return to earth. If there is one, it would have to be here: "l'amor che move il sole e l'altre stelle."

In a sense, to have found God is already to have returned, even if the return is to the city of Ravenna. In a boundless but finite world, any linear trajectory ultimately returns to its point of origin, because space/

time itself is curved. In Dante's poem, all of the universe is contained in the mind of God: "non ha altro 'dove' che la mente divina" (no other "where" than the mind of God) (*Par.* 27.109). Moreover, if God is both center and circumference, the distinction between inside and out is obliterated. It is as if we imagined the pilgrim's traveling around one of those circular ribbons of the *Timaeus*, or a hoop of the armillary sphere wrapped around the closed world of antiquity. If that band were given a single 180 degree twist, it would be transformed from a two-sided strip into a single surface, where it became impossible to distinguish the inside from the outside. In topology, such a figure is called a "Möbius strip." In more humble terms, it is like a conveyor belt, given a single twist so as to wear evenly along its single side. In terms of the theme, it would be like an autobiographical novel that claims to be true and definitive, a linear progression toward its own origin.

There remain the few words of the last clause, dependent on "Amore," as is heaven and all of nature (*Par.* 28.42). I would like to suggest that the brief phrase is a "dying fall," back to earth. The term, "dying fall," comes from Shakespeare in *Twelfth Night*, the play that begins with Duke Orsino listening to his consort's music: "That strain agen, it had a dying fall." The noun translates Latin *cadentia* or Italian *cadenza* but the poignant adverb, "dying," made it irresistible in English poetry from Pope to Eliot and subsequently turned it into a cliché. Earl Wasserman discusses it in his essay on Pope's "Ode to Musick," in which he associates it with Orpheus. The memorable lines in Pope's poem give an example of the cadence in terms that denote it: "Exulting in triumph now swell the bold notes, / In broken air, trembling, the wild music floats; / Till by degrees, remote and small, / The strains decay, / and melt away / in a dying, dying fall."

In spite of its overuse, "dying fall" seems especially appropriate for Dante's last clause. It begins with the resounding first word, after which there is a mandatory pause. The secondary accent then falls on the word "sole" and then fades away with the soft liquids of "altre stelle." The phrase ends on the same word that ended *Inferno* and *Purgatorio*. Here, it suggests calm resignation. "Dying" brings together all of the overtones of ending: the vision, the poem, his life, which was to last only a few days more. The clause hits exactly the right note of nostalgia—for heaven, this time, the true homeland—with which *Paradiso* is suffused.

Wasserman tells us that the "dying fall" was a technical term in music and, taking him at his word, we find even more relevance for the theme of the poem. On any singing, the first word, "Amor" is resoundingly tonic and must be followed by a pause for breath. Five notes, or syllables, after the tonic comes the dominant, or fifth of the key, the word "Sole," the sun, at the center of the verse. By design or fortunate circumstance, in the scale of Guido d'Arezzo, derived in the eleventh century from the first words of a hymn sung at vespers (Ut, Re, Mi, Fa, Sol, La, Si), the dominant note is *Sol*, and so it is in the text we have before us, before the unaccented hemistich brings us to silence and the final tonic resolution.

# The Fig Tree and the Laurel

After six hundred years, Petrarch's reputation as the first humanist remains unshaken. Cultural historians have generally accepted his own estimate of himself as the man who inaugurated a new era, leaving behind him what he called "the dark ages." His reputation as poet is equally secure, at least in the literary histories; he is in many respects the most influential poet in the history of Western literature. Critics have failed, however, to define adequately the ways in which his poetry was as revolutionary as his humanistic writings. The poetics of the *Canzoniere* remain as elusive as the person that emerges from its lyrics. The purpose of this chapter is to offer a tentative definition and to suggest the ways in which Petrarch's greatest work deserves its reputation as the precursor of modern poetry.

Petrarch's poetic achievements, for all of its grandeur, would appear to be decidedly conservative with respect to the Middle Ages. Far from repudiating the verse forms of his predecessors, he brought them to technical perfection and established them as models for future generations of poets. The poems of the *Canzoniere* seem to be crystallizations of previously invented verse forms: the sonnet, the sestina, the Dantesque *canzone*. In content, they are equally familiar, not to say banal, for they elaborate with spectacular variations a tired theme of courtly love: the idolatrous and unrequited passion for a beautiful and sometimes cruel lady. Apart from the extensive use of classical myth, there is little that is radically new in the thematics of the *Canzoniere*.

The extraordinary innovation in the *Canzoniere* is rather to be found in what the verses leave unsaid, in the blank spaces separating these lyric "fragments," as they were called, from each other. The persona created by the serial juxtaposition of dimensionless lyric moments is as illusory as the animation of a film strip, the product of the reader's imagination as much as of the poet's craft; yet, the resultant portrait of an eternally weeping lover remains Petrarch's most distinctive poetic achievement. Because it is a composite of lyric instants, the portrait has no temporality; only the most naïve reader would take it for authentic autobiography. For the same reason, it is immune from the ravages of time, a mood given a fictive *durée* by the temporality of the reader, or a score to be performed by generations of readers from the Renaissance to the Romantics. It remained for centuries the model of poetic self-creation even for poets who, in matters of form, thought of themselves as anti-Petrarchan.

Literary self-creation in the Middle Ages could not fail to evoke the name of Augustine, the founder of the genre. The *Confessions*, Petrarch's favorite book, is at the same time the model for much of Petrarch's description of the lover as sinner. Both stories are ostensibly attempts to recapture a former self in a retrospective literary structure, a narrative of conversion (*Canz.* 1.4: "quand'era in parte altr'uom da quel ch'i'sono" [when I was in part another man from what I am now]), but Petrarch makes no claim to reality or to moral witness. Instead, he uses Augustinian principles in order to create a totally autonomous portrait of the artist, devoid of any ontological claim. The moral struggle and the spiritual torment described in the *Canzoniere* are, as we shall see, part of a poetic strategy. When the spiritual struggle is demystified, its poetic mechanism is revealed: the petrified idolatrous lover is an immutable monument to Petrarch, his creator and namesake. In this sense, the laurel, the emblem both of the lover's enthrallment and of the poet's triumph, is the antitype of Augustine's fig tree, under which his own conversion took place. The fig tree was already a scriptural emblem of conversion before Augustine used the image in his *Confessions* to represent the manifestation of the pattern of universal history in his own life. Petrarch's laurel, on the other hand, has no such moral dimension of meaning. It stands for a poetry whose real subject matter is its own act and whose creation is its own author.

The two emblems, the fig tree and the laurel, may be said to stand respectively, as we shall see, for different modes of signification: the allegorical and the autoreflexive. The first is the mode characteristic of Christian typology, while the second, extended over the course of the entire narrative, is Petrarch's own. The fig tree and the laurel stand for the two poles of a verbal universe whose principles were shared by Augustine and the poet. Before defining the differences between them more precisely, we must turn to review some of those principles.

For Augustine, consciousness begins in desire. To discover the self is to discover it as in some sense lacking, absent to itself, and desire is the soul's reaching out to fill the void. The reaching out toward an as yet unspecified object is at the same time the birth of language, or at least of the paralanguage of gesticulation, literally a reaching out toward signification. The first chapters of the *Confessions* represent language and desire as indistinguishable, perhaps even coextensive. The child learns to speak in order to express its desire; at the same time, however, it learns what to desire from a world of objects that adults have named. Language is not only the vehicle of desire, it is also in some sense its creator, first through the agency of others, the mother and the nurse, and ultimately, sometimes insidiously, through the power of literary suggestion. From the first words of the child to the final utterance, the process remains essentially the same: far from being the sole interpreters of the words we use, we are at the same time interpreted by them. For Augustine, then, as for contemporary semiologists, man *is* his own language, for his desires and his words are inseparable.

If this is so, it follows that the end term of both language and desire are one and the same, and so it is, inevitably, in a theology of the Word. The ultimate end of desire is God, in Whom the soul finds its satisfaction. The ultimate end of signification is a principle of intelligibility whereby all things may be understood. God the Word is at once the end of all desire and the interpretant of all discourse. In the ninth book of the *Confessions*, just before the death of Monica, Augustine speaks of language in terms of desire and of desire in terms of language:

> If, for any man, the tumult of the flesh were silent, if the images of the earth, the waters and the air were silent: if the poles were silent; if the soul itself were silent and transcended itself by not thinking about itself . . . if they were silent and He spoke . . . by Himself, Whom we love in these things; were we to hear Him without them and if it continued like this, would it not be entering into the joy of the Lord?
>
> *Conf.* 9.10

All of creation is a discourse leading to Love, just as all desire is ultimately a desire for the Word. The theology of the Word binds together language and desire by ordering both to God, in Whom they are grounded. From a naturalistic standpoint, it is impossible to say whether human discourse is a reflection of the Word or whether the idea of God is simply a metaphoric application of linguistic theory. Whether we accept Augustine's theology in some form or translate it into what might be called a semiology of desire, we remain without a verbal universe, reaching out for a silent terminal point that lies outside the system.

The Word, the silence that subtends the system, grounds both desire and language. In its absence, however, both threaten to become an infinite regression, approaching ultimate satisfaction and ultimate significance as an unreachable limit. This is probably most clear in terms of Augustinian desire, which is insatiable in human terms. Each of the successive desires of life are in fact desires for selfhood, expressed metonymically in an ascending hierarchy of abstraction: nourishment for the child, sex for the adolescent, fame for the adult. In an Augustinian world, there is no escape from desire short of God: "Our heart is unquiet until it rests in you" (*Confessions* 1.1).

As all desire is ultimately a desire for God, so all signs point ultimately to the Word. In a world without ultimate significance, there is no escape from the infinite referentiality of signs. Signs, like desire, continually point beyond themselves. In the *De Magistro*, for example, Augustine says that signs cannot convince an unbeliever, but can only point in the direction of reality. For him to perceive the Truth, Christ must teach the unbeliever from within. Short of the Word made flesh, there can be no bridge between words and things: "All other things may be expressed in some way; He alone is ineffable, Who spoke and all things were made. He spoke and we were made; but we are unable to speak of Him. His Word, by Whom we were spoken, is His Son. He was made weak, so that He might be spoken by us, despite our weakness" (*De Magistro* 10.33f).[1] Like the intentionality of a sentence that preexists its utterance and emerges concretely, in retrospect, from that utterance, the uncreated Word produces its signifier and is in turn made manifest by it. Like language itself, the redemptive process is tautology, ending where it began.

In our own day, we have learned about the infinite referentiality of signs, "unlimited semiosis," from Saussure and from Peirce, among others. Anterior to the written text is the spoken text, anterior to that is the acoustic image, in turn dependent upon a concept that is itself linguistically structures. Our attempt to make the leap from words to things seems doomed to a continual feedback that looks like infinite regression. C. S. Peirce speaks of the phenomenon in terms that are reminiscent of the *De Magistro*:

> The object of representation can be nothing but a representation of which the first representation is the interpretant. But an endless series of representations, each representing the one behind it, may be conceived to have an absolute object at its limit . . . Finally, the interpretant is nothing but another representation to which the torch of truth is handed along; and as representation, it has its interpretant again. Lo, another infinite series.[2]

For Augustine, the central metaphor of Christianity provided the grounding for this infinite regression. Reality itself is linguistically structured. It is God's book, having Him for both its Author and its subject matter. Words point to things, but those things are themselves signs pointing to God, the ultimately signified. The metaphor of God's book halts the infinite series by ordering all signs to itself. In germ, this is the foundation of Christian allegory and of salvation history.

The fig tree, in Augustine's narrative, is a sign, just as it is in the Gospels when Christ says to his disciples that they must look to the fig tree if they would read the signs of the Apocalyptic time. The fig tree in the garden of Milan, in the eighth book of the *Confessions*, for all of its historicity, is at the same time meant to represent the broader pattern of salvation history for all Christians. The moment represents the revelation of God's Word at a particular time and place, recapitulating the Christ event in an individual soul. Behind that fig tree stands a whole series of anterior images pointing backward to Genesis; Augustine's reader is meant to prolong the trajectory by applying it to his own life and extending it proleptically toward the ending of time.

In the Old Testament, the prophet Micah looks forward to the day when the promise will be fulfilled: "He shall sit every man under his vine and under his fig tree" (Book of Micah 4:4). The hope of the Jews, their nationhood, is represented by the same tree that in Genesis suggested their estrangement from God. At the beginning of the Gospel of John, the words of the prophet are perhaps recalled when Nathanael is called out from under the fig tree by the Messiah: "Before Philip called thee, when thou wast under the fig tree, I saw thee" (John 1:48). So in the *Confessions*, Augustine's calling, in the voices of children who sing "tolle, lege," takes place under the tree of Micah and Nathanael, whatever its botanical species. The paradigm of salvation history is made manifest at the end of an historical evolution and provides another "testament" to the interpretation of a man by God's Word.

Because Augustine's narrative is patterned after the same model that he took to be the principle of intelligibility in all human reality, the question of its historicity is meaningless. We have already seen that the redemption itself depends upon a literary understanding of God's relationship to the world: the manifestation, at the end of a syntagmatic chain, of a significance present from the beginning. Exactly the same relationship exists between Augustine's narrative and the reality it presumably represents. Is the story that we read a faithful portrayal of a life interpreted by God, or is that conversion experience the illusory feedback of plot structure in a narrative of the self? Conversion demands that there be both a continuity and a discontinuity between the self that *is* and the self that *was*; similarly, a narrative of the self demands that author and persona be distinguished until they are fused at the narrative's culminating moment. Just as it is impossible to say whether God's presence is the reality of the Bible or the illusory projection of it, so it is impossible to say whether the conversion experience is the cause or the creature of the narrative that we read. When language in some form, however metaphorical, is the ultimate reality, we must be content with words upon words.

It must not be imagined that this is a modern distortion of Augustine's conception of his enterprise. In the text of the *Confessions*, conversion is always a literary event, a gloss on an anterior text. He correctly interprets the voices of the children to be a command to pick up the Bible and read a passage at random because he remembered Ponticianus's story of the two men who read the life of Antony and were thereupon converted. Anthony himself, he remembered, "happened to go into a church while the gospel was being read and had taken it as a counsel addressed to himself when he heard the words, 'Go home and sell all that belongs to you . . . and follow me.' By this divine pronouncement he had at once been converted to you" (*Conf.* 8.12). So Augustine picks up the Bible and reads the passage that interprets him and is thereby converted. The following moment points to his newly acquired vocation, for he then passes the Bible to his friend Alypius, thereby suggesting that his own text is to be applied metaleptically to the reader himself as part of the continual unfolding of God's Word in time. Consequently, the "truth-value" of Augustine's narrative depends, not upon its hypothetical conformity to brute "fact," supposing such a thing to exist, nor upon the illusory projection of human representation, but upon the arbitrary privilege granted to God's Word as the ultimate interpretant of all discourse. The fig tree, under the shade of which all of this takes place, stands for a tradition of textual anteriority that extends backward in time to the Logos and forward to the same Logos at time's ending, when both desire and words are finally fulfilled: "Justi et sancti fruuntur Verbo Dei sine lectione, sine litteris" (The just and the holy enjoy the Word of God without reading, without letters) (*Enarrationes et Psalmos* 119:6).[3]

We must turn now, for contrast, to a passage in the first book of Petrarch's *Secretum*, in which Francesco is scolded by his fictive interlocutor, Augustine, for a moral weakness with which they were both familiar: a certain paralysis of the will. Augustine reassures Francesco by describing his own conversion:

> Yet, for all that, I remained the man I had been before, when finally a profound meditation brought before my eyes all of my unhappiness. Thus, from the moment that I willed it fully and completely, I found the power to do it, and with a marvelous and joyful rapidity, I was transformed into another Augustine, whose story I believe you know from my *Confessions*.
>
> Francesco: I know it, of course: nor can I ever forget that life-giving fig tree, under whose shadow this miracle happened to you.
>
> Augustine: I should hope not, for neither myrtle nor ivy, nor even that laurel dear (so they say) to Phoebus, should be so welcome to you. Even if the entire chorus of poets should yearn for that laurel and you above all, who alone among all of your contemporaries were worthy to have its sought-after leaves as your crown, yet the remembrance of that fig tree should be dearer, if, after many tempests you one day arrive in port, for it portends a sure hope of correction and pardon.
>
> *Secretum* 1.1

The note of preciosity, here as elsewhere in the *Secretum*, derives from the fact that since both voices are Petrarch's, the inconclusive conversation about moral paralysis constitutes an elegant dramatization of its own subject matter. Like the historical Augustine whom he so much admired, Petrarch was expert at drawing real literary strength from fictionalized moral flaws. Of much more interest, however, is the very un-Augustinian homage that Augustine pays to the poet laureate, thereby betraying the real point of the exchange. Francesco compliments Augustine for the *Confessions* and acknowledges the fig tree as an example for all men. The laurel, however, the symbol of poetic supremacy, is his alone. We must turn now to the implications of Petrarch's claim.

We have seen that the fig tree is an allegorical sign. It stands for a referential series of anterior texts grounded in the Logos. It is at once unique, as the letter must be, and yet referential, pointing to a truth beyond itself, a spiritual sense. While it is true that the being of the letter cannot be doubted, its meaning transcends it in importance. As all signs point ultimately to God, so it may be said that all books, for the Augustinian, are in some sense copies of God's book. When Dante affirms that he is simply a scribe, copying down the words that love dictates to him, he is echoing this theory. On the other hand, for the laurel to be truly unique, it cannot *mean* anything: Its referentiality must be neutralized if it is to remain the property of its creator. Petrarch makes of it the emblem of the mirror relationship *Laura-Lauro*, which is to say, the poetic lady created by the poet, who in turn creates him as poet laureate. This circularity forecloses all referentiality and in its self-contained dynamism resembles the inner life of the Trinity as the Church fathers imagined it. One could scarcely suppose a greater autonomy. This poetic strategy corresponds, in the theological order, to the sin of idolatry.

In his *Religion of Israel*, Yehezkel Kaufman has shown that the Jews' conception of idolatry was of a kind of fetishism, the worship of reified signs devoid of significance.[4] The gods of the gentiles were coextensive with their representations, as though they dwelt not on Olympus or in the skies, but within a golden calf, a stone or a piece of wood. Signs point to an absence or a significance yet to come; they are in this sense allegorical. Idols, as the Jews understood them, like fetishes, were a desperate attempt to render presence, a reified sign, one might almost say a metaphor.[5] It is almost as if the gentiles, in the Jews' reading, sought to evade the temporality inherent in the human condition by reifying their signs and thereby eternalizing significance in the here and now. Stones are mute, but as a compensation they last forever.

This theological problematic has its exact counterpart in the linguistic realm, except that its terms are reversed: In order to create an autonomous universe of autoreflexive signs without reference to an anterior Logos—the dream of almost every poet since Petrarch—it is necessary that the thematic of such poetry be equally autoreflexive and self-contained, which is to say, that it be idolatrous in the Augustinian sense. The idolatrous love for Laura, however self-abasing it may seem, has the effect of creating a thoroughly autonomous portrait of the poet laureate. Because the laurel stands at once for a unique love and for the poet who creates it, its circular referentiality, like that of the Trinity (Father, Son, and the Love that binds them), cannot be transcended at a higher order. The laurel lives forever, no matter what happened to Francesco. This is the human strategy, the demystification of Petrarch's deliberately idolatrous pose. If the gentiles, in the Jews' interpretation of them, sought to make their gods present by reifying their signs, then we might say that Petrarch sought to reify his signs, objectify his poetic work, by making his "god," the lady Laura, the object of his worship. Critics given to psychologizing have repeatedly tried to reconstruct Petrarch's spiritual torment from his verses; where language is the only reality, however, it would be more prudent to see the spiritual torment simply as the reflection, the thematic translation of his autoreflexive poetics.

We may observe in passing that the semiological meaning of idolatry, that is, the reification of the sign in an attempt to create poetic presence, is consonant with Augustine's sign theory. In the first chapter of *De Doctrina Christiana* (1.2), in the middle of a discussion of the referentiality of signs, he introduces his famous distinction concerning human desire: God alone is to be enjoyed [*frui*], all other things are to be used [*uti*]. Sin consists in enjoying that which should be used. The distinction seems somewhat out of place until we recall that all things are signs and that God is the terminal point on a referential chain. Once language is equated with desire, then it is clear that to deprive signs of their referentiality and to treat a poetic statement as autonomous, an end in itself, is the definition of idolatry.

Perhaps the most obvious example of Petrarch's attempt to short-circuit the referentiality of his signs is to be found in the sestina numbered 30 in the *Canzoniere*: "Giovene donna sotto un verde lauro." Augustine's conversion took place in a single moment, the *kairos*, in the shadow of the fig tree. Petrarch transforms the moment into a cyclical lifetime in the shadow of the laurel:

seguirò l'ombra di quel dolce lauro
per lo più ardent sole e per la neve,
fine che l'ultimo dì chiuda quest'occhi.

*Canzoniere* 30.16–18

I shall follow the shadow of that sweet laurel
in the most ardent sun or through the snow
until the last day closes these eyes.

The *lauro* here represents the lady, whose shadow the lover will follow all the days of his life, just as the lover in Dante's sestina, from which Petrarch's is derived, spends all of his time searching "do[ve] suoi panni fanno ombra" (where her skirts cast a shadow).[6] Because Petrarch's *lauro* is literally a tree, however, that symbolic search is a turning around in a circle, following the shadow cast by the tree through the hours of the day and the seasons of the year. The exterior quest has become an internal obsession: the image of the beloved [*idolo*] is quite literally an idol: "l'idolo mio scolpito in vivo lauro" (my idol carved in living laurel).

In his brilliant article on this sestina, Robert Durling has produced further evidence of the idolatrous quality of its content.[7] It is, he reminds us, an anniversary poem celebrating the poet's meeting with Laura. Since this occurred on Good Friday, a private liturgy of love is here substituted for the liturgy of the cross. Moreover, the laurel, with its branches of diamond, has become an idolatrous cross of glory. In other words, the most significant of Christianity's *signs* has become virtually a proper name. The pun, underscoring the opacity of the sign (*Laura/lauro*), makes any mediation impossible.

There is a further point to be made about this sestina, concerning its last lines:

l'auro e i topacii al sol sopra la neve
vincon le bionde chiome presso agli occhi
che menan gli anni miei sì tosto a riva.

*Canzoniere* 30.37–9

Gold and topaz in the sun above the snow
are vanquished by the golden locks next to those eyes
that lead my years so quickly to shore.

The comparison of Laura's face to gold and topaz on the snow, sparking in the sun, is not only reified and coldly beautiful, it is radically fragmentary in a way that scarcely seems accidental. One of the consequences of treating a signifier as an absolute is that its integrity cannot be maintained. Without a principle of intelligibility, an interpretant, a collection of signs threatens to break down into its component parts. To put the matter in medieval terms, we may say that the Spirit is the "form" of the letter in the same way that the soul is the form of the body. In the absence of such a principle of anteriority, signs lose their connection to each other. So it is with Laura. Her virtues and her beauties are scattered like the objects of fetish worship: Her eyes and hair are like gold and topaz on the snow, while the outline of her face is lost; her fingers are like ivory and roses or oriental pearls, her eyes are the pole stars, her arms are branches of diamond. Like the poetry that celebrates her, she gains immortality at the price of vitality and historicity. Each part of her has the significance of her entire person; it remains the task of the reader to string together her gemlike qualities into an idealized unity.

The same may be said of the unity of the *Canzoniere*. In order to remove from the poems all traces of temporality and contingency, poetic instants are strung together like pearls on an invisible strand. The lyrics themselves counterfeit a *durée* by their physical proximity and so create a symbolic time, free of the threat of closure. The arrangement of these *rime sparse*, whatever its rationale, may be thought of as an attempt to spatialize time and so to introduce a narrative element in a way that does not threaten to exceed the carefully delimited confines of the text. It is reminiscent to us of cinematographic art, a counterfeit of time wherein a series of images are spatially juxtaposed, awaiting a temporality that will give them life from the outside. Since Petrarch's day, the strategy has been used by innumerable authors of sonnet sequences, so that it remains one of the most familiar devices of literary self-portraiture.

I have spoken repeatedly of Petrarch's *attempt* to exclude referentiality from his text. His success, of course, was only relative. Not only is referentiality intrinsic to all language, but also there towered behind him the figure of Dante, to whom all love poetry, especially in Italian, would forever after be referred, if only by contrast.[8] Beatrice is in many senses the opposite of Laura. She was a mediatrix, continually pointing beyond herself to God. Throughout most of *Paradiso*, for example, the pilgrim looks into her eyes only obliquely so that he sees what lies beyond her. Laura's eyes, by contrast, are "homicidal mirrors" in which her narcissistic lover finds spiritual death. When we translate that theme into poetic terms, we conclude that the lady celebrated by Petrarch is a brilliant surface, a pure signifier whose momentary exteriority to the poet serves as an Archimedean point from which he can create himself.

One of the Dantesque themes that most clearly suggests Beatrice's epistemological function as a sign is the theme of her veil, used extensively in the last cantos of *Purgatorio*. Her unveiling of her face is peculiarly apt to illustrate the parallelism of language and desire in the Augustinian tradition, for the motif is at once erotic and semiotic: her feminine beauty *revealed* with the context of an intellectual and doctrinal *re-velation*. In the canto of the Medusa ("Sotto il velame de li versi strani" [Beneath the veil of strange verses] *Inf.* 9.63), Dante had already referred to the significance of his poem with the same figure: His verses were a *veil* to his meaning. It seems likely that in analogous passages, most notably that of the Siren (*Purg.* 19.63), we are meant to perceive this metalinguistic dimension of meaning. Even in our own day, the figure is still used to describe the process of representation. C. S. Peirce, in the passage cited above, makes suggestive use of it: "The meaning of a representation can be nothing but a representation. In fact, it is nothing but the representation itself conceived as stripped of irrelevant clothing. But this clothing can never be completely stripped off; it is only changed for something more diaphanous. So there is an infinite regression here."[9] The Freudian (or neo-Freudian) implications do not concern us here; the point is that from St. Paul to Dante the veil covering a radiant face was used as a figure for the relationship of the sign to its referent.[10] In the light of this tradition, it can hardly be fortuitous that Laura's veil, though also a covering, was at times her only reality.

This is the significance, I believe, of what seems otherwise to be simply a charming madrigal:

> Non al suo amante più Diana piacque
> quando per tal ventura tutta ignuda
> la vide in mezzo de le gelide acque,
> ch'a me la pastorella alpestra et cruda
> posta a bagnar un leggiadretto velo,
> ch'a l'aura il vago et biondo capel chiuda.
>
> *Canzoniere* 52.1–6

> Not so much did Diana please her lover when, by a similar
> chance, he saw her all naked amid the icy waters,

as did the cruel mountain shepherdess please me, set to wash a
pretty veil that keeps her lovely blond head from the breeze.

Laura's name, hidden in the pun of the last line, is her only presence in these verses, just as her veil is her only presence in the charming
anecdote. Her veil, bathed in the water like the naked goddess seen by
Acteon, functions as a fetish, an erotic signifier of a referent whose
absence the lover refuses to acknowledge. So poetically, the reified verbal sign, wrenched free of its semantic context (*l'aura / Laura*), must be
read as an affirmation of poetic presence, the *word* (and by extension
the poem) as its own sole and sufficient meaning. For all of its light-
heartedness, the poem illustrates the fundamental strategy of the *Canzoniere*: the *thematics* of idolatry transformed into the *poetics* of presence.

I do not mean to imply that the sin idolatry exhausts the thematics
of the *Canzoniere*. Many of the later poems suggest that the love for
Laura was ennobling, at least in a literary or humanistic sense. My
point is simply that idolatry, however repugnant to an Augustinian
moralist, is at the linguistic level the essence of poetic autonomy.
Because language and desire are indistinguishable in a literary text, we
may say that by accusing his persona of an idolatrous passion Petrarch
was affirming his own autonomy as a poetic creator. To psychologize
about "spiritual torment" in the *Canzoniere* is to live the illusion that
Petrarch was perhaps the first to create.

Many more studies of this length would be required to illustrate
the full implications of this affirmation for the history of love poetry.
In germ, it suggests that all of the fictions of courtly love have their
semiotic justifications: The love must be idolatrous for its poetic expression to be autonomous; the idolatry cannot be unconflicted, any more
than a sign can be completely nonreferential if it is to communicate
anything at all. Spiritual struggle stands for the dialectic of literary
creation, somewhere between opaque carnality and transparent tran-
scendency. Finally, it might be suggested that the illicit or even adulterous nature of the passion has its counterpart in the "anxiety of
influence": Communication demands that our signs be appropriated;
poetic creation often requires that they be stolen. Petrarch's prodigious
originality, as I hope to show in future studies, is that he was entirely
self-conscious about the principles of which his predecessors were only
dimly aware. By transforming the Augustinian analysis of sin into a
new aesthetic, he made self-alienation in life the mark of self-creation

in literature and so established a literary tradition that has yet to be exhausted.

The *Canzoniere* ends with a prayer to the Virgin for forgiveness. Laura, he says, was a Medusa who turned him into a man of stone. Nevertheless, I have shown that the dead-end nature of that passion is a sign of the poetry's monumentality. In the same poem, he addresses the Virgin as the antitype of his beloved, affirming that the Queen of Heaven is the only true mediatrix: *Vera beatrice*. At one level, of course, his refusal to capitalize that familiar word suggests that Dante too had his problems with idolatry and reification. At another level, however, it identifies his own beloved with that of his literary ancestor. On that ambiguous note, both the passion and the poem are concluded and Petrarchism is born.

# Medusa and the Madonna of Forlì

## *Political Sexuality in Machiavelli*

O ne *usually* thinks of Machiavelli as the political theorist who unmasked the political myths of his predecessors by treating politics as an autonomous realm, not subject to ethical or moral considerations. *Il Principe* is concerned with what he called "effective truth"—that is, truth that is operative in the real world, in spite of the efforts of those in power to mask it from their subjects. By openly acknowledging the usefulness of force and fraud and by dispelling the myths and cant surrounding issues of power and legitimacy, Machiavelli stated what had always been obvious to successful tyrants, but rarely to their victims. His candor earned for him not only the opprobrium of moralists, but the gratitude of patriots as well.

Nevertheless, there is a trace of "political theology" that shows remarkable persistence even in the work of so great a demythologizer: the myth of the state as a political body. It is true that the corporate metaphor pervades our languages, however vestigial the concept of the "body politic" may be. We are scarcely conscious of the original physical sense of the word "member," just as the words "head" or "chief" in the context of social organization no longer seem figurative. In political rhetoric, the dormant figure is revived when necessary to persuade individual "members" to act against their self-interest for the good of the "head."[1] What interests us here, however, is Machiavelli's speculative use of the figure to lend a certain vitality to the political entities to which he applies it. The "state" described by such a corporate metaphor can no longer be thought of as a passive object—the prince's *estate*— but assumes by implication a separate identity.[2] Moreover, the body is gendered: The state or the realm is like a spouse to the ruler who possesses her. Commentators are sometimes embarrassed by Machiavelli's sexual aggressivity and dismiss it as though it were irrelevant to his politics. We shall see, however, that because of the metaphor of the state as female, there is in his work a certain homology between sexual politics and political sexuality. His apparently "sexist" remarks about *Fortuna*, for example, have political implications that cannot be dismissed as simply as the distasteful allegory by which they are conveyed.

The corporate fiction appears throughout Machiavelli's work, not always with mythic force, but often with more than merely etymological resonance. Class distinctions are regularly referred to as "humors" and disorders are described as wounds, sores, or disease.[3] In *Discorsi*, the metaphoric body of Rome is said to have been a healthy organism, with a life of its own; its heart and vital organs were armed, even when its extremities were not (3.30). In *Il Principe*, however, contemporary Italy seemed to have strength in its members but not in its head (26). It was a body beaten, enslaved, and very nearly, dead:

> Italia si riducessi ne' termini presenti . . . piú stiava che li ebrei, piú serva ch'è persi . . . senza capo, sanza ordine, battuta, spogliata, lacera, corsa, e avessi sopportato d'ogni sorte ruina . . . rimasa come sanza vita, aspetta quale possa essere quello che sani la sua ferite . . . e la guarisca da quelle sue piache già per lungo tempo infistolite. Vedesi come la prieda Iddio che li mandi qualcuno che la redima da queste crudeltà e insolenzie barbare. Vedesi ancora tutta ponta e disposta a seguire una bandiera, pur che ci sia uno che la pigli.

> Italy [has been] reduced to her present state; . . . she [is] more enslaved than the Hebrews, more abject than the Persians . . . headless, orderless, beaten, stripped, scarred, overrun, and plagued by every sort of disaster . . . Left almost lifeless, [she] waits for a leader who will heal her wounds . . . and minister to those sores of hers that have been festering so long. Behold how she prays God to send someone to free her from the cruel insolence of the barbarians; see how ready and eager she is to follow a banner joyously, if only someone will raise it up.[4]

This impassioned appeal is addressed to a prince who, like a new Moses, is called upon to deliver from bondage an Italy that is clearly a woman.

Traditional rhetoric had established the figure of the "body politic" regally clothed, chaste, and, of course, female. Without a legitimate

Caesar, however, she was not a lady but a whore: "non donna di provincie, ma bordello!" Machiavelli's enslaved Italy was a direct descendant of Dante's *serva Italia*, but unlike Dante, the Florentine secretary would not be content merely to pray for an imperial savior to marry her with God's blessings. Italy, like Lady Fortune, was there for the taking. It was up to the would-be prince to seize and possess her.

There is a considerable difference between coming to the rescue of Italy and assaulting Lady Fortune because Fortune is not a *woman*, in spite of recent assertions to the contrary, but has traditionally been a courtly *lady*.

> Io iudico bene questo, che sia meglio essere impetuoso che respettivo: perché la fortuna è donna ed è necessario, volendola tenere sotto, batterla e urtarla. E si vede che la si lascia piú vincere da questi, che da quegli che freddamente procedono: e però sempre, come donna, è amica de' giovani, perché sono meno respettivi, piú feroci e con piú audacia la comandano.

> But I do feel this: that it is better to be rash than timid, for Fortune is a [lady] and the man who wishes to hold her down must beat and bully her. We see that she yields more often to men of this stripe than to those who come coldly toward her. Like a [lady] too, she is always a friend of the young, because they are less timid, more brutal, and take charge of her more recklessly.[5]

> *Il Principe* 25

Italy is a Cinderella whom the prince is urged to make into a lady. Where there is no king, one can become a prince by seizing someone else's lady.

Sexuality is, for Machiavelli, the emblem of the insatiability of human appetite, which is by nature able to desire all things and by fortune limited to the acquisition of very few.[6] This thoroughly Augustinian contradiction is the source of all discontent and envy. We may perhaps discern a hint of Machiavelli's private experience in the bitter remark about the lady's preference for younger men—one is reminded of the painful and hollow laughter in *Clizia*—but the fantasy rape of Lady Fortune is more than just the expression of sexual aggressivity. It is also the metaphorical assault of a political arriviste on the established social order. In the absence of traditional structures of legitimacy, the prince establishes his authority by taking what he wants.

In chapter 26 of Book 3 of *Discorsi*, entitled "How Women [*femine*] Can Be the Cause of the Ruin of the State," Machiavelli surveys occasions on which the catalyst for social revolution was the possession or loss of a woman. It is important to point out that "cause" in this context means *proximate* cause—that is, the *occasion* for the ruin of the state. The women he discusses are clearly pawns rather than instigators of violent struggle. The first occasion was a struggle between patricians and plebeians in the city of Ardea over whether an orphaned noblewoman should be given in marriage to a noble or to a plebeian, after she had been offered to both. The second was the rape of Lucretia, which led to the downfall of the Tarquins, and the last was the rape of Virginia, which caused the overthrow of the decemvirate. The rhetoric of Machiavelli's invitation to Lady Fortune by force must be read against the background of these myths of violation.

By placing these three stories together, Machiavelli makes it clear that rape (including forced marriage) is both the subjugation of another human being and a violation of the prerogatives of the males to whom she belongs in the class structure. Revolution breaks out in the instance of the orphaned noblewoman, but not as it does in the case of Lucretia and Virginia—that is, not because a family or a class is dishonored, but rather because it is not clear to whom she belongs. She is the occasion for a struggle between social classes in a city at war with itself, a pretext for social transgression. In these examples, sexual violence is a social crime, a seizure of property rather than an exchange.

If one carries this analysis further, the allegorical rape of Lady Fortune would also appear to be an attack on class structure. She is a *lady* because medieval tradition granted her that station as a sign of her inviolability. The proper response to a lady was to long for her from afar; yearning valorized the social barrier and distance preserved it. In this context, sexual violence against a metaphoric "donna" stands for a defiance of the social structure within which erotic etiquette is inscribed. It is a brutal figure for the refusal of Christian resignation.

In a text that Machiavelli knew well, Dante struck the analogy between erotic distance and resignation to the social status quo. In *Inferno* 7.94, he portrays Lady Fortune as a courtly lady oblivious to the vulgarity of her suitors: "Ella *si* è beata e ciò non ode" (She is blessed *unto herself* and doesn't hear these things). Here Dante uses the same untranslatable reflexive verb that he had used to describe the passage of

Beatrice in his earlier love poetry: "Ella *si* va, sentendosi laudare" (She goes off *by herself*, hearing herself praised) (*Vita nuova* 26, my emphasis). The presence of the reflexive of separation—*si*—in both verses underscores the analogy between erotic yearning and social aspiration: Fortune is as unmoved by the attention of her suitors as Beatrice was unmoved by Dante's youthful sighs. Machiavelli's violent rhetoric accepts the analogy but rejects the resignation dictated by courtly convention. The force of the argument is directed against the notion that one's place is fixed by birth rather than by ambition. It presses a Dantesque line of reasoning to a radical conclusion. If, as Dante has argued in *Convivio* 4, nobility is not a function of aristocratic birth, then neither is the power that nobility wields; anyone can dare to be prince. From a modern perspective, we may say that the offensive courtly code that transforms a woman into a prize is made more offensive by urging that the prize is there to be seized.

The coarseness of this imagery is deliberately meant to contrast with Dante's political rhetoric, to which *Il Principe*'s rhetoric has a close, if ambivalent, relationship. The Latin title and subtitles of *Il Principe* might have led Machiavelli's first readers to expect a treatise written in conformance with conventional decorum and that shocking or obscene details would thus be passed over in silence. Such *reticentia* had the effect of addressing, or indeed creating, a community of the like-minded, like a wink or a nudge in the ribs. To speak the horror or the obscenity is to refuse membership in such a community and to address those who are outside it. Often these are its victims. This is the substance of Antonio Gramsci's reading of *Il Principe*: a work about political power addressed to those "who do not know" because they have never had it.[7] For Gramsci, Machiavelli's rhetoric serves to create a new, demystified audience in which he places his hopes for the liberation of Italy.

Although it contrasts with traditional political rhetoric, Machiavelli's use of obscenity and horror for shock value is not without precedent. A famous episode in *Il Principe* is startlingly reminiscent of Dante's *Inferno*, although the execution of Remirro de Orco is meant to illustrate Borgia's political technique, rather than the Divine Will. Cesare had apparently ordered his lieutenant to repress the people of Cesena. He soon became so good at his task that he earned the enmity of the people:

E perché conosceva le rigorosità passate avergli generato qualche odio, per purgare li animi di quelli populi e guadagnarseli in tutto, volse mostrare che, se crudeltà alcuna era seguita, non era causata da lui ma da la acerba natura del ministro. E presa sopra a questa occasione, lo fece, a Cesena, una mattina mettere in dua pezzi in su la piazza, con uno pezzo di legne e uno coltello sanguinoso accanto: la ferocità del quale spettacolo fece quegli populi in uno tempo rimanere satisfatti e stupidi.

And because [the duke] knew that the recent harshness had generated some hatred [against him], in order to clear the minds of the people and gain them over to his cause completely, he determined to make plain that whatever cruelty had occurred had come, not from him, but from the brutal character of the minister. Taking proper occasion, therefore, he had him placed on the public square of Cesena one morning, in two pieces, with a piece of wood beside him and a bloody knife. The ferocity of this scene left the people at once stunned and satisfied.

*Il Principe* 7

The sundered body of Borgia's minister recalls the cloven bodies of Dante's sowers of discord or the crucified body of Caiaphas, who was guilty of precisely the kind of conspiracy Machiavelli espouses. Caiaphas told the Pharisees that it would be fitting to put one man to death to save an entire people (*Inf.* 23.117), a principle echoed approvingly in *Discorsi* when the subject is the rape of Lucretia. So too, Mosca incited his cohorts to murder with a lapidary phrase that rivals Machiavelli's terrible candor: "capo ha cosa fatta" (a thing done has an end) (*Inf.* 28.107), memorably rendered in the words of Macbeth: "If it were done when 'tis done, then 'twere well it were done quickly." Texts such as these give voice to what are supposed to be unspeakable secrets of political power.

The horror that Machiavelli dares to speak is the horror of politics in the real world. If we are no longer shocked by it, it is largely thanks to his exposé. His cynicism sometimes seems a mask for outraged idealism, a cry of pain rather than a dispassionate analysis. By his own logic, the maxims Machiavelli offers must always have seemed self-evident to those who have held power. It is unlikely, for example, that any successful ruler would need to be told that "the injury done to a man should be of such a nature as to make vengeance impossible," any more than a businessman would have to be reminded of Augustine's ironic advice: "Buy cheap, sell dear" (*De Trinitate* 13.3). However valid strategically, such principles are of limited tactical value. They are shocking, however, because they are offered without fear or embarrassment, as though they were infernal confidences, uttered out of the world's earshot.

Long before Machiavelli, Dante sought in *Inferno* to break the conspiracy of silence concerning the acquisition of political power. In canto 27 of *Inferno*, Guido da Montefeltro is portrayed as willing to reveal the secrets of his subversive art because he no longer fears public exposure. Guido's remarks constitute Dante's demystification of political authority in general and papal authority in particular. At the same time, they provide an example of the irony of *Inferno*, where all is as in real life, except that shameful secrets are revealed and injustice is punished. It was perhaps to evoke the tradition of infernal revelation that T. S. Eliot used these verses to introduce "The Love Song of J. Alfred Prufrock":

> S'i' credesse che mia risposta fosse
> > a persona che mai tornasse al mondo,
> > questa fiamma staria senza più scosse:
> Ma però che già mai di questo fondo
> > non tornò vivo alcun, s'i'odo il vero,
> > sanza tema d'infamia ti rispondo.
>
> *Inf.* 27.61–6

If I thought my reply were to one who might ever return to the world, this flame would be still; but since no one has ever returned alive from this depth, if what I hear is true, I shall answer you without fear of infamy.

Coaxed by a power-drunk pope into telling him how to overthrow the city of Palestrina, the condottiere replied, "Promise much, deliver little." This single phrase synthesizes endless intrigue and pronounces a moral judgment that is clear, although silent. Machiavelli's aphorisms are written in the same tradition, except that they are not framed in the context of an infernal journey. Unlike *Inferno*, Renaissance Italy provides no place to stand from which a moral standard might be applied to such advice. It is as if we were all in hell.

There are several other details in canto 27 that seem to be evoked by *Il Principe*. For one thing, Machiavelli's celebrated reference to the lion and the fox is usually ascribed to his reading of Cicero, but it also occurs in Guido's definition of his own political guile. The advice he gives is referred to as "fraudulent counsel," not because it does not work—on the contrary it is completely efficacious—but because it advocates the commission of fraud, as does *Il Principe*. Guido's slyness extends to God's judgment, which he tried to evade by his last-minute conversion. "It might have worked" (*giovato sarebbe*), he says, had he not been outsmarted by the Pope, whom he calls a prince (*principe*) of the new Pharisees. We may observe in passing that Machiavelli's last example in *Il Principe* of a leader with *virtù* is also a Pope: Julius II. Reading the canto of Guido with Machiavelli in mind produces the anachronistic and uncanny impression that Dante is seeking to refute Machiavelli's concern for "what works"—"la verità effettuale."

In this most ironic of cantos, the prescriptive value of infernal secrets is undercut by infernal condemnation; this is, after all, hell. The surroundings call into question every assertion of the damned. Without such a framework, the conversation between Guido and the Pope would be indistinguishable from what we could imagine to have been the dialogue between Machiavelli and the aspiring leader whom he may have been addressing. Guido's story is clearly ironized by the infernal framework. By further ironizing it, *removing* the infernal framework and giving the advice "straight," Machiavelli doubles the negation and yields a deceptively positive portrait. In hell, Machiavelli's advice makes perfect sense.[8]

A further parallel between the two texts brings us back to the political body. In Guido's infernal monologue, he tells us that Pope Boniface came to seek his advice as physician:

> Ma come Costantin chiese Silvestro
> d'entro Siratti a guerir de la lebbre,
> così mi chiese questi per maestro
> a guerir de la sua superba febbre.

*Inf.* 27.94–7

But as Constantine sought out Sylvester within Soracte to cure his leprosy, so this one sought me out as the doctor to cure the fever of his pride.

This moment marks for Dante the beginning of the infection that has always afflicted Italy: the donation of the empire by Constantine to the Church. It is the disease from which Italy still suffered in Machiavelli's day, with a complication that could prove fatal: the invasion of foreign bodies. So too, it is as physician to the *stato* that Machiavelli offers his advice:

E' quali non solamente hanno ad avere riguardo alli scandoli presenti, ma a' futuri, e a quelli con ogni industria ovviare; perché, prevedendosi discosto, vi si rimedia facilmente, ma, aspettando che ti si appressino, la medicina non è a tempo, perché la malattia è diventata incurabile; e interviene di questa, come dicono e' fisici dello etico . . . non la avendo nel principio conosciuta né medicata, diventa facile a conoscere e difficile a curare.

You have to keep an eye, not only on present troubles, but on those of the future, and make every effort to avoid them. When you see the trouble in advance, it is easily remedied, but when you wait till it is on top of you, the antidote is useless, the disease has become incurable. What the doctors say about consumption applies here: in early stages, if you have done nothing about it, it becomes easy to recognize and hard to cure.

*Il Principe* 3

Politics is thus the art of medicine, rather than ethics, as it was in the Quattrocento.[9] It is a praxis requiring interventions that are sometimes cruel and violent, but always dispassionate. In *Discorsi*, the subject is "health maintenance" in ancient Rome. In *Il Principe*, however, it is emergency medicine for contemporary Italy.

The distinction between the two kinds of medicine is at the heart of the difference between Machiavelli's two great works. In the early 1950s, Jacques Maritain observed that there was no trace of duration in *Il Principe*, no distinction between the temporality of the individual and the temporality of the state. Neither posterity, which is extension in time, nor the human community, which is extension in space, seemed to enter into the calculations of *Il Principe*.[10] J. G. A. Pocock, in *The Machiavellian Moment*, describes the political emergency for which *Il Principe* was written.[11] His title points to its timeless "punctuality." To turn from *Il Principe* to *Discorsi*, however, is to turn from a political moment to historical time, from a no-man's-land to the Roman republic, where the emphasis is on the continuity between the past and the future. The commentary focuses on Machiavellian *duration* in Republican Rome. The character of the prince, his *virtù*, is decisive, surgical, and timely. Given the etymology of the words, from *virtus* and *vir*, it inevitably carries with it masculine or even phallic associations. In contrast, *Discorsi* are less concerned with phallic *virtù* than with survival and posterity.

A passage in the third book of *Discorsi* is notorious for its grotesque quality and for its questionable verisimilitude. After the myth of the prince himself it constitutes, according to Gramsci, the most important of Machiavelli's political myths.[12] In the dialectic of concealment and revelation of political secrets, it represents an extreme case. The anecdote serves as an emblem of the widowed state without a prince—no longer enslaved and abject, as was Dante's Rome, but rather possessed with a potential energy enabling her to survive.

Caterina Sforza is mentioned in chapter 20 of *Il Principe* as the Lady of Forlì. The context is a discussion of the relative usefulness of fortresses to rulers under siege. Machiavelli's conclusion, which he reaches from an analysis of Caterina's fate on two separate occasions when she sought refuge in her fortress, once successfully and once not, is that "the best fortress that there is is not to be hated by the people." This passage identifies Caterina as an emblem of the people, in spite of her aristocratic birth. It is as such that she reappears in *Discorsi* 3.6:

> Ammazzarono, alcuni congiurati Forlivesi, il conte Girolamo loro signore, presono la moglie e i suoi figliuoli che erano piccoli, e non parendo loro potere vivere sicuri se non si insignorivano della fortezza e non volendo il castellano darla loro, Madonna Caterina (che così si chiamava la contessa) promise ai congiurati che, se la lasciavano entrare in quella, di farla consegnare loro, e che ritenessero a presso di loro i suoi figliuoli per istatichi. Costoro sotto questa fede ve la lasciarono entrare; la quale, come fu dentro, dalle mura rimproverò loro la morte del marito e minacciogli d'ogni qualità di vendetta. E per mostrare che de' suoi figliuoli non si curava, mostrò loro le membra genitali, dicendo che aveva ancora il modo a rifarne. Così costoro, scarsi di consiglio e tardi avvedutisi del loro errore, con un perpetuo esilio patirono pene della poca prudenza loro.

> Some conspirators who were citizens of Forlì, killed Count Girolamo, their Lord, and took prisoner his wife and his children, who were little ones. It seemed to them, however, that their lives would scarce be safe unless they could get hold of the citadel, which its governor declined to hand over. So [Lady (*Madonna*)] Caterina, as the countess was called, promised the conspirators that, if they would let her go to the citadel, she would arrange for it to be handed over to them. Meanwhile they were to keep her children as hostages. On this understanding, the conspirators let her go to the citadel, from the walls of which, when she got inside, she reproached them with killing her husband and threatened

them with vengeance in every shape and form. And to convince them that she did not mind about her children she exposed her [genital members] and said that she was still capable of bearing more. The conspirators, dumbfounded, realized their mistake too late, and paid the penalty for their lack of prudence by suffering perpetual banishment.[13]

The scene calls to mind, if only by contrast, a familiar literary theme associating a woman's body with the walls of a castle or city. In the *Chanson de Roland*, the assault of a castle of city is figured as rape (Charlemagne is said to have ravaged Spain: "The castles taken, the cities violated");[14] in the *Roman de la Rose*, sexual assault is allegorized as the storming of a fortress. It would be difficult to imagine a more radical departure from such a literary conventions than Caterina's gesture. Rather than submit to her captors, the Lady of Forlì first beguiles and then terrifies them with her reproductive power.

Caterina's gesture is analogous to the phallic taunt of an ancient warrior, but her vengeance is prophetic rather than immediate. She, in fact, remarried and gave birth to Giovanni della Bande Nere, the romantic soldier of fortune who was to replace Cesare Borgia in the hopes and the esteem of Machiavelli after the duke's death. For Gramsci, however, her power was not so much historic as it was mythic. The image of Caterina was to him an emblem of the *matrix* from which future generations would proceed in sufficient numbers to overwhelm their oppressors.

The passage in *Il Principe* just quoted associated the historical Caterina with both fortresses and the people. By extending that association, Gramsci transformed her into an inexorable force, an allegory, rather than a person. Whatever human grief she might have felt was, like Medea's, insufficient to deter her from her purpose, which Gramsci identified, in his most impassioned moment, with history itself. It did not seem to matter to him that she was by no means a woman of the people; he was able to transform her historic identity into political myth by interpreting her reproductive power as a social force. Two mythic figures loomed up from Machiavelli's text: the Prince, emblem of the revolutionary party, and Madonna Caterina, which is to say, history itself. For Gramsci, she was a more appropriate emblem of the struggle of the Italian people than either the brutalized female slave figure in the last chapter of *Il Principe* or the ridiculous nineteenth-century personification dressed in a peplum, and carrying a scepter.[15]

There are folkloric elements in this narrative that are thoroughly consistent with such a mythic interpretation, yet they derive from a cultural context so far removed from Machiavelli as to suggest that Gramsci may have had parody in mind. The characterization of Caterina as the archetypal mother evokes the more traditional version of that image: the Virgin Mary as *Mater Omnium*. Caterina may be thought of as a fierce caricature of those images of divine maternity found on medieval walls and city gates, welcoming outsiders and offering sanctuary to those within.[16] Perhaps the most familiar of such representations is *La Madonna della Misericordia*, opening wide her mantle to expose the spiritual progeny clustered around her (see Figure 6). Caterina seems in Gramsci's reading to be a secular version of that liminal icon, fierce rather than comforting, displaying her reproductive power not proleptically, in terms of the children she would one day produce, but with brutal directness. In accordance with literary convention, her body stands metonymically for the fortress, but its power is apotropaic; she is more like a Medusa than a mother.

In at least one instance, popular piety could depict the Virgin proudly exhibiting her reproductive power rather than simply nurturing her son. The pose captured by Piero della Francesca in *La Madonna del Parto*, of a pregnant woman about to open her gown with her right hand, her left hand placed somewhat aggressively on her hip, strikes an obvious, almost anatomical, analogy between Mary's garment and her body (see Figure 7). It is a decorous and metaphoric version of Caterina's gesture.

Both of these gestures are *revelations* (*re-velatio*, "un-veiling") in the sense given to the word by Saint Paul, when he refers to the coming of Christ as an "unveiling" of the radian face of Moses (II Cor. 3:12–16). The parting of the Virgin's gown is a figure for the interpretation of Christianity's central mystery, a stripping away of successive veils of significance, from the tent, with its anatomically symmetrical angels, to her body, the last veil covering the unborn child at the center of the painting ("tent" is from the Latin *tabernaculum*, that is, *tabernaculum Dei*, the "Virgin's body").[17] Similarly, Caterina's "unveiling" of herself reveals an as yet nameless power, not unlike the messianic Moses so fervently entreated in the last chapter of *Il Principe*, in whom Machiavelli placed his hope for Italy's deliverance.

To speak of unveiling and of the apotropaic obstacle at the gates is, for the student of Italian literature, inevitably to recall the moment in

FIGURE 6. Piero della Francesca, *La Madonna della Misericordia*. Museo Civico, Sansepolcro, 1460–62. Photo: HIP / Art Resource, New York.

FIGURE 7.  Piero della Francesca, *La Madonna fra due Angeli, detta del Parto*. Monterchi, Cappella del Cimitero, 1460–62. Photo: Alinari / Art Resource, New York.

canto 9 of Dante's *Inferno* when the pilgrim and his guide try to enter the city of Dis and are repulsed by demons who threaten from the ramparts to summon the Gorgon. The threat of the Medusa in the action of the narrative seems to trigger a pause in the story and what is perhaps the most famous of Dante's addresses to his readers:

O Voi ch'avete li intelletti sani,
mirate la dottrina che s'asconde
sotto 'l velame de li versi strani.

*Inf.* 9.61–3

O you who have sound understanding, mark the doctrine that is hidden under the veil of the strange verses!

The significance of the passage for Dante's poetics arises from the importance of vision in erotic poetry. The Medusa represents the glance that once enamored and now stuns the observer, a demystification of poetic seduction as it was represented, for instance, in the *Roman de la Rose* or in Dante's own earlier love poetry. We shall see that what makes this episode particularly relevant to Machiavelli's anecdote is that a subsequent passage in the poem, relating the dream of the Siren, indirectly associates the Medusa with the sight of the female sex.

The Medusa figures a rejection of the themes that Dante celebrated in his youth. The poet of *Inferno* seems to regard the eros that once beguiled him as now constituting an obstacle to his spiritual progress: "Se 'l Gorgon si mostra e tu 'l vedessi, / nulla sarebbe di tornar mai suso" (If the Gorgon shows herself and you should see her, never would you return to the world above) (*Inf.* 9.56–7). The same threat is repeatedly recalled in the poem—indeed, one could characterize the love poetry of the *Commedia* as erotic revisionism[18]—but most pointedly in a dream in *Purgatorio*, where it is represented not by the Medusa but rather by the Siren's womb (*Purg.* 19.1–33). The pilgrim dreams of her song and is bewitched until Virgil strips away her clothing revealing her horrible sex: "mostravimi il ventre." The dramatic and verbal echoes suggest that the Medusa and the Siren are both images of a male terror of the female sex, but the implied misogyny is not peculiar to Dante or to the Middle Ages. It is, in fact, rooted in the most ancient of mythological traditions. A. A. Barb, bemused by the scandal provoked by Freud's reading of the Medusa, demonstrated that the Medusa and the Siren were related in antiquity precisely as alternate representations of the primordial womb, the *Diva Matrix*.[19]

If the connection to the episode of the Siren suggests an indirect allusion to female sexuality in Dante's Medusa, there is conversely something of the Medusa in Caterina's sex, discernible perhaps in a few anomalies in the text of *Discorsi*. First, the phrase *le membra genitali* is odd as a description of the female sex. Not only is the word "member" unexpected but the plural number is perplexing. The equivalent Latin phrase usually describes only the male sex. In written Italian before Machiavelli, there seems to have been only one recorded usage that applied to females, in a medical treatise of the fourteenth century, but modern dictionaries usually cite Machiavelli as the earliest example. Second, there is an almost obsessive use of alliteration in the last lines. It is true that prose stylists of the Cinquecento were especially fond of this device, but in the description of Caterina's gesture, there are no fewer than eight external alliterations in *m* and two internal: "dalle mura . . . rimproverò . . . la morte del marito . . . minacciogli . . . mostrare . . . mostrò le membra genitali . . . modo." The horrified reaction of the conspirators to this gesture is also described with obsessive alliteration: "perpetuo . . . patirono . . . pene . . . poca prudenza." The key word in the alliterative description of Caterina's gesture seems to be *mostrò*, the word that recurs in Dante's similar "revelations," as we have seen; the word that is highlighted in the second group of alliterations is *pene*. Whether intentionally or not, these words are indistinguishable from the words for "monster" and for the male organ.

Caterina's appearance at the castle wall is meant to ward off would-be assailants precisely as the head of the Medusa was meant to ward off potential attackers from ancient cities and fortifications. An attempt to evoke that emblem with its fearsome snakes could account for the bizarre plural "members," as well as for the alliterations that are, on some level, iconic. We recognize in the insistent return of these primal sounds, *m* and *p*, the phonic image of the mother and the father, as Roman Jakobson has suggested, phonic images that would also serve to identify *M*edusa, the mother's usually terrifying counterpart, and *P*erseus, her less-than-formidable enemy.[20]

The association of mother and Medusa is by now a commonplace of psychoanalytic literature, since it was first suggested by Freud, to whom it represented the terror of castration, caused by the boy's first sight of his mother's genitals:

> The terror of Medusa is thus a terror of castration that is linked to the sight . . . of the female genitals . . . surrounded by hair . . . The hair upon Medusa's head is frequently represented in works of art in the form of snakes, and these are once again derived from the castration complex. It is a remarkable fact that, however, frightening they may be in themselves, they nevertheless serve actually as the mitigation of the horror, for they replace the penis, the absence of which is the cause of

the horror. This is a confirmation of the technical rule according to which a multiplication of penis symbols signifies castration.[21]

Freud here interprets the myth of the Medusa as though it corresponded to a specific event in the life of any male child, a primal sight inspiring a terror of castration. The sight of Caterina's genitals also inspires fear, but for very different reasons. Her sex is the proleptic representation of her vengeance, an emblem or political survival through reproductive power.

For Machiavelli, the Medusa's face is not the horror that it would appear to be in the traditional male imagination or to Freud himself, who under the circumstances finds even a nest of snakes reassuring.[22] The multiplicity of heads of members that provides the basis for Freud's sexual interpretation of the Medusa gives the myth a possible applicability in the political realm. The importance of the use of the Italian feminine plural for a neuter Latin noun, *membrum*, is that it signifies a collectivity: specifically, the unity of a body with a plurality of members. The neuter pronoun *unum* in the motto of the United States, "E pluribus unum," points unmistakably to the neuter noun *corpus*, and thus to the persistence of the rhetorical commonplace with which I began this essay, the "body politic." The body's gender is crucial, however, for the *membra* of a woman's body include the future, as well as the past. Caterina stands for such a collectivity. She is without a husband, but is far from being the disconsolate widow that Dante had used to portray Rome.[23] On the contrary, her autonomy is her strength, sufficient to discourage her would-be possessors.

In the Renaissance, rulers had a political reason to fear the Medusa, apart from the usual psychosexual anxieties. About five years after the death of Machiavelli, Benvenuto Cellini cast the masterpiece of his lifetime, the bronze Perseus that was to be erected in the Loggia dei Lanzi in Florence. Several pages of his autobiography are devoted to recounting how he cast the statue at the insistence of Cosimo I, the grand duke of Tuscany. Mythographers traditionally identified the Medusa as *Discordia*, but according to one of Cellini's editors in the nineteenth century, the duke meant the statue to have a political significance: He imagined himself to be a Perseus, putting down the Medusa of republicanism. The statue was therefore meant as a warning against any attempt to usurp his power. *Discordia* in the political order seems close to what Machiavelli would have called "tumult," a form of civic strife that is sometimes of benefit to the state, no matter how tyrants feel about it.[24] In any case, Machiavelli was spared any knowledge of the statue or of the fact that the grand duke who commissioned it was the son of Giovanni delle Bande Nere and the grandson of Caterina Sforza.

To see the Medusa's face in the body of Caterina is to read historical significance into the reproductive force of nature. It is also to see in the body of a woman no longer the passive sign of political power, an object to be possessed, but rather an autonomous force waiting for a husband to minister to her. We cannot attribute to Machiavelli an anachronistically enlightened view of women in society any more than we can credit him with a democratic spirit, yet it is undeniable that he saw in Caterina Italy's only hope, in the absence of a prince.

# Donne's "Valediction: Forbidding Mourning"

As virtuous men passe mildly'away,
     And whisper to their soules, to goe,
Whilst some of their sad friends doe say,
     The breath goes now, and some say, no:

So let us melt, and make no noise,
     No teare-floods, nor sigh-tempests move,
'Twere prophanation of our joyes
     To tell the layetie our love.

Moving of th'earth brings harmes and feares,
     Men reckon what it did and meant,
But trepidation of the spheares,
     Though greater farre, is innocent.

Dull sublunary lovers love
     (Whose soule is sense) cannot admit
Absence, because it doth remove
     Those things which elemented it.

But we by'a love, so much refin'd,
     That our selves know not what it is,
Inter—assured of the mind,
     Care lesse, eyes, lips, and hands to misse.

Our two soules therefore, which are one,
     Though I must goe, endure not yet
breach, but an expansion,
     Like gold to ayery thinnesse beate.

If they be two, they are two so
    As stiffe twin compasses are two,
Thy soule the fixt foot, makes no show
    To move, but doth, if th'other doe.

And though it in the center sit,
    Yet when the other far doth rome,
It leanes, and hearkens after it,
    And growes erect, as it comes home.

Such wilt thou be to mee, who must
    Like th'other foot, obliquely runne;
Thy firmnes draws my circle just,
    And makes me end, where I begunne.[1]

I n the twelfth chapter of Dante's *Vita nuova*, Love appears to the poet in the form of an angel and gives himself a mystic definition: "I am as the center of a circle, to which all part of the circumference stand in equal relation; *you, however, are not so*" (*Vita nuova* 12.21–3, my emphasis).[2] For Dante, as for most thinkers of his time, the spatial and temporal perfection represented by the circle precluded its use as a symbol for anything human. The perfect circularity of *Paradiso* was a gift awaiting the man who had been through Hell; it could never be considered a birthright, for perfect circles transcend the human just as the heavens transcend the earth. So great was the gap between perfection and humanity that it could be spanned only by the Incarnation.

Dante and the early Florentine humanists were the last Italians for several centuries to take Love's admonition very seriously. Later thinkers of the *Quattrocento* would not accept any such limitation and with their rhetoric attempted to set man free from the great chain, which bound him to the angels above and to the beasts below. By attributing to the human soul an angelic perfection, they attempted to divorce it from its body, which they were prepared to leave to the protective custody of Lorenzo de' Medici. While they claimed for the soul eternity's symbol, the infinite circle, they surrendered to *Il Magnifico* the more limited space around the Square of the *Signoria*, thus making of God's circular hieroglyph not only an emblem of man's dignity, but also of his solipsism. This metamorphosis of the circle from the transcendent to the mundane, recently and brilliantly traced by Georges Poulet, was historically coincident, at least in Italy, with the metamorphosis of the human soul from incarnate reality, to angelic abstraction, to poetic fiction.[3] The beast that was left behind, however, remained substantially unchanged.

Among English poets who underwent the influence of Italian love poetry of the Renaissance, John Donne stands out as one who sought to reconcile the errant soul to its body once more. This meant rescuing human love from both the angelic mysticism and the erotic formalism of the Italian tradition and restoring it to its proper domain: humanity. Donne was primarily concerned neither with the angel nor with the beast, but rather with the battlefield separating them, long since vacated by the Italians; insofar as he defended that middle ground in the question of human love, his poetry marked a return to a more "medieval" sensibility. It is the thesis of this chapter that his most famous image, that of the compass in "A Valediction: Forbidding Mourning," protests, precisely in the name of incarnation, against the neo-Petrarchan and Neoplatonic dehumanization of love. It makes substantially the same point made by Love to the young Dante three hundred years before: Angelic love is a perfect circle, while beasts move directly and insatiably to the center: *tu autem non sic.*

Human love is neither because it is both; it pulsates between the eternal perfection of circularity and the linear extension of space and time. The compass that Donne uses to symbolize it, therefore, traces not merely a circle but a dynamic process, the "swerving serpentine" of Donne's poetry and of his thought.[4] This is the essence of the love celebrated in the "Valediction: Forbidding Mourning," a vortical reconciliation of body and soul. At the end of its gyre, on the summit where time and eternity meet, stands the lovers' Truth: "hee that will / Reach her, about must, and about must goe . . ." (*Satyre* 3.80–1). Because Love's truth is incarnate, however, its celestial apex is at the same time the profound center of an interior cosmos that is governed by its own laws and bounded by the lovers' embrace. For such lovers there can be no breach between the macrocosm of space and time and the microcosm of Love because all of reality is circumscribed by the point upon which their Love is centered. With its whirling motion, Love's compass describes the expansion of the lovers' spirit from eternity to time and back again.

This motion is the archetypal pattern of Love's universe, the principle of coherence joining matter and spirit throughout all levels of reality. The first part of this study will show that this is the motion traced by the compass. We shall see that the principle of motion in

Love's universe is patterned upon what was considered the principle of motion in all of reality. By itself, however, this principle is purely formal. The image of the compass cannot convey the vital reality that underlies it and gives to the poem its symbolic substance. The second part of this study is therefore concerned with describing the "vehicle" itself, the "spirit" of Love to which motion is imparted. Finally, the last part of this study will examine the literal significance of the symbolic statement in terms of the relationship of the lover to his beloved.

In his sermons, Donne expresses the incarnate dynamism of humanity with the figure of married love: "As farre as man is immortall, he is a married man still, still in posession of a soule, and a body too" (*Sermons* 7.257). "Death," he tells us, "is the Divorce of body and soule; Resurrection is the Re-union. . . ." (6.71).[5] It is from this exegetical commonplace that the argument of the "Valediction: Forbidding Mourning" derives its force. If incarnation is not simply an abstraction, but rather the informing principle of reality, then the terms of the analogy are reversible and the union of body and soul may serve as a figure for the love of husband and wife. Donne the preacher wrote of death and resurrection in figurative terms of the separation and reunion of husband and wife; as a lover, in the poem I am about to discuss, he had written to his beloved of their separation and eventual reunion in figurative terms of death and resurrection: "As virtuous men passe mildly away . . . So let us melt. . . ." The poem reversed a traditional figure and gave to the neo-Petrarchan dialectic of presence and absence a new metaphysical meaning. As the soul is indissolubly linked to the body, so the husband is linked to his faithful wife. The "Valediction" is a *congé d'amour* that precludes grief in the same way that the death of a virtuous man *forbids mourning*; that is, the simile with which the poem begins glosses the poem's title by hinting that, just as the righteous soul will at the Last Judgment return to its glorified body, so the voyager will return to his beloved.

The ironic reversal of a traditional theme is not mere flippancy. Donne characteristically pushes the analogy to a fine philosophical point. If the union of husband and wife, their love, is like the union of body and soul, then it too is a "hylomorphic" entity that cannot be simply reduced to the carnality or to the spirituality of which it is nevertheless composed. It is Love incarnate, possessed of a single soul ("our two soules . . . which are one") and, in its perfection, of a single body:

Adam and Eve cleave unto each other and are one flesh (Genesis 2:24). The doctrine of the Resurrection can be of little comfort to lovers whom death parts, since there is no marriage in heaven (Matthew 22:30; Mark 12:25; Luke 20:35). In the case of these lovers, however, who part only temporarily, the Resurrection lends considerable force to the poetic statement of their inseparability because, by inverting the whole theological structure and balancing it on a personification—the body and soul of Love—Donne gives the entire weight of Revelation to his promise to return. Love dies a physical death when the lovers part, for their bodies "elemented" its body. Its soul lives on, however, in the comfort of the Resurrection, when husband and wife, the components of Love's body, will cleave together once more. It is because their Love is like a just man that it can "passe mildly away," "care lesse" (but like the lovers still *care*) to miss its body, knowing that it will end where it began, reconciled to the flesh once more.

The beginning of the poem states the relationship of the lover to his beloved in terms of the union of body and soul. The ending of the poem traces the emblem of that union, the geometric image of a soul that cannot be perfect while it remains disembodied and therefore cannot be represented in the same way that Dante represented angelic love. In other words, the "circle" that ends the poem is no circle in the ordinary sense, but is rather a circle joined to the rectilinear "otherness" distinguishing man from the angels. This explains the apparent inconsistency in Donne's image, a poetic inconsistency, it would seem, compounding the obscurity of the final verses. Two difference movements are executed by the compass:

> And though it in the center sit,
> > Yet when the other far doth rome,
> It leanes and hearkens after it,
> > And growes erect as that comes home.

These verses clearly describe motion along a radius, from a center to a circumference and back to the center again. On the other hand, the last stanza of the poem clearly describes circular motion:

> Such wilt thou be to mee, who must
> > Like th'other foot, obliquely runne;
> They firmnes drawes my circle just,
> > And makes me end, where I begunne.

Together these two movements comprise the dynamism of humanity. With its whirling motion, the compass synthesizes the linear extension of time and space with the circularity of eternity.

The metaphysical importance of the geometrical problem presented by these verses becomes apparent when we examine a passage from the sermons in which Donne distinguishes between the circle of eternity and the human circle, which is in the making: "this life is a Circle, made with a Compasse, that passes from point to point; That life is a Circle stamped with a print, endlesse, and perfect Circle, as soone as it begins" (2.200).[6] We are not told what the radius of eternity's circle is, for the stamp is merely intended to convey its simultaneity, not its dimensions. No finite circle can express the all-encompassing dimensions of eternity, nor can any localized center give a hint of its omnipresence. Like the God of the mystics, eternity is an infinite circle whose center is everywhere, circumference nowhere. In terms of earthly coordinates, it can be represented only by the dimensionless point, which is both a center and a circumference. The human circle, on the other hand, has its limits. Both its radius and its sweep are measured by time and space. Nevertheless, it tends toward eternity as its goal. Geometrically speaking, then, it moves toward the circular perfection of the center; when the circle is finally closed, its radius will no longer have finite extension but will coincide with the limitless point of eternity. The compass of the human soul opens with time and closes toward eternity all the while that it whirls around the central point, which is both its beginning and its end.

The epigrammatic quality of the last verse suggests that the harmonization of the circle and the line is indeed complete and that both motions end at their point of departure. Like Plato's star-soul (*Timaeus* 44c–d), the soul of Love ends with the perfect circularity with which it began. Its movement is therefore a pulsation, a contraction following an expansion ("Our two soules . . . endure not yet / A breach, but an expansion . . ."), a synthesis of two distinct motions: circular, but with an ever-increasing radius until a maximum circumference is described, whereupon the radius decreases and the circle contracts, approaching the point as its limit ("Thy firmness drawes my circle just"). The word "just" certainly refers to circular perfection; at the same time, however, it recalls the virtuous men of the first stanza and therefore underscores the analogy between the soul of Love and the soul of a "just" man. The dimensionless *point* of dying coincides with the central point of return, the transition between a "just" life and the infinite circle of glory. Thus, like the Aristotelian circle (*De caelo* 269.b.1; 286.b.15),[7] Donne's has no beginning or end along its circumference, but is rather contracted and expanded along its radius, so that the beginning and end of its pulsation coincide at the center. Were it otherwise, we would have difficulty applying the resultant image to the two lovers who part and are reunited. If we were to take "end" to mean some point on the circumference, then the feet of the compass would remain equidistant throughout such an image, whereas the meaning is that the lover begins from the center, beside his beloved, is separated from her and finally will return. No matter how far he "romes," however, his thoughts revolve about her. Such a movement is at once linear and circular.

In antiquity, the spiral was considered to be the harmonization of rectilinear motion with circularity. Chalcidius, in his commentary on the *Timaeus*, describes spiral motion precisely in terms of the two-fold movement of a compass: radial, from center to circumference, and circular, around the circumference. This passage is probably the ultimate source of Donne's compass image:

> We usually call "spiral" that genus of circle which is described when one foot of a compass is fixed and the compass is either stretched out or closed up, either by chance or intentionally, so that circles are described such that not only does the extremity of the circular line not return to its place or origin but is even deflected a given amount either above or below the previous circular line so as to make either wider or narrower circles.
>
> *Timaeus a Calcidio translatus* 160

The spiral is therefore a kind of circle whose outline is unfixed until outward motion ceases and inward motion begins, retracing the same gyre in the opposite direction toward the central point of origin. When we consider the figure, our attention is directed toward the center as beginning and end of all movement, while the periphery remains undefined and vague. So in the poem, our attention is directed not toward Donne's destination abroad but rather toward his wife, to whom he will return, no matter how far he roams.

A similar focus is characteristic of most of the *lemmata* that were illustrated in Donne's day with the emblem of the compass. "Donec ad idem," for instance, stands for a meditation on death and its accompanying compass image serves to illustrate God's condemnation of Adam, that he will end where he began: "donec revertaris in terram" (till you return to the ground) (Gen. 3:19). The poet or preacher's promise to return to his central theme is pictorially represented with the compass and the *lemma*: "non vagus vagor" (I do not wander uncertainly). Even the Jesuit missionary's obedience to his superior can be similarly illustrated: "si jusseris, ibit in orbem" (if you so order it, he will return to the world).[8] Most of the similes in love poetry of the sixteenth century that are based on the compass also stress central constancy in spite of circumstantial vicissitudes. So the explicit compass image from Guarini's madrigal: "un piede in voi quasi mio centro i'fermo,/l'altro patisce di fortuna i giri" (I place one foot in you, almost at my center, while the other suffers the turns of fortune)[9] or the submerged compass image of Maurice Scève, of which we shall have more to say later: ". . . ma pensée, à peu pres s'y transmue, Bien que ma foy, sans suyvre mon project, Çà et là tourne, et point ne se remue" (*Délie* 132).[10] Insofar as these compasses have their origin in the tradition of Chalcidius's image, they trace spirals, whether their authors knew it or not.

We can, however, be sure that John Donne knew it. The word "rome" in the verse, "Yet when the other far doth rome," cannot refer to circular motion, anymore than can the finite verb "vagor" in the emblem books, for a circle does not wander. Donne used the compass image in precisely the same way that Chalcidius used it in the passage I have quoted—that is, to describe a wandering path which is nevertheless rooted in circular regularity. The exemplar of all such orbits is the path described by the planets, or "wandering" stars.

Plato used the movements of the heavenly bodies in order to "spatialize" his conception of intellectual process; it was in this way that he managed to give to his idea of *paideia* a symbolically dynamic dimension. In his microcosmic analogy, the perfect circling of the fixed stars represented the perfect movement of the speculative reason, whereas the rectilinear motion characteristic of the elements represented the lowest human faculties. Between these upper and lower limits of human potentiality there lay the human composite itself, a synthesis of both circle and line. Like the planets, the human soul partakes of the movements of both the outermost sphere, rationality, and of the sublunary world of matter.[11]

Planetary movement was considered to be spiral because it seemed to be composed of at least two opposing movements. Like the sun and moon, the planets rise and set each day, moving from east to west. At the same time, they move along the Zodiac from west to east. The resolution of these two motions, from the perspective of the earth, described a slow-moving spiral from one tropic to the other. In other words, from what we know to be the earth's rotation and revolution, the sun, moon, and planets seem to follow a spiral course (see Figure 8). Chalcidius continues the passage containing the compass image as follows:

> . . . [Plato] has correctly called them [the planets] errant stars, rotating in a spiral, because of the inconstant and unequal circular movement. If, for example, the star of Venus is in the sign of Aries and then is rapt by the course of the universe so that it is carried further and further away from its previous progression, there will certainly be some declination away from Aries; and as many more turnings as it makes, so much the more will it descend from Aries to Pisces, the next sign, and from there it will be impelled to Aquarius. On the other hand, if it were rapt the other way it would proceed from Aries to Taurus and thence to Gemini and Cancer, its gyre becoming ever smaller in due measure; which gyre the Greeks call *helix* . . .

In most of the redactions of Chalcidius's commentary, this passage is accompanied by a diagram of Venus's orbit, viewed from the pole and projected onto the plane of the ecliptic (see Figure 9).[12]

The word "rome" suggests the planetary, or at least "wandering," character of the lover's journey away from his beloved. We shall see that

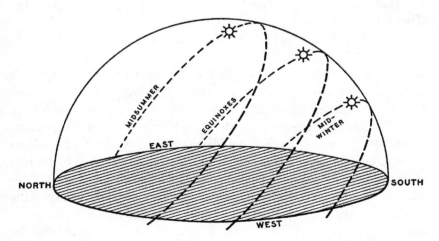

FIGURE 8. The Path of the Sun, after a sketch by M. A. Orr, *Dante and the Early Astronomers* (London, 1913), 23.

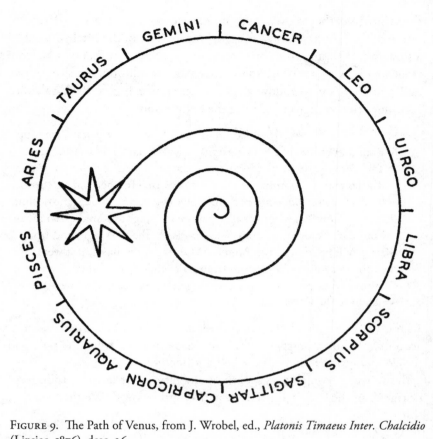

FIGURE 9. The Path of Venus, from J. Wrobel, ed., *Platonis Timaeus Inter. Chalcidio* (Lipsiae, 1876), desc. 26.

several other words in Donne's last verses prove that the imagery is basically astronomical. For the moment, our suggestion seems confirmed by a phrase in the second verse of the last stanza, "obliquely runne." This phrase not only describes planetary motion quite accurately, but also points toward the Platonic analogy, which I have been discussing, and hence to the significance of the spiral form. In the first place, the word "oblique" is still used as a substantive in English to denote the ecliptic, the imaginary line that runs along the center of the Zodiac and traces the path of the planets, sun, and moon. In the Middle Ages, Dante used a form of the word as an adjective to describe the ecliptic: "l'oblico cerchio che i pianeti porta" (the oblique circle that bears the planets) (*Par.* 10.14) while in the Renaissance Théophile de

Viau speaks of the sun's path as an "oblique tour" in "Le matin,"[13] thereby giving to the word the meaning of "spiral," at least implicitly. Of particular interest to us, however, is that Donne here uses an adverbial form, "obliquely," which indicates not a path or a line but a *kind* of motion, the motion that in the Latin Neoplatonic tradition was referred to as the *motus obliquus.*

Plato's geometric analogy for the three "motions" of soul—circular (divine), spiral (human), and rectilinear (animal)—from which is derived his theory of microcosm and macrocosm, enjoyed a great vogue in subsequent Neoplatonic writings. According to the pseudo-Dionysius, for instance, the three "conversions" were characteristic not only of the heavens and of the human soul, but also of the angels. The highest order of angels moves circularly around God and the lowest order moves directly toward man. Between these, the middle order rotates around God while at the same time pursuing its terrestrial missions. In like manner, the human soul can turn directly to God by divine intuition (*supra nos*, St. Bonaventure was later to say), or to the outside world (*extra nos*); but since the "unitive" way is given to few men, most must proceed to God with a combination of those two movements (*intra nos*). This last movement, the spiral, is emblematic of the soul incarnate, of the soul whose inner life is a continual contemplation of God in spite of worldly vicissitudes (*De divinis nominibus* 4.8–9).[14]

In the Latin translations of the Dionysian corpus, from the ninth to the fifteenth centuries, the translation usually offered to describe the "spiral motion" of the human soul is the Latin adverb "oblique."[15] Marsilio Ficinio comments upon the three movements of the soul under the rubric, "De motu angeli et animae triplici, id est, circulari, recto, obliquo" (On the angular three-part motion of the soul, which is to say, circular, erect, oblique).[16] Elsewhere, he uses the same words to describe celestial movement. The planets, he tells us, move "sinuosa quadam obliquitate, velut in spiram" (curving with a certain obliqueness, which is to say, spiral).[17] It seems most likely that this tradition, at once astronomical and mystical, underlies Donne's use of the words "obliquely runne." If this is the case, then Donne himself alludes to the geometrical solution of the problem presented by his own lines. A compass can lean or grow erect *at the same time* that it describes a circle only if that "circle" is in fact a spiral. The next to the last line of the poem does indeed indicate diurnal, circular motion, the fixity of love, while the last refers to a diastolic and systolic pulsation, the "zodiacal" exigencies of life, for these two patterns are combined in the figure that "obliquely" runs.

To return to our summary of the strategy of the poem, with which I began this essay, we said that the "body" of Love dies when the lovers part and is "resurrected" when they are reunited. The compass image manages to span these two moments and thus provides us with an emblem of duration, a fixity of being (insofar as it is a single image) in the process of becoming (insofar as it moves). That duration is literally the time of the lovers' separation from each other and figuratively the history of the disembodied soul of Love, awaiting its glorification at the end of time. In the universe of Love, the time measured by the compass's whirling is the *marking* of time between one moment of eternity and the next, between the creation of time and its dissolution. It cannot be a circle for it is as yet incomplete, as the soul is incomplete without its body, as the lover is incomplete without his beloved. When the restoration is finally achieved, however, the lovers will be reunited, the soul of Love will be reconciled to the body of Love and the planets will end their wandering at their points of origin.

To a modern reader, planetary imagery may seem gratuitous in a poem that is primarily concerned with the relationship of body and soul as a figure for the relationship of two lovers. To thinkers of the Renaissance, however, there seemed to be an intimate connection between the life of the cosmos and the life of man. The exile of the soul from its body was thought to last precisely as long as the exile of the planet from its home. According to the doctrine of "universal restoral," which is Platonic in origin, the life of the entire universe is measured by the Cosmic Year.[18] All of the heavenly bodies will return to precisely the same positions from which they began at the end of 36,000 solar years. Ausonius is one among many in antiquity who describe this *apocatastasis*; his verses call to mind the *lemma* of Death's compass, "donec ad idem":

> Donec consumpto, magnus qui dicitur, anno,
> Rursus in antiquum veniant vaga sidera cursum
> Qualia dispositi steterant ab origine mundi.[19]

Before that which they call the great year reaches its close, and the wandering stars return to their ancient course, just as they had stood at the beginning of the ordered universe.

By an association that seemed to Christian astrologers inevitable, in spite of the protestations of critics such as Pico della Mirandolo, the *apocatastasis* of the ancient was taken to be coincident with the Christian Apocalypse and hence with the resurrection of the body.[20] Thus, when the human soul ends where it began, the planets, *vaga sidera*, will return to the positions they occupied at the Creation. Marsilio Ficino, characteristically, defends the religious doctrine with the astrological "fact" in order to bolster his own somewhat shaky belief in the Resurrection:

> Nor should it appear absurd that souls, after they have left their natural state, should return again to the same place, for indeed the planets leave their natural homes [*domicilia*] and seek them again. Further, particles of elements which are expelled from their natural place return again to it. Nor is it difficult for the infinite virtue of God, which is everywhere present, which created everything *ex nihilo*, to bring together those elements of a body which had once been dissolved.[21]

The homes of the planets, their *domicilia* or *klairoi* in the celestial sphere, mark the beginning and end of planetary motion. Donne the lover, metamorphosed into a planet wandering from his beloved, also begins and ends at "home" (line four, stanza eight). The poet has once more reversed a traditional argument, reversing signifier and thing signified and interposing a concrete image increasing the distance between them. As the soul will return to the body, so the soul of Love (the lovers' two souls) will return to its body (the lovers' two bodies) as the planets come "home."[22]

If our contention that the compass image has primarily astronomical reference is correct, then there is a series of words in the next to last stanza that still require interpretation. The stanza says of "Thy soule the fixt foot":

> And though it in the center sit,
> > Yet when the other far doth rome,
> It leanes, and hearkens after it,
> > And growes erect, as that comes home.

I have suggested that "rome" characterizes the motion of the wandering stars and that "home" designates their *klairoi* or *domicilia*. Another position that astrologers felt obliged to determine was the planetary *exaltatio*, or as the word is still translated, the "erect" position.[23] Vittoria Colonna, for example, describing the auspicious moment of her lover's birth, says that the planets were in that position:

> Gli almi pianeti in propria sede eretti
> Mostravan lieti quei benigni aspetti,
> Che instillan le virtù nei cor più rari . . .[24]

> The noble planets erect in each their own seat happily demonstrate
> those benign aspects that the virtues instill in the most rare hearts

In the history of astrology there was considerable disagreement about how the "homes" and the "exaltations" of the planets were measured. According to Pliny in the passage that is the *locus classicus* for the discussion of the *exaltatio* of the planets, the critical point on the Zodiac was reached by the planet when its orbital arc was at its highest elevation from the center of the earth. Using this criterion, he provided a catalogue of planetary domiciles: "Igitur a terrae centro apsides altissimae sunt Saturno in scorpione, Iovi in vergine, Marti in leone . . . [etc.]" (Therefore the planetary arcs are at their highest point from the center of the earth for Saturn in Scorpio, for Jove in Virgo, and Mars in Leo) (*Naturalis historiae* 2:16). Later thinkers, and especially the Arabs, disagreed, and insisted that the measurement of the *altitudo* was to be taken not from the earth but from the center of the Zodiac to the zodiacal sign. From this new form of calculation they put together a totally different catalogue of "exaltations."[25] For our purposes, however, it should be noted that the measurements themselves, according to a probably spurious passage in the text of Pliny, were taken precisely by means of the compass: "Omnia autem haec constant *ratione circini* semper indubitata" (moreover all of these things are made clear by the always infallible reason of the compass).[26] The point on the Zodiac diametrically opposed to a planet's *exaltatio* is the point of *deiectio*; if the former can be described in terms of a compass that is tracing a spiral and is at its maximum erection, then the *deiectio* will be the point of the compass's maximum depression.[27] It is at this point that the compass "leanes," when the moving foot is at its greatest distance from the foot fixed in the orbit's center. In the context of the "Valediction," the suspicious lines "It leanes, and hearkens after it, / And growes erect as that comes home" are primarily a geometric indication that, at the end of the exile of Love's soul, the planets will be exalted in their homes, awaiting the final consummation and the lovers' eternity.

A word must be said here about the literal meaning of the phrase "It leanes . . . and growes erect" as it applies to the woman, in order to lay to rest the erotic interpretation sometimes given it. Whatever else the poem may be, it obviously constitutes a song of praise to the woman. In the Middle Ages, the most of such *encomia* was the praise of the virtuous wife taken from Proverbs 31:10–31: "Who can find a virtuous woman . . . for her price is far above rubies." The verses in the original form an acrostic, each verse beginning with a letter of the alphabet in order from Aleph to Sin. Verse 20 reads: "She stretcheth out her hand to the poor." Albertus Magnus in his *De muliere forti* notes that the verse begins with the letter Kaph (כ), which he interprets inclinatio, referring to the compassion that inclines the hardness of the heart (*De muliere forti* 11.1). Verse 24, "She maketh fine linen," is introduced by the letter Samech (ס), which he interprets *erectio*, the hope that raises us up (*De muliere forti* 15.1). Donne may have been using the words "lean" and "erect" as similar compliments to his faithful beloved; this would explain why he uses the words with respect to her in spite of the fact that the purely literal meaning of the words is necessarily applicable to both legs of the compass. More interesting, however, is the fact that the Hebrew letters standing for the words "inclinatio" and "erectio" constitute ingenious hieroglyphs for separation and reunion. Kaph, the broken circle (כ), marks the separation of the feet of the compass, whereas Samech brings them together and closes the circle (ס) as the compass becomes erect. This interpretation of the words has the advantage of doing violence neither to the poem nor to its context and, if it strains our credulity about how much Donne could put into a single line, it at least avoids the physiological naiveté required for an erotic interpretation of the words.

We have seen that the souls of the lover and the beloved together constitute the soul of Love, tracing humanity's emblem in a spiral course around the center, which is their common possession, much like a planetary orbit around the axis of the universe. It happens that the gyre of the planetary soul is the archetype of motion in the human soul as well. The compass stands for a principal of motion that is common to humanity and to the heavens.[28] It is this analogy that relates the beginning of the poem to its ending, for if the soul of Love moves like a planet, it also moves like a *human* soul. Further, once we understand this movement, we shall also understand how a soul can be one and yet logically two-fold ("Our two soules . . . which are one") in literal, as well as figurative terms. We shall have to discover why the compass is a perfect image of the soul.

In order to clarify the interrelationship of the cognitive and appetitive powers of the soul, Aristotle in *De anima* described its workings mechanistically in terms that recall "stiffe twin compasses."[29] All movement consists of three factors: 1) that which originates movements; 2) the means whereby it originates it; 3) that which is moved. In locomotion, the origin of movement is the soul, working through the heart (1). The means (2) are the vital spirits, pushing and pulling against a stationary point, which provides thrust: the "fixt foot" (stanza 8 of the "Valediction"). The thing that is moved is the other foot. If we analyze the origin of motion, the heart, we find that it is where the beginning and end of motion coincide, the center of articulation, a joint between two extremities. Aristotle compares it to a ball-and-socket joint (*gigglimus*), or to the elbow (*De anima* 3.10.433b).[30] This is because it is the mid-point between the alternate movements of pushing and pulling in the motions of an animal. When a human being walks, one side remains fixed while the other moves, the latter in turn becoming fixed while the former moves. An interesting poetic description of the first steps of Adam is given to us in the *Microcosme* of Maurice Scève, where the word for "measure," *compas*, is perhaps used as a pun:

> Dresseé sur piés branchus, une jambe en avant,
> L'autre restant, se vit à cheminer savant,
> Et se conduire droit en tous lieux pas à pas
> Mesurant son alleure avec grave compas.[31]

According to Averroes, the pushing and pulling movements are not precisely straight because the vital spirits themselves, which are responsible for transmitting the heart's impulses to the limbs, move in a gyre: a *motus gyrativus* around the heart.[32]

The movement of the soul is precisely analogous to the local motion of the body. It is the appetitive faculty, the will, which, like the left foot, provides thrust, while the reason steps out first, like the right foot. They are joined to each other by the faculty of choice itself, whose "highest" point came to be called the *apex mentis*.[33] The link between all of these and the body is *pneuma* or *spiritus*, the mysterious substance that is the locus of contact between body and soul. If the *apex mentis* is like the heart, the joint of a compass, then the will is its fixed foot while the reason is the other. The *pneuma*, which joins them, traces its gyre on the plain of human action.

In the compass of the human soul, it is the will that remains fixed in its constancy while the reason moves out. So in Scève's submerged compass image, the lover's "pensée" may be diverted, but "ma foy, sans suyvre mon project, / Ça et là tourne, et point ne se remue."[34] So too, the Plantin device serves as an image of constancy in action: "Labore et constantia."[35] To this is doubtless related Cesare Ripa's use of the compass as an emblem for "practica," by which he probably means the practical reason.[36] Donne chose to compliment his beloved on her constancy, her faith, with this emblem. At the same time, he consoled her by suggesting that they were as the will and reason respectively of a single soul, "inter-assured" of the apex of the mind. For all of its dazzling virtuosity, the conceit is analogous to an ancient exegetical commonplace. As Adam represents *ratio*, or the highest faculty of the soul, so Eve represents *appetitus*, which is in direct contact with the body. Together, they are one.[37]

We have so far been concerned with establishing the principle that governs the movement of the poem, symbolized by the compass image. It is this universal principle that gives the "Valediction" its coherence upon so many analogical levels of reality. In the second part of this paper, we shall turn to a close reading of the poem in order to examine its multileveled coherence. Before we proceed, however, something must be said of the poem's relationship to the literary tradition from which it takes its point of departure. It will be seen that Donne's originality here, as so often, consists in the startlingly new form that he bestows upon time-worn banalities. Thematically, the "Valediction: Forbidding Mourning" resembles the medieval *congé d'amour*, wherein a lover takes leave of his lady and consoles her by claiming that they are not really two individuals, but rather affirms that they are one, or that he has left with her his heart.[38] In Renaissance treatments of the presence-absence antithesis, elements of the *congé* are combined with Petrarchan and stilnovistic themes and often expressed in terms of Plotinian theories of ecstasy, as has been pointed out by Merritt Hughes.[39] Among the *trattati d'amore* of the *Cinquecento*, Sperone Speroni's is almost exclusively concerned with the antithesis of presence and absence, although he does not mention the Resurrection, as does

Marsilio Ficino in a similar context.[40] Nor is the consolation of a reunion at the end of a cosmic year entirely original; Giordano Bruno, in a rare fabulist mood, pokes fun at the idea of "universal restoral" and Plotinian ecstasy with a bizarre *congé d'amour* of his own, written thirty years before Donne's poem:

> The flea, which had been educated according to the dogma of the divine Plato, was consoling the bedbug with loving words from the height of the roof, while a cruel fate was dividing the two companions: the chamber-boy, shaking the mattress, was already at the point of casting them down and throwing them off to diverse fates, for he was rolling up the sleeve of his shirt from his naked arm. The bedbug's face was lined with tears as it said: "Not my fate, not my cruel fate bothers me, that this my spirit should abandon these ugly and miserable members, but rather does that violent separation disturb me because you, dear Flea, are forced by iniquitous fates to leave me, fates which tear me away and cannot give you back to me." The flea answered, "Do not torment yourself, for this your torment transfixes me, consumes me and makes me unhappy. My spirit and yours are not twin, o bedbug of one soul with me, for you are more intimate to me than I am to myself; wherefore my worry for you bothers me while I have no worry for myself. Therefore, even if thundering Jove himself separate these our two bodies iniquitously, nevertheless, only when he makes me leave my very self can he cause my spirit to leave you, my fate, my death, once my life and my hope. But even making me forgetful of myself, I find it difficult to believe that he can make me forgetful of you. Weep not, my life's blood, I know certainly that our two bodies will one day be together again. I should like to say more, but already we are torn apart. Ahi! ahi! Now farewell, sweet love! After two times, three times, one hundred thousand years, added to which two other times three and two times three hundred thousand (which I hope will come to pass auspiciously and happily), you will look for me a second time and I myself will see you a second time."
>
> *De immenso et innumerabilibus* 3.7[41]

It is, however, the Resurrection, not the cosmic year, that Donne offers to his wife as a consolation forbidding mourning. This is not simply an attempt to adapt a Platonic banality to the Christian revelation, but rather has the effect of transposing the theme of "restoration" from the universe of space and time to an interior dimension. The criticism of Bruno, which is to say the criticism of the "layetie" who do not understand that the entire universe and its mystery are recapitulated in the microcosm of Love, is groundless here; the "Valediction" establishes a *symbolic* cosmology, Love's universe, where time begins at the lovers' parting and ends at their reunion. The poem and the duration it spans seem at first to be a breach of eternity's circle; as we read, however, we come to realize that time is eternity's moving image—its end is its beginning—and the 36,000 years of its reign (measured in Donne's 36 verses) constitutes merely a pause for lovers who are eternally one. Similarly, space is transcended in Love's symbolic cosmos by the assurance that, thanks to the constancy of Love's faith, the centrifugality of any separation will be overcome by the centripetal force that binds all of reality to the same Center.

The neo-Petrarchan antithesis of presence and absence underlies the simile of the dying man with which the poem begins, but its banality is here transcended by what Albert Béguin has called love's "chemin vers l'intérieur."[42] As each of the lovers is the life of the other, separation is tantamount to the death of their superficial identity. The absence of his beloved forces the lover into himself to begin the spiral descent toward the void where his life once was. At the center of his being, he discovers, not his heart, nor even the heart of his beloved, but rather the "heart" of the entire universe, the Center about which all of reality revolves. It is here, in the depths of his subjectivity, that death is transcended and the whole universe interiorized around the pole-star of Love.[43] Upon this transcendence, the death "intra nos" that ultimately leads "supra nos," a new, more authentic identity is established. The miracle of Love's *askesis* is that in thought, by participation in the "mind," which transcends them, man and woman are joined together and transmuted above the sphere of the moon, "refin'd" to await their glorious reunion. All of the heavens are embraced by the soul of their love, for at Love's center is the point that is, in fact, a cosmic circumference.

Insofar as the compass stands for the archetypal movement of the soul (whether celestial or human), it is a symbol a formal image standing for the instrumentality whereby spiritual movement is accomplished. It is the rational principle underlying that movement, or its formal cause. The movement itself, however, must be a movement of *something*; it is to this something that we must now turn our attention. Just as scientists, before the theory of relativity, believed that motion in the cosmos had to be through some sort of vehicle that they called *aether*, so metaphysicians believed that the interaction of soul and body had to be through a medium that combined the properties of both. This medium they called *pneuma*. Similarly, in Donne's poem, a symbolic pneuma joins the body and the soul of Love, and therefore is the symbolic medium through which the poem moves.

The vital reality underlying the compass image is *pneuma*, or *spiritus*, the mysterious substance that was considered to be the medium of the soul's action on the body, as well as the medium of the planetary soul's action on the heavenly body. In effect, this "breath of the universe" represented antiquity's attempt to find a single explanation for all movement in the cosmos, a primordial "field theory," which the Stoics used to interpret the pulsations of both air and aether and which the Christians did not hesitate to associate with the God-head.[44] It was because pneuma represented the locus of contact between body and soul that its movement was composed "ex recto et circulari," a movement that Averroes chose to call the "motus gyrativus" (*In Aristotelis de anima* III 3.55).[45] The vital "spirits" move in their gyre around the heart as the planetary aether moves around its soul. Albertus Magnus equates the two movements: "Motus autem horum spirituum in corpore sunt sicut motus luminarium in mundo" (Moreover, the movement of the spirits in the body are just like those of the stars in the sky) (*Summae de creaturis* 2.2, q. 78). "Breath" was for the ancients the *hegemonikon* of the universe; in Donne's poem, it is the pulsating reality. The compass is an image that stands for an archetypal movement as universal as the heavens and as commonplace as respiration. We may turn now to see *what* it is that actually moves.

The poem opens with an important statement that identifies the "spirit" of Love by comparing it to life's "pneumatic" principle:

> As virtuous men passe mildly away,
>     And whisper to their soules, to goe,
> Whilst some of their sad friends doe say
>     The breath goes now, and some say, no:

Virtuous men pass away mildly because they are convinced that their death is no definitive separation; it is simply a pause in the life of body and soul. The resurrected body is precisely the same body, but glorified and made immortal; the soul that leaves it, therefore, endures "not yet / A breach, but an expansion," since an ideal link (however tenuous) still joins the two. We shall see that this subtle link, of "ayery thinnesse," is the *pneuma* of Love's cosmos, the "spiritus" of Love, refined from the sublunary world to the heavens.

The sad friends of virtuous men lack an intimate assurance of the Resurrection and therefore cannot be sure that they will ever see the dying man again. This may well be the moment of definitive separation and it therefore seems a matter of some importance to watch the purely material breath (which is all they can perceive) as it leaves its body once and for all. Their debates are, however, irrelevant to the dying man who, like the historian of ideas, knows that the "breath," which is expired in time, is intimately connected with the soul, which is "inspired" in eternity.[46] With a confidence he cannot communicate to the "layetie," he whispers his *congé* to his soul. The effect of that whisper is that it gives substance to his soul and spirituality to his breath. His last breath is impressed with the seal of rationality, the *words* that are the physical manifestation of thought, a link between body and soul. Material breath is transformed by speech into *spiritus*, the God-given *efflatus* (Gen. 2:7), which is the symbol of humanity.[47] Were it not for this link, the body could say nothing—a man whose soul departs is no longer a man but a corpse. The point is that here there is no separation. Body and soul are eternally related to each other by the "pneumatic" whisper that is "exhaled" to a cosmic dimension before coming home. We shall have more to say of this sublime mystery.

The expansion and contraction of this breath are the diastole and the systole of both human and cosmic life, the *motus gyrativus* of man and the planets. This is the analogical link between the opening and the closing of the poem. Marsilio Ficino describes the mechanics of "breath":

> [The body's extension in space and time] might cause it to be drawn apart in rectilinear fashion [i.e., centrifugally], so that it would perhaps dissipate itself were it not drawn back by the intellectual soul. Hence, nature gives it a propensity to circularity. Think of the heavenly body in the same way, as if it were the breath [*spiritus*] expelled by the soul's exhalation, most certainly subject in the same way to rectilinear dispersion, but alternately contained again immediately afterward by the soul's inhalation. Therefore, since the soul cannot ever cease its breathing, it is necessary that [the heavenly body] be turned back within the heavens around the soul and, indeed, within it.[48]

The analogical structure of *pneuma* accounts for the poetic connection between the expiration of virtuous men and planetary movement. The rectilinear impulsion of the heavenly *spiritus* is overcome by the circular force of the Soul in the same way that the human soul holds sway over the vital spirits. These cycles are mechanically recapitulated in every human breath. In Donne's poem, however, the analogous structure is not simply a static juxtaposition of the two opposite states of *pneuma*, a simile comparing the breath of man to the "breath" of the universe; it is rather a dynamic continuum joining the two poles. As the soul leaves the body, the *spiritus* is gradually released from the flesh, which contains it, rises by a continual refinement to the celestial dwelling-place of the soul and joins the heavenly *spiritus* in the cosmic "respiration."[49] When the planets return to their starting place at the end of the cosmic year, the soul then descends to the glorified body, gradually contracting its *pneuma* so that both may again be contained within the resurrected flesh. Because of the doctrine of the Resurrection, then, the final breath of an expiring soul is separated by a cosmic diffusion from the first breath of the glorified body. Nevertheless, they are simply the two phases of a single cycle. In the odor of sanctity, the last breath of time virtually coincides with the first breath of eternity.[50]

The third stanza of the poem is the macrocosmic counterpart of the first, for it contrasts definitive separation with the diastole and systole of death and Resurrection:

> Moving of th'earth brings harmes and feares,
>     Men reckon what it did and meant,
> But trepidation of the spheares,
>     Though greater farre, is innocent.

C. M. Coffin was incorrect when he supposed that this stanza was a juxtaposition of the old cosmology with the new, a Copernican moving of the center of the earth with the Ptolomeic trepidation of the spheres.[51] "Moving of th'earth" is simply Donne's translation of *terrae motus*, the earthquake, believed to be caused by a violent expulsion of winds (*pneuma*) trapped within the earth. According to Aristotle, it is the macrocosmic parallel of death: in both cases, the *pneuma* is expelled by the separation of the body's elements (*Meteorologica* 366b).[52] The parallel is implicit in a passage from *Henry IV*, part 1:

Diseased nature oftentimes breaks forth
In strange eruptions; oft the teeming earth
Is with a kind of colic pinch'd and vex'd
By the imprisioning of unruly wind
Within her womb; which for enlargement striving
Shakes the old beldam earth, and topples down
Steeples and moss-grown towers.

*Henry IV* 3.1.31

It is therefore a definitive rupture of "body" and spirit, a *breach* full of evil portents (which is the point of the passage in the context of Shakespeare's play) and calamitous consequences. Since it is a departure of "breath," the men who reckon its consequences are much like the sad friends of the first stanza, who see death from a purely earthbound perspective and similarly discuss what seems to them an imminent breach ("Some . . . doe say, / The breath goes now, and some say, no"). Moreover, earthquakes are caused by the same pneumatic turbulence that is responsible for flood and tempests, a point worth remembering for our discussion of the lovers' silent parting in the last section of this chapter ("No teare-floods, no sigh-tempests move"). In all of these ways, but above all *spatially*, moving of the earth is the antithesis of trepidation of the spheres.

The essential difference between the trembling of the earth and the "trembling" of the eighth sphere is that the latter movement is no break, but simply a going and coming, an "access and recess."[53] The two movements differ in exactly the same way that a purely physical death in the sublunary world differs from the death of a virtuous man seen from the perspective of eternity. The first is an occasion for sadness and "feares"; the second, which measures the universe's life in a single pulsation of immense extension in space and time, can do no harm ("is innocent") to the man who virtuously submits to it, who has no reason to fear the end of time and the Last Judgment. When, after thousands of years, the pole of the heavens returns to the true pole in its sinuous curve, all of creation will arise from death.[54] The *pneuma* that leaves the body (of men or of the world) joins the cosmic respiration until the Resurrection.[55]

Because its pulsation rules both the microcosm and the macrocosm, the "spirit" of Love is the vital bond that gives to the lover's universe its coherence and its continuity. That universe is purely poetic and Donne therefore has license to disregard contemporary cosmology and to take liberties with contemporary theology when he describes Love's *hegemonikon*. Nevertheless, the assertion of a universal continuity, in an epoch that had long since been shaken from such dreams, seems painfully naive even when its validity is restricted to the closed world of human love. Furthermore, the poem seems poetically unsatisfying while its fundamental principle lacks the symbolic concreteness that we have come to expect from Donne. Finally, unless the "spirit" of Love is somehow rooted to the real world, the hope and consolation that it offers seem equally insubstantial and purely poetic.

There was at least one science in Donne's time, however, that still held to a theoretical continuity between matter and spirit: the science of alchemy. Donne borrowed some of its principles in order to give a symbolic consistency to his "Valediction: Forbidding Mourning." An allegory based upon the Hermetic science resolves the complexity of the poem into a unified and poetically meaningful statement because it gives to the "spirit" of Love a symbolic grounding by equating it with something real and—very nearly—tangible. The allegory is a subtle answer in kind to the cynicism of "Loves Alchymie."

We have seen that the first and third stanzas of Donne's poem trace the expansion of "breath" from the world of time to the heavens and back again in a diastolic-systolic movement of death and resurrection. The poet refers to this process indirectly as a refinement, for he compares it with the refinement of the two lovers ("But we by a love, so much refin'd"): as virtuous men pass away, so let us melt and be refined to celestial expansion, "Like gold to ayery thinnesse beate." This refinement is exactly analogous to the refinement of sublimation practiced by the alchemists in their search for the philosophers' stone. The volatile "spirit" of a metal is extracted by liquefaction, transmuted by sublimation and subsequently "fixed" by settling. The all-important sublimation was considered to be a transmutation of the "spirit" of a metal from one level of reality to another; what made it possible was the alchemist's unshakeable faith in the doctrine of *pneuma*. Because alchemy was a "child of Greek philosophy," it regarded all of reality as a continuum between the poles of mind and matter, or of body and soul. *Pneuma* was considered to be the universal link, at once the substance of the heavens and the "breath" of the human soul, marking the transition between the two by its varying degrees of subtlety.[56] According to a commonplace as old as Diodorus Siculus, it was the Quintessence, ontologically located between the four elements and pure immateriality.[57] Ever since Aristotle, men had believed that metals were produced by the action of *pneuma* trapped within the bowels of the earth; it followed that *pneuma* could bring any metal to the perfection of pure gold.[58] All that was necessary was to solidify *pneuma* into usable form: the Philosophers' Stone.

Because the doctrine of *pneuma* was historically not only a physical and metaphysical principle, but also a religious tenet, a description of it was perforce three-fold in its reference. To discuss the nature of *pneuma* was to discuss not only the relationship of body to soul, but also the relationship of the earth to the heavens and even the relationship of the universe to God, the Holy Spirit. This accounts for the almost limitless possibilities at the disposal of the practical alchemist to hide his true meaning under the guise of cosmic or religious allegories. Thus, the removal of the volatile "spirit" from a metal was the severing of body and soul, the chemical "death" necessary in order to bring about the "resurrection" of the philosopher's gold. The vehicle of this process was the "breath" of the universe; its principles were repulsion, attraction and circularity. The end product was a gold of such subtlety, incorruptibility and purity that it could be compared only to the glorified body.[59]

J. A. Mazzeo has discussed Donne's reversal of signifier and signified in these alchemical allegories and has quoted several examples of Donne's "spiritual alchemy" in the sermons.[60] It should be stressed that the reversibility of spiritual and chemical orders was built into the language of all of the alchemists. I cite Nicholas Flamel as one example among many:

> You should also know that in our Art we distinguish two things—
> the body and the spirit; the former being constant, or fixed, while the
> other is volatile. These two must be changed, the one into the other
> ... Then the body loses all its grossness, and becomes new and pure;
> nor can this body and soul ever die, seeing that they have entered into
> a eternal union, such as the union of our bodies and souls shall be at
> the last day.[61]

By a further association, which I first noted at the beginning of this paper, the relationship of the body to the soul was itself allegorized in terms of the relationship of man and woman, or husband and wife. So, too, in alchemy, where a kind of generation or birth was the object of the art, an additional allegorical dimension was provided by sexuality, the physical analogue of all generation or birth was the object of the art, an additional allegorical dimension was provided by sexuality, the physical analogue of all generation in the cosmos. Albertus Magnus, for instance, discussing the components of all metals, reduces them to two, mercury and sulfur, and says of them: "quasi universalia metalorum sunt sicut pater et mater." In later alchemical works, we find that the union, dissolution, and subsequent restoration of chemical elements is allegorized by death and resurrection in both the spiritual and the sexual senses of the words.[62]

The process of refinement must be attended by both water and air, in very careful measure. Giano Lacinio says, "the experience of sigh is essential." Too much air and floods of water will produce a tempestuous condition and ruin the experiment:

> For though the soul of the metal has to be extracted, it must not be killed in the operation; and the extraction of the living soul, which has to be reunited to the glorified body, must be carried on in a way very different from the violent method commonly prevailing among alchemists.[63]

The "death" of the metal must therefore be like the death of a Christian, accompanied, not by "teare-floods" or "sigh-tempests," but by a faith in the Resurrection:

> This separation of body and soul is brought about by a spiritual dying. For as the dissolution of body and soul is performed in the regenerated gold, where body and soul are separated from one another, and yet remain close together in the same phial, the soul daily refreshing the body from above, and preserving it from final destruction, until a set time: so the decaying and half-dead bodily part of man is not entirely deserted by the soul in the furnace of the Cross, but is refreshed by the spirit from above . . . (for our temporal death, which is the wages of sin, is not a real death, but only a *natural and gentle serving of body and soul*). The indissoluble union and conjunction of the Spirit of God, and the soul of the Christian, are a real and abiding fact.[64]

This is the profound mystery that sad friends, "layetie," and "dull sublunary lovers" will never understand. The recipe was considered so great a secret by some alchemists that it could be whispered by the philosopher only on his death-bed.[65]

It remains now, before discussing the literal meaning of the poem, to show how Donne's alchemical allegory is related to the geometric statement with which the poem ends. W. A. Murray has shown that the current symbol for gold in Donne's time suggests the compass image: ☉.[66] The lovers are therefore compared to a circle "to ayery thin-nesse beate," or, as I have stated the matter, to a circle that is expanded and ultimately contracted with two fold-movement: radially, from center to circumference, and circularly, with an ever increasing circum-ference. Because the lovers begin as gold and "endure not yet a breach, but an expansion" until they come together as glorified gold, their move-ment is a regular expansion of a small circle and a regular contraction back to it. Because the terminal point coincides with the lovers' eternity, however, the final circle approaches the minimum point, the center, which the mystics identified with the infinite circle of eternity.[67] In the world of space and time, the only way that such a movement can be formally represented with a mathematical figure that captures both its essence and its duration is by means of a compass whose circlings never cease (the fixity of Love) while its radius expands and contracts (the exigencies of life).

I have, however, shown that the compass traces a planetary orbit, and not just any regular spiral. It is obvious to even the most casual student of alchemy that the continuity of *pneuma* throughout the cos-mos had the effect of linking experiments on earth with the movement of the heavenly bodies. The philosophers' Quintessence (which I have called the "spirit" of Love) was itself considered to be the incorruptible material of which the heavenly bodies are composed.[68] In a general way then, one would have expected Donne to give a cosmic circumference to the poetic refinement represented in his poem. It is Donne's genius, however, never to leave the matter at a merely general stage of coher-ence. His poetic precision narrowed the focus to a particular planet and thereby linked the symbolic statements to the real world. In order to demonstrate this, we must return for a moment to our analysis of plan-etary movement in the first part of this paper.

I have tried to show that Donne used the words "erect" and "home" in a technical sense to indicate the *exaltatio* and *domicilium* respectively of his planetary orbit. These are two different points of the planetary course through the Zodiac. The "home" of a planet is always the mid-point of an arbitrary constellation in which the planet was believed to have been at the moment of creation. Since the arc of a constellation is 30, the "home" of a planet is always 15 of the given constellation. On the other hand, the *exaltatio* is mathematically determined. The point of the Sun's erection, for instance, is 19 Aries, of the Moon 3 Taurus, of Saturn 11 Libra, etc. Of only one planet is it true that the point of *exaltatio* coincides exactly with the planetary *domicilium*, and that is the planet Mercury. Its *exaltatio* is 15 Virgo; its "home" is in the same constellation—at 15 Virgo. Only of a mercurial orbit may it be said that its altitude ". . . growes erect as that [i.e., the planet itself] comes home." The movement of the "spirit" of Love therefore moves as does the "subtle" Mercury, the "Hermaphrodite" planet.[69]

Since the lovers begin and end as gold, it is clear that their "spirit" must be the "spirit" of gold, the tincture. In the blundering confusion of formulae and recipes in the history of alchemy, the importance of mercury as a constituent of all metals remains constant. In medieval metallurgy all metals were considered to be composed of sulfur and mercury, the latter being the volatile principle. Gold's purity and uniformity was due to the purity and the perfect homogeneity of its elements; its "spirit" was identified with *spiritus* itself, the fifth essence. Thus, in the fifteenth and sixteenth centuries, mercury was considered the essential element in the production of the "spirit" of gold and of the "philosophers' stone."[70] Paracelsus's famous innovation, the theory of the *tria prima*, which made such an impact on Donne, did not shake mercury's pre-eminent position; on the contrary, his assertion that all of matter was composed of sulfur, salt, and mercury made of the last substance the perfect analogue of bodily and heavenly *pneuma*. Mazzeo states the analogy succinctly: "To the mystical interpreters of the 'tria prima' mercury became the human spiritual principle [i.e., *pneuma*] and sulfur and salt corresponded to the human body and its soul."[71] By having his compass trace a mercurial orbit, Donne identified the *pneuma* of Love's universe with the *Mercurius Philosophorum*. Its quintessential *motus gyrativus* contains within it all of reality, for "est in Mercurio quicquid quaerunt Sapientes."[72] Thanks to celestial Mercury, the "spirit" of Love (". . . we by a love so much refin'd . . ."), the earthly gold of the two lovers is refined into the immortal and incorruptible gold of the glorified body and soul.

It may be useful to recapitulate the alchemical process that Donne uses as an allegory of his love. The homogeneous mixture of mercury and sulfur, which is gold, is prepared by being beaten into gold-leaf. It is melted gently and carefully in the presence of some air and some moisture. Its mercurial "spirit" and its soul are thereby extracted gently from the body, but remain in contact with it from afar, refreshing it from time to time. In some experiments, the "spirit" of mercury was sometimes "refined" by being whirled in a spherical container; in Donne's macrocosm, the container is of course the vault of heaven, while "Trepidation of the spheares" is the gentle whirling of refinement.[73] When the "spirit" reaches its point of celestial purity, both it and the soul return to the body, which is thereby coagulated, "fixed" in the form of celestial, glorified gold, now capable of turning into gold all that it touches. It is gold's *pneuma*, the "breath" of the two lovers, which has undergone a cosmic expansion and contraction.

To conclude this reading of the poem, it will now be necessary to determine the literal terms of the contrast between the initiate-lovers and the dull sublunary "layetie." This contrast is at the heart of the poem's literal meaning.

The first two stanzas are a simile comparing the death of virtuous men to the parting of the two lovers. Another simile, antithetical to the first, is also presented in the first two stanzas: sad friends who cannot determine when the separation is definitive because they cannot discern the breathing are like the "layetie" who cannot understand the mystery of love. The use of the word "layetie," however, suggests that the process is hermetic and therefore associates both the soul's whisper and love's whisper with the secret of "refinement" in the alchemist's art. The third stanza shifts the focus of attention to the macrocosm rather abruptly by adding still another set of dichotomies to the poem's dialectic. The spatial tension that it introduces (earth-spheres) matches the logical tensions we have just examined. Moving of the earth, the earthquake, is a fortuitous breach in the sublunary world, which brings with it tempests and floods. It is a macrocosmic analogue of death in the purely physical sense and an analogue of the separation of elements in ruined or "flooded" experiments. Trepidation of the spheres, however, is an access and recess, a departure followed by a return. The analogue is metaphysically apt, for the movement measures the life of the cosmos and of the soul from the moment of death to the Resurrection: It is a harmless ("innocent") respiration. Its alchemical equivalent is also a necessary trembling, for the gentle whirling of the "spirit" of gold in a spherical container is the refinement prior to a fixation in the glorified composite. The problem seems to be with the relevance of this stanza to the literal situation.

The cosmic restatement of the third stanza is a development that is familiar to us within the context of both physical and metaphysical statements. Because of the doctrine of *pneuma* and the universal continuity that it implies, any alchemical occurrence has a dimension of meaning in the universe. Similarly, because of the theory of macrocosm and microcosm, the soul's processes have their universal counterparts. These multiple associations, however, are scarcely enough to account for the abruptness of the transition between the first two stanzas and the third. Logic seems to require an amplification of the first simile as it applies to the two lovers rather than a shift to a universal dimension. This is, in fact, what Donne provides. His macrocosmic language simply underscores the importance he gives to the laws of Love and serves to make a universe of the two lovers. In order to make his literal meaning apparent, it will be necessary to reverse his procedure and reduce the statement to microcosmic proportions, interpolating what he says of the world's body to apply to the body of Love.

This is clear in retrospect when we come to the fourth stanza. The phrase "Dull sublunary lovers love" telescopes microcosm and macrocosm and brings to the surface the submerged literal meaning of the preceding stanza. The earthquake is the love of sublunary lovers "because it doth remove those things which elemented it." It is a "fatal" release of *pneuma*, which culminates in absence. Lovers who are merely carnal couple only to separate; their violent coming together can have disastrous consequences. Coitus is a collision of "elements" accompanied by floods and outbursts of noise, the *strepitus* which is the sign of the animal.[74] It is ended in an orgasmic death, which, like the earthquake, is a burst of *pneuma* from the organic depths of the body, a definitive "going."[75] This is how sad friends conceive of death and how dull sublunary lovers love—only with their earthly selves.

If the "earth" of a lover is his body, then his "sphere" is his head. The analogy between the spherical shape of the head and the spherical shape of the celestial vault is probably the origin of Plato's theory of macrocosm and microcosm.[76] It is, at any rate, the most familiar of the *Timaeus's* analogies. So in Donne's poem, the spheres stand for the highest part of incarnate, rational lovers. In spite of their physical separation, they are still joined by the mind, the pivot of Love's compass. Because of its rational quality, their love is a "virtuous" melting: an "innocent" trepidation of "breath." It is a blending of souls in an ecstatic whisper: the farewell kiss of rational lovers. In a famous passage of the fourth book of the *Courtier*, Castiglione analyzes the kiss in rational love:

> For since a kiss is the union of body and soul, there is danger that the sensual lover may incline more in the direction of body than in that of soul; whereas the rational lover sees that, although the mouth is part of the body, nevertheless it emits words, which are the interpreters of the soul, and that inward breath which is itself called soul. Hence, a man delights in joining his mouth to that of his beloved in a kiss, not in order to bring himself to any unseemly desire, but because he feels that that bond is the opening of mutual access to their souls, which, being each drawn by desire for the other, pour themselves each into the other's body by turn, and mingle so together that each of them has two souls; and a single soul, composed thus of these two, rules as it were over two bodies. Hence, a kiss may be said to be a joining of souls rather than of bodies, because it has such power over the soul that it withdraws to itself and separates it from the body. For this reason all chaste lovers desire the kiss as a union of souls; and thus the divinely enamored Plato says that, in kissing the soul came to his lips in order to escape from his body. And since the separation of the soul from sensible things and its complete union with intelligible things can be signified by the kiss, Solomon, in his divine book of the Song, says: "Let him kiss me with the kiss of his mouth," to signify the wish that his soul be transported through divine love to the contemplation of heavenly beauty in such manner that, in uniting itself closely therewith, it might forsake the body.
>
> *The Book of the Courtier* 4.64[77]

This is the ecstasy that Donne and his beloved enjoy, precisely like the ecstasy of a virtuous man dying. According to a tradition of the *Midrash*, which entered Renaissance treatises of love through Pico della Mirandola, virtuous men die like Moses: "Thereupon God kissed Moses and took away his soul with the kiss of his mouth."[78] They "melt" ecstatically in the same way ("So let us melt . . ."), with a tenderness that releases their *spiritus* from their mouths in the form of a kiss.[79] They whisper into each other the quintessence of their love and begin their physical separation. That quintessence recapitulates the gyre of their lives in the "spiraculum vitae," which joins them for all time of exile in the universe of Love. At the end of that exile, the lover's journey, their refined soul will reanimate a glorified body in the perfect golden circularity of an eternal embrace.

The vortex of John Donne's poem has no carefully defined and static structure, but is simply a repetition of its basic theme through all the analogous planes of reality. It obliterates space by pulsating from a center of consciousness toward an infinity in which it might perhaps be dissipated, were it not for its point of fixity. Similarly, it has no time, for its 36 verses divide a circumference that constitutes both an instant and a sidereal period of 36,000 years. It whirls around in its path the wreckage of the poetry and philosophy of three centuries and, like the kaleidoscope, gives a simple form to the complex of its pieces only by shaking them together. Part of its complexity is the work of history; our reading has been at times involved because it was necessary to reconstruct a pattern of thought before identifying its fragments. In part, however, its complexity is a deliberate reflection of the love of the poet, in all of its vital historicity. Underlying the fragile complexity, however, the bewildering flux rests on an ontological certainty. At the center of the human vortex, in profundity, is the Center of all reality. Because the poem rests on that Center, it is safe, as long as Love is safe, from the angels that would flatten it to circular perfection and from the best, which tightens the coils. Like the kiss that is its emblem, it is an incarnate (although ephemeral) reality, neither pure body nor pure soul. In this way, it resembles both the man who wrote it and, as far as I can tell, the men who read it.

# Zeno's Last Cigarette

Que si maintenant quelque romancier hardi, déchirant la toile habilement tissée de notre moi conventionnel, nous montre sous cette logique apparente une absurdité fondamentale, sous cette juxtaposition d'états simples une pénétration infinie de mille impressions diverses qui ont déjà cessé d'être au moment où on les nomme, nous le louons de nous avoir mieux connus que nous ne nous connaissons nous-mêmes.

—HENRI BERGSON, *Essai sur les données immédiates de la conscience*

A written confession," Zeno remarks, "is always a lie." For this reason, literature is most false precisely when it aspires to being most true: when it attempts to tell the story of the author's life. Inevitably, the attempt to abstract self from self and to make the past in each of its successive moments somehow consistent with the present distorts the image that was the object of the search. Any "portrait of the artist," if it is to be an image at all, must be set off at a distance from the dynamic present—as a *young* man, Joyce insisted—as though there were an unbridgeable gap between then and now, and as though time were not a continuum connecting the present with both birth and death. Analysis presupposes the detachment of the writer from his subject, a perspective impossible to achieve when the subject is the self. Thus, for a writer to speak of his childhood or of his senility, the successive images of which his life seems to be composed, is to speak of empty abstractions, which cannot be observed from the flow of his consciousness.

The titles of Italo Svevo's novels hint at this, his central preoccupation: *Una Vita, Senilità, La coscienza di Zeno*, all seem to be meditations upon the attempt to capture the essence of his life in retrospect—meditations ending with the realization that to recapture the past is to falsify it, to invent it as though it had belonged to someone else. In Svevo's last novel, his whimsical *persona*, Zeno, begins his written attempt to recapture his childhood at the insistence of a somewhat obtuse psychiatrist, Dr. S., who does not believe that the problem has its roots in metaphysics rather than in psychology. Zeno's first words state his problem succinctly:

> Vedere la mia infanzia? Più di dieci lustri me ne separano e i miei occhi presbiti forse potrebbero arrivarci se la luce che ancora ne riverbera non fosse tagliata da ostacoli d'ogni genere, vere alte montagne: i miei anni e qualche mia ora . . . il presente imperioso risorge ed offusca il passato.

> See my childhood? Now that I am separated from it by over fifty years my presbyopic eyes might perhaps reach to it if the light were not obscured by so many obstacles. The years like impassable mountains rise between me and it, my past years and a few brief hours in my life . . . The present surges up and dominates me, the past is blotted out.
>
> *Coscienza di Zeno* 57–8; 3

In Zeno's purely spatial imagination, the present moment is conditioned by the one that went before, that one in turn conditioned by its predecessor, and so on, back into the past, toward the origin of the individual and of the species. In a sense, then, the past exists in the present and moves with it into the future. This continuous chain is life itself, and consciousness *is* the present moment, the spearhead of the past thrust into the future. Because one cannot stop the trajectory, and because the present carries with it all that went before, one cannot speak of one's past without a vantage point from which retrospective abstractions can be made. Zeno attempts to construct for himself a place to stand in his effort to find the cause of his disease, chain-smoking, and his attempt results in the creation of a lie-literature:

> È così che a forza di correr dietro a quelle immagini, io le raggiunsi. Ora so di averle inventate. Ma inventare è una creazione, non già una menzogna . . . credetti che quelle immagini fossero delle vere riproduzioni di giorni lontani . . . Le ricordavo come si ricorda il fatto raccontato da chi non vi assistette.

> And by dint of pursuing these memory-pictures, I at last really overtook them. I know now that I invented them. But invention is a creative act,

not merely a lie. . . . I thought my dream-pictures really were an actual reproduction of the past. . . . I remembered them as one remembers an event one has been told by somebody who was not present at it.

*Coscienza* 443; 384–5

Zeno's consciousness converts memory-pictures into dream-pictures, perception into creation, and thereby constructs of barren truth a rational lie. He chooses elements from his experience in order to construct an essence, to "characterize" himself in a plot of his own choosing, omitting the myriad irreducible details that add nothing to the portrait, or indeed seek to obfuscate its general outlines. Like the novel it so closely resembles, Zeno's lie is a work of art.

In a sense, a novelist is at once a creature and a creator, for the story he tells is necessarily his own invention, yet it must be drawn from his own experience. He must be within it in order for it to be "alive," yet in another sense he must be outside of it in order to understand. It is the use of a fictional plot that enables him to know the story's end before its beginning and to stand to his own experience like the medieval God Who was *auctor naturae*, able to take in past and future with his synoptic view. This transcendent foreknowledge gives his characters a rationale and an inner consistency that makes them intelligible. At the same time, however, that foreknowledge foreordains the characters and deprives them of the liberty that real persons seem to possess. They are oppressed by their destiny, or by what Pirandello would call their "form," unable to assert themselves against the crushing exigencies of plot. The dialectic of the novel is then the struggle between the freedom of a God-like novelist to write the plot as he chooses, and the resistance of his experience, seeking to establish its own true, although chaotic, liberty. So it is with Zeno's confession: The truth of his story varies inversely with its degree of intelligibility. By the act of making his own experience (which he cannot understand) into a *story* (which he understands for having invented it), Zeno rationalizes away the history of his own freedom and with the miracle of the lie becomes his own God, seeking to justify, at least in the world of fiction, the flesh-and-blood reality from which he has abstracted himself.

The traditional novelist of the self turns from life to literature and in his fiction takes the place of the God *manqué* in his life. But just as the God of tradition has been reproached for the tyranny of predestination, so in recent times the existentialists, recapitulating the history of theology in their phenomenology of the novel, reproach the novelist for knowing what his characters are about. They revive (perhaps without knowing it) the medieval analogy between the author of a book and the Author of the Cosmos, and attempt to banish the former as the Enlightenment banished the latter. So anxious are they to preserve human freedom even in the world of fiction that they suggest the abdication of the author from his own experience in favor of the liberty of his creatures. If it were possible for the novelist to be *manqué* in the same way that God is missing from the world, then the new novel would indeed hold up a mirror to life: a mass of senseless detail, signifying nothing. Its characterless characters would be doomed, just as Pirandello's six characters are doomed, to wait for an author, possessed of the absolute liberty of indeterminancy. Unlike the world, however, an authorless novel cannot come into existence: The *anti-roman* of Robbe-Grillet remains the written record of some other author's refusal to write a novel, as the play of Pirandello remains the successful dramatization of some other author's refusal to write a play.

Curiously enough, however, while the theorists of the novel have been seeking to make it resemble their image of life, ordinary men like Zeno have turned away from that life and behave as though they were searching in their lives for the logic and plot of the hack novel. The liberty of indeterminancy given by the author-*manqué* to his novelistic creatures is a *tour-de-force*; in everyday life, however, the same gift is a source of anguish. The underground man of our time attempts to withdraw from himself in order to superimpose a logical pattern upon the unrelated fragments culled from his imagination, and with an act of *mauvaise foi* that the psychologists call "rationalization," paints a reasonable portrait of himself with the gray pigments of his life. The objective is always the same: in Zeno's words, "an excuse for doing what I wanted or which would prevent my doing it." The unfortunate (and inescapable) secondary effect of the novelist's art, the negation of his characters' freedom, is for Zeno the primary objective. His intention is precisely the reverse of Svevo's.

Justification is the object of Zeno's literary rationalization, just as it is always the object of the stereotyped romantic "confession." It is achieved by retrospectively denying one's freedom and therefore one's responsibility. From the perspective that he invents for himself, Zeno sees all that has happened as something that *had* to happen, given his image of himself and his self-imposed novelistic destiny. The historic

Zeno was a mere puppet, "understandable" and therefore blameless. Or so we might be led to believe were this a simple trial of the accused before the gullible jury of a literary audience—were this a nineteenth-century novel of confession. We are able to see through Zeno's literary subterfuge, however, for we have a place to stand, outside of his life and his lie, from which the ironic gap between the two can be measured. Dr. S., the psychiatrist who is Svevo's naïve surrogate, introduces Zeno's story with a few remarks that succeed in casting into doubt all of that which is to follow: "Se sapesse quante sorprese potrebbero risultargli dal commento delle tante verità e bugie ch'egli ha qui accumulate" (He little knows what surprises lie in wait for him, if someone were to set about analyzing the mass of truths and falsehoods that he has collected here) (*Coscienza* 56; vii). The ironic introduction makes of the confession a novel-within-a-novel, precisely in order to reveal the mechanism of rationalization for what it is: the creative lie of defense. Svevo's technique is much like Dostoyevsky's biting satire: Both *The Confessions of Zeno* and *Notes from the Underground* are directed against the vanity of those who, like Rousseau, would seek to prove their innocence by a process traditionally reserved for the admission of guilt. Specifically, it accuses the man who would paint the truth after his own image of himself.

Before he embarks on his writing adventure, Dostoyevsky's man from the underground meditates upon his sincerity along the same lines (and with the same degree of sincerity) as Zeno:

> In any case, I have not long since decided to recall to mind some of my former adventures; up until now, I had avoided them, not without a certain uneasiness. At this moment, however, while I am evoking them and even writing them down, I am trying an experiment: Is it possible to be frank and sincere, at least with oneself, and can one tell oneself the whole truth? I note in this regard that Heine assures us that there can be no such thing as an accurate autobiography and that a man always lies when he is talking about himself. Rousseau, according to him, surely deceived us, even deliberately, in his *Confessions*, out of sheer vanity. I am sure Heine is right . . . but [he] had in mind public confessions; I am writing only for myself, and I wish to make clear once and for all that if I seem to be addressing a reader it is merely for convenience.[1]

His greatest lie is that his confession is not public. Since the whole point of confession, whether theological or novelistic, is justification, it becomes difficult to imagine how it can succeed without a judge from whose perspective the penitent can be absolved, or, more correctly, acquitted. In the ordinary literature of confession of the nineteenth century, by the process of publication, we the readers are judges before whom the author attempts to exculpate himself. It is the genius of Dostoyevsky, however, and of Svevo after him, to put us at one remove from the trial scene, so that we have some other testimony besides that of the accused, and may see each of his lies for what it is. In a profound sense, it may be said that the novel-within-the-novel is the novelist's indictment of all public confession, particularly (and this explains the savagery of the attack) of his own. The novelist who *is*, confessing his guilt, accuses the novelist who *was*, seeking to proclaim his innocence. We must pause to discuss the gap that separates them.

The novel of justification, the false confession enclosed within the novels of both Dostoyevsky and Svevo, can never succeed because it can never end. Zeno abandons his attempt at writing his confessions when the war breaks out; and the man from the underground, we are told, would go on interminably were he not interrupted by Dostoyevsky. The audience may be taken in by the lie within the temporal and spatial confines of the novel; in real life, however, the neurotic must go on and on in order to convince himself. The moment he ceases to abstract he must once more take up the tedious task of living, and he then realizes that he has attempted to judge and to justify a life that he is still in the process of creating. Paradoxically, he knows that he can never fully be all that he is until he ceases to be; he can never know his own essence until he dies, when he will have ceased to know anything at all. Only death will provide the necessary gap between the man and an accurate self-portrait.

Death has many faces, however—one of which, we have to learn from the existentialists, is purely epistemological. The act of reflecting upon one's own consciousness is a type of death of the self that involves no physical decomposition: *je pense, donc je ne suis pas.* The great novelists extend the process of Sartre's *pour-soi* throughout a whole novelistic duration and become all-knowing impersonal observers. What Sartre has not seen, however, is that death of the self, in order to be more than simply a striking metaphor, must be complete, and if complete, can permit of no return to "the old man." The gap that exists in the novel-within-a-novel between the lying *persona* and the novelist (Dr. S[vevo]., Dostoyevsky) who accuses him is a kind of absolute separation between the experience of the novelist who *was* and the novelist who *is*. If this were a merely temporary and purely epistemological separation, then the novel-within-a-novel would also be a lie, capable of being in turn inserted into another novel (and another and another) in an infinite regression of false journals in the manner of Gide, the sum total of which might approach but never reach the truth as a limit, and the purpose of which would always be to justify, because of the essential vital continuity of subject and object. On the contrary, however, the sincerity of a Dostoyevsky or of a Svevo points to the seriousness of their undertaking, and proclaims the absolute truth of their perspective. Thus the death of their former selves is total and complete, and their own works can be described only as a kind of resurrection. Such a process of spiritual death and resurrection has a traditional name— "conversion"—and the early history of the written record of such conversions is intimately linked to the history of the novel.

From the perspective of Augustine, the inventor of the genre, it was possible to believe that an autobiography could be the truth, that one could discover a principle of intelligibility in one's life and need not invent it. This is not to say that Augustine was unaware of the fundamental problem; he knew as well as any modern novelist how futile is the attempt to make a verbal abstraction from the flow of time, and his meditation was a lesson to all who would discover themselves in the present moment. "The present," he wrote, "occupies no space." The moment one attempts to transfix time, to set off the past and eternalize the self in the present moment, that moment has slipped by from proximate future to proximate past. The present progressive is an abstraction, a mere grammatical convention when applied to the self, for the self is perpetually changing. In order to capture its essence in retrospect, one must establish a gap between then and now; in order to take stock, all transactions must first be concluded; in order to have the static word correspond to the dynamic flesh it seeks to express, one must die and be born again. In effect, the Augustinian solution of the epistemological problem of confession was identical with the Pauline solution of the moral problem facing all Christians. All confession, literary or sacramental, is either a lie or the record of a conversion, a descent into Hell, while self-expression in its profoundest sense is necessarily re-birth.

For the Middle Ages, in order to make one's confession (or to write one's "confessions"), one needed a point of Being in the stream of becoming. Such a point could only be provided by grace, a sacramental place to stand outside of time from which the *ek-static* penitent might examine his conscience, from which the "novelist" might analyze his consciousness (the two processes are one for Augustine, as they are in the "*Coscienza*" of Zeno). The miracle could be brought about only by the God who had Himself died and been reborn, the Word made flesh, and its effect was so profound that it was said to mark the beginning of what St. Paul termed a "New Life." Similarly, the novelist of today seeks to reconcile a stable principle of intelligibility, his ontological "word," to the liberty and flow of life. This too can only be brought about with a kind of conversion, and in the greatest of novelists, with a kind of "incarnation romanesque," to use the expression of René Girard. But Zeno's hilarious attempt to stop smoking, which is presumably his search for a conversion to a "new life," is an act of bad faith, for his self-accusation, like Rousseau's and like that of the man from the underground, is in reality self-justification. Zeno's frustration is the ironic proof of the fact that in Svevo's eyes, such a conversion is impossible in human terms. Augustine, presented with a similar situation, might have quoted the Psalms: "In the sight of God shall no man living be justified." Zeno looks everywhere for his moment of truth, except within himself.

It must not be imagined that this is merely a fanciful application of moral theology to esthetic phenomenology; the fashionable literary theology of the existentialists is at least as old as Dante. The *Vita nuova*, a spiritual biography that owes much to Augustine, records the poet's transition from old to new life, from inferior poet to great artist, through the grace of his lady, in the language of conversion that Zeno parodies in his first chapter. The scholarly arguments about the "reality" of Beatrice and the more recent refusals to see her as an analogue of Christ betray at once a modern misunderstanding of the Middle Ages and an old-fashioned misunderstanding of the profundities of literary creation. She is Dante's Word and flesh, his death and resurrection, his perspective on himself, necessary for the Christian and the artist.

So closely does Zeno's search for salvation parody the language of conversion in the *Vita nuova* that we must pause to recall a few essential features of the latter story. Dante's book begins in a moment of calm recollection:

> In quella parte del libro de la mia memoria dinanzi a la quale poco si potrebbe leggere, si trova una rubrica la quale dice: *Incipit vita nova*.

Sotto la quale rubrica io trovo scritte le parole le quali è mio intendi-
mento d'assemplare in questo libello; e se non tutte, almeno la loro
sentenzia.

In that part of the book of my memory, before which there would be
little to read, I find a rubric which says; "*Incipit Vita nova.*"—here
begins the New Life. Beneath that rubric I find written the words
which I intend to copy into this little book, and if not all of them, at
least their substance.

*Vita nuova* 1.1

The substance of a book of memory, it would seem, is the essence
of a life, distilled in memory out of many seemingly unrelated fragments and expressed with the serenity of artistic and psychological
detachment. The poet believed that his new life had begun in a
moment of Grace made sacred by the powers of the number three
when he first met Beatrice: "Nove fiate già appresso lo mio nascimento
era tornato lo cielo de la luce quasi a uno medesimo punto, quanto a la
sua propria girazione, quando a li miei occhi apparve prima la gloriosa
donna de la mia mente . . ." (Nine times already since my birth had the
heaven of light returned to the same point with respect to its own
revolution, when the glorious lady of my mind first appeared to my
eyes. . . .) (*Vita nuova* 2.1). The stars themselves seemed to mark the
moment, as if heaven and earth, God Himself, had pre-ordained this
meeting of two nine-year old children, which began the poet's
authentic life and one of the world's great love stories. Dante's tiresome insistence upon the numerically exact moment is explained by
the conviction, formulated by the poet as he looks backward over his
life, that his love for Beatrice made time stand still, and gave the new
life its meaning.

But precisely because of that story's neatness, it would strike Zeno
as a poetic lie. Dante glosses a book of memory that seems already a
creation of the imagination; the real book of memory, to Zeno, is his
dictionary, whose order is the arbitrary alphabet, a pure convention
applied to an amorphous mass of detail heaped up by the passing of
time.

Sul frontispizio di un vocabolario trovo questa mia registrazione fatta
con bella scrittura e qualche ornato: "Oggi, 2 Febbraio 1886, passo dagli
studii di legge a quelli di chimica. Ultima sigaretta!!"

I find the following entry on the front page of a dictionary, beautifully written and adorned with a good many flourishes: "2 February, 1886. Today I finish my law studies and take up chemistry. Last cigarette!!"

*Coscienza* 64; 9

With confidence in himself, a sense of victory, with "hope for strength and health in the future," he smoked his interminable last cigarettes, one very much like another, at each moment renewing his vow to begin a new life. Somehow he seemed out of touch with whatever cosmic force makes moments propitious and presents each of us with his salvation in the form of a last cigarette, last puerility or weakness:

> Certe date erano da me preferite per la concordanza delle cifre. Del secolo passato ricordo una data che mi parve dovesse sigillare per sempre la bara in cui volevo mettere il mio vizio: "Nono giorno del nono mese del 1899." Significativa nevvero? Il secolo nuovo m'apportò delle date ben altrimenti musicali: "Primo giorno del primo mese del 1901." Ancora mi pare che se quella data potesse ripetersi, io saprei iniziare una nuova vita.

> I had a partiality for certain dates because their figures went well together. I remember one of the last century which seemed as if it must be the final monument to my vice: "Ninth day of the ninth month in the year 1899." Surely a most significant date! The new century furnished me with dates equally harmonious, though in a different way. "First day of the first month in the year 1901." Even today I feel that if only that date could repeat itself I should be able to begin a new life.

*Coscienza* 64; 11

But he waits for a new life, a conversion in a propitious moment, which is no more likely to come than is the next year 1901. He passes from cigarette to resolution and back to cigarette again, searching for the key to his destiny from the mass of possible permutations: "Third day of the sixth month, in the year 1912, at 24 o'clock," or even a date that is striking because of its very inconsequence: "third day of the second month of the 1905 at six o'clock!" But one date is very much like another, as one cigarette or one bead of time is much like another, and in a world where any number may serve as the mystic key, no number will do. Zeno the *persona* will not achieve the detachment of Svevo the author until death overtakes him.

But if there is no number, there is at least the dictionary—the alphabet—and for a man so desperate for order it suffices. Zeno finds

his wife, not as Dante found his Beatrice, through an apparently chance
encounter that had in reality been planned by God Himself, nor again
by the merest accident, as one suspects that healthy men do, regardless
of the rationalizations they construct in retrospect, but rather through
a systematic, rational, and therefore ludicrous search, in alphabetical
order. Or so he would have us believe:

> Si chiamavano (seppi subito a mente quei nomi): Ada, Augusta, Alberta
> e Anna. A quel tavolo si disse anche che tutt'e quattro erano belle.
> Quell'iniziale mi colpì molto più di quanto meritasse. Sognai di quelle
> quattro fanciulle legate tanto bene insieme dal loro nome. Pareva fos-
> sero da consegnarsi in fascio. L'iniziale diceva anche qualche cosa d'al-
> tro. Io mi chiamo Zeno ed avevo perciò il sentimento che stessi per
> prendere moglie lontano dal mio paese.

> Their names, which I immediately committed to memory, were Ada,
> Augusta, Alberta and Anna. I was also told that they were all
> good-looking. That initial seemed to me more significant than it really
> was. I dreamt about those four girls linked together so closely by their
> names. I almost felt they were a bunch of flowers. But that initial meant
> something else too. My name is Zeno, and I felt as if I were about to
> choose a wife from a far country.

> *Coscienza* 122; 64

He proposes to the sisters in alphabetical order, skipping only the
infant Anna: Ada, Alberta, and then Augusta, who finally accepts:
"Devo poi confessare che in quel moment fui pervaso da una soddis-
fazione che m'allargò il petto. Non avevo più da risolvere niente, perché
tutto era stato risolto. Questa era la vera chiarezza" (I don't mind confessing that at that moment a feeling of immense satisfaction pervaded
me. I had no longer any decision to make. Everything was decided for
me. At last I had obtained certainty) (186; 127–8). Later, when the adulterous Zeno must face the decision to leave his mistress, again his
emblematic dictionary serves as a book of memory: "Fu marcata in
quelle ore angosciose in caratteri grandi nel mio vocabolario alla lettera
C (Carla) la data di quel giorno con l'annotazione: 'ultimo tradimento'"
(During those hours of torment I wrote the date of the day in my dictionary against the letter C (Carla) with the comment: "Last Betrayal")
(253; 194).

The dictionary is the intellect's parody of the book of memory, the
result of the mind's attempt to transcend itself and to give order to

chaos with its own static "word" in an imitation of the divine process. Ideally, it represents the sum total of all of reality bound up in a single volume, with a sequential order (and therefore an apparent continuity) and an apparent rationale. Only a madman would mistake it for the meaningful account of a life and thus be taken in by the obvious counterfeit; yet the lie that the dictionary represents is little worse than the lie of the completely contrived plot. It is dead because it is a spatial, discontinuous order, lacking the temporal flow of life just as the intellect is dead for analyzing atoms and for not being able to account for change. In the process of retrospective reconstruction the intellect attempts to capture life, but intellect and life, the fragmentary dictionary and the flow, are inalterably opposed because they pull in opposite directions, the first seeking the scientific certainty of dead determinism, the other seeking the future flow of liberty. This incompatibility is at the source of Zeno's paradoxical nature, for even the healthiest organism would appear pure mechanism under the scrutiny of the intellect's retrospective gaze.

Zeno's book of memory has no essence; the dictionary has many characters but no plot, for the course of life has had no rationale and no privileged moments that he can observe in retrospect: One cigarette is exactly like another. Together all those cigarettes go to make up his life, measured out in discontinuous parcels, which disappear as they are lived, leaving behind an ash that mingles with all the ashes of history. We live in this world with our ashes, which each of us carries with him. In order to recall, Zeno must invoke "l'assistenza delle sigarette tutte tanto somiglianti a quella che ho in mano" (the aid of all those many cigarettes I have smoked, identical with the one I have in my hand now) (60; 5). But even this one is gradually disappearing and in a moment will belong to the past. Zeno cannot stand still in the course of life, and yet it is precisely this that he must do in order to remember. One cannot recall the past while one is creating it; one cannot begin a new life while continuing to smoke. Zeno's homely, sensible wife unknowingly stumbles upon the truth when she remarks that "il fumo non era altro che un modo . . . non troppo noioso di vivere" (smoking is one way of living, and not such a bad one, either) (73; 17). One day, Zeno will quit smoking: when the chain comes to an end and he finally succumbs to (and thus is cured of) the disease that afflicts him—life itself—the only disease, he tells us, which is always fatal.

Authentic life, true health, is no more aware of itself than is perfect vision, perfect movement, or perfect breathing. Life is a rhythm into which one must enter; it is recapitulated "dal suono piú rudimentale, quello dell'onda del mare, che, dacché si forma muta od ogni istante finché non muore" (in the most rudimentary of sounds, that of a sea-wave, which from the moment it is born until it expires is in a state of continual change) (114–5; 57). Like music, its whole substance is rhythm—*tempo*—time itself, and not the string of beads that Zeno imagines. Guido, Zeno's rival in love, improvises upon Bach and produces beautiful music—"un organismo equilibrato" (the rhythm of a healthy organism). "Quando la faró cosí," Zeno remarks, " saró guarito" (When I can play like that I shall be cured) (166; 108). In spite of his theoretical knowledge of music, however, or perhaps because of it, his violin will produce only cacophony. His intelligence is acute but mechanical, and like his eyes, it can never focus on the present—that which is at hand. A friend tells Zeno about the mechanics of walking:

> Mi raccontà ridendo che quando si cammina con passo rapido, il tempo in cui si svolge un passo non supera il mezzo secondo e che in quel mezzo secondo si muovevano nientemeno che cinquantaquattro muscoli. Trasecolai e subito corsi col pensiero alle mie gambe a cercarvi la macchina mostruosa. Io credo di avercela trovata. Naturalmente non riscontrai cinquantaquattro ordigni, ma una complicazione enorme che perdette il suo ordine dacché io vi ficcai la mia attenzione. Uscii da quel caffè zoppicando . . .

> He told me with amusement that when one is walking rapidly each step takes no more than half a second, and that in that half second no fewer than fifty-four muscles are set in motion. I listened in bewilderment. I at once directed my attention to my legs and tried to discover the infernal machine. I thought I had succeeded in finding it. I could not of course distinguish all its fifty-four parts, but I discovered something terrifically complicated which seemed to get out of order directly I began thinking about it. I limped as I left the café. . . .
>
> *Coscienza* 155–6; 98

If Zeno is ridiculous, it is because in telling his story he would apply his cinematographic intelligence to the flow and change of life, hoping desperately to reproduce movement from separate and isolated states, like a machine imitating life. Unfortunately, the moving-picture camera of the mind cannot work quite fast enough, and even if it could, we would not be taken in by our own illusion: In this Bergsonian world, the myopic man of science and the farsighted philosopher alike fall flat on their faces.

Zeno's wife, with her crossed eyes and her animal health, lives in the present without a thought of birth or death, attached to those stationary objects—jewelry or furniture—which prevent men from becoming seasick in a world perpetually turning. For the far-sighted, chain-smoking Zeno, on the other hand, the present lies just beyond his last cigarette, a present into which his intelligence, or at least his imagination, plunges, leaving behind the will-less creature rooted to life by his past and by the weed that is burning in his hand.

> Compresi finalmente che cosa fosse la perfetta salute umana quando indovinai che il presente per lei era una verità tangibile in cui si poteva segregarsi e starci caldi. Cercai di esservi ammesso e tentai di soggiarnarvi risoluto di non deridere me e lei, perché questo conato non poteva essere altro che la mia malattia ed io dovevo almeno guardarmi dall'infettare chi a me s'era confidato. Anche perciò, nello sforzo di proteggere lei, seppi per qualche tempo movermi come un uomo sano.

> I understood at last the meaning of perfect health in a human being, when I realized that for her [Augusta] the present was a tangible reality in which we could take shelter and be near together. I tried to be admitted to this sanctuary and to stay there, resolved not to laugh either at myself or her; for my skepticism would only be a symptom of disease, and I must at least beware of infecting someone who had given her life into my keeping. It was my desire to protect her that made me act for a while like a normal human being.

> *Coscienza* 207; 147

It is Zeno's intelligence that converts the rhythm of life into disease, by analyzing and dissecting, by searching for stability in the present and substituting self-consciousness for action, chain-smoking for life. It is his delusion that he can find himself, capture his ego, undergo a conversion, and thus elude the pressure of his past forcing him along a predestined track. His intelligence dupes him into believing that he can stand still, outside of himself, and begin anew from a clean slate in the present moment. His cigarettes represent his discontinuous duration, his connection with the past, and his direction in the future. To make one of them the last, while such a resolution might satisfy the mind's desire to fix reality in static images and thus render it intelligible, would never-theless result in breaking the continuity, in fixing life only by ending it. To renew the resolution each moment, however, and *then* to break it, would be to satisfy the life instinct while throwing the intellect its nec-essary bone. But this double operation leaves time for nothing else, and brings with it only paralysis. Zeno's dilemma is that he would walk and know that *he* is walking, would live and know that *he* is living, endure and know that *he* is enduring. He would be the man defining his own ego, giving direction and purpose to his life, ignoring the dictionary dragging behind him that is his past (and the past of his father and of his species), in order to begin a new life a moment from now, to be determined only by himself. It cannot be done, for to think is to kill reality by freezing it, to live is unconsciously to flow. The last cigarette is a desperate, compulsive attempt at a compromise between action and thought:

> Mi ero arrabbiato col diritto canonico che mi pareva tanto lontano dalla vita stessa benché ridotta in un matraccio. Quell'ultima sigaretta significava proprio il desiderio di attività (anche manuale) e di sereno pensiero sobrio e sodo.

> I was irritated by canon law, which seemed to me so remote from life, and I fled to science in the hope of finding life itself, though imprisoned in a retort. That last cigarette was emblem of my desire for activity (even manual) *and* for calm, clear, sober thought.
>
> *Coscienza* 65; 9

He is then two men: an intellect perceiving separate, disjointed states, powerless to control an organism whose liberty is gained only by following its trajectory. A "last" cigarette satisfies both the hope of the intellect and the demand of the organism:

> Per diminuire l'apparenza balorda tentai di dare un contenuto filosofico alla malattia dell'ultima sigaretta. Si dice con un bellissimo atteggia-mento: "mai più!" Ma dove va l'atteggiamento se si tiene la promessa? L'atteggiamento non è possibile di averlo che quando si deve rinnovare il proposito. Eppoi il tempo, per me, non è quella cosa impensabile che non s'arresta mai. Da me, solo da me, ritorna.

> In order to make it seem a little less foolish I tried to give a philosophic content to the malady of the "last cigarette." You strike a noble attitude and say: "Never again!" But what becomes of the attitude if you keep

your word? You can only preserve it if you keep on renewing your resolution. And then Time, for me, is not that imaginable thing that never
stops. For me, but only for me, it comes again.

*Coscienza* 67; 11

The attitude, a pose struck for the moment, is a pause in the stream
of life. In the next moment, a new pause, a new resolution. But because
time, like nature, abhors a vacuum, something must fill the gap between
these instants. Imagining a third moment will not do, for this only succeeds in halving the instant, as a fourth and fifth will only succeed in
quartering it. No quantity of renewed resolutions will succeed in working the qualitative change from spatially fixed points, the time that
"comes again," to the stream of authentic time. Zeno tells his formerly
fat friends why dieting is so much easier than curing the smoking habit:

> Gli spiegai che a me pareva piú facile di non mangiare per tre volte al
> giorno che di non fumare le innumerevoli sigarette per cui sarebbe stato
> necessario di prendere la stessa affaticante risoluzione ad ogni istante.
> Avendo una simile risoluzione nella mente non c'è tempo per fare altro
> perché il solo Giulio Cesare sapeva fare piú cose nel medesimo istante.

> I explained to him that giving up three meals a day seemed to me noth-
> ing compared with the task of making a fresh resolution every moment
> not to smoke another cigarette. If you use up all your time making res-
> olutions you have no time for anything else, for it takes a Julius Caesar
> to be able to do two things at once.

*Coscienza* 71; 15

The intellectual desire to know liberty leads to the paralysis of discontinuous time—disease, Zeno calls it—whereas the flow and rhythm
of animal health preclude the exercise of what is distinctively human—
thought. The closest thing to freedom that he can reach is a compromise between the two—Zeno can play the violin only on the condition
that he beat out the rhythm with his foot. Perfect liberty would entail
the reconciliation of separate points with a continuous line, making of
discrete perceptions of the self the smooth trajectory of life.

The first chapter of Zeno's novel presents us with an old paradox in
unique form: How can one reconcile the movement of life, animal
health, with the transversal static cuts made by the intellect? How can
one *be* and know that he is being? The paradox is a form of the ancient
paradox of Zeno of Elea, transposed from the mysteries of space and

motion to those of Augustinian duration and time. Svevo has called his character Zeno, surely a strange name for an Italian, precisely because his character is an embodiment of the spirit of the Eleatic, seeking to reconcile reality to reason. The effect of transposing the puzzle from space to human time, however, is to make of the conundrum the anguish of a soul.

The puzzle of Zeno of Elea may be stated in one of its forms in the following manner: If we imagine the trajectory of an arrow flying through space, it must be said that at any given moment it occupies a given space and is therefore momentarily motionless, requiring another moment before it can occupy the next successive position. Hence the trajectory is made up of an infinity of successive moments for the gradual transition from place to place. But these infinite moments cannot be said ever to reach the continuity that we perceive. Motion itself cannot be deduced. At each separate moment the arrow is motionless, all the time it is moving. Just as one can never place enough mathematical points side by side in order to make up a straight line, it is impossible to deduce the trajectory of the arrow from the logical stages, the transversal cuts, that go to make it up. It will never reach it target.

If we substitute for the arrow the present moment, the spearhead of consciousness moving from past to future, we have the paradox in Svevo's terms. Bergson himself transposed it to a temporal dimension. In *Creative Evolution* the philosopher wrote:

> Nothing would be easier, now, than to extend Zeno's argument to qualitative becoming and to evolutionary becoming. We should find the same contradictions in these. That the child can become a youth, ripen to maturity and decline to old age, we understand when we consider that vital evolution is here the reality itself. Infancy, adolescence, maturity, old age, are mere views of the mind, *possible stops* imagined by us, from without, along the continuity of a progress. On the contrary, let childhood adolescence, maturity and old age be given as integral parts of the evolution, they becomes *real stops*, and we can no longer conceive how evolution is possible, for rests placed besides rests will never be equivalent to movement. How, with what is made, can we reconstitute what is being made?[2]

Svevo suggested the paradox in several different ways. One would have appealed to Zeno of Elea, had he known about it. Zeno has a kind of hallucination when he attempts to recall the past:

Vedo, intravvedo delle immagini bizzarre che non possono avere
nessuna relazione col mio passato: una locomotiva che sbuffa su una
salita trascinando delle innumerevoli vetture; chissà donde venga e dove
vada e perché sia ora capitata qui!

I dimly see certain strange images that seem to have no connection
with my past; an engine puffing up a steep incline dragging endless
coaches after it. Where can it all come from? Where is it going? How
did it get there at all?

*Coscienza* 58; 4

Its significance becomes clear at his father's deathbed:

Scopro che l'immagine che m'ossessionò al primo mio tentativo di
vedere nel mio passato, quella locomotiva che trascina una sequela di
vagoni su per un'erta, io l'ebbi per la prima volta ascoltando da quel sofà
il respiro di mio padre. Vanno così le locomotive che tracinano dei pesi
enormi: emettono degli sbuffi regolari che po s'accelerano e finiscono in
una sosta, anche quella una sosta minacciosa perché chi ascolta può
temere di veder finire la macchina e il suo taino a precipizio a valle.

I realize that the image that obsessed me at the first attempt to look
into my past—the image of an engine drawing a string of coaches up a
hill—came to me for the first time while I lay on the sofa listening to
my father's breathing. That's just what engines do when drawing an
enormous weight: they emit regular puffs, which then become faster
and finally stop altogether; and that pause seems dangerous too,
because as you listen you cannot help fearing that the engine and the
train must go tumbling head over heels down into the valley.

*Coscienza* 99; 43

Zeno's attempt to go back to his childhood is to retrace his steps,
coach by coach from the present moment, "invoking the aid of all those
cigarettes." With the mistake characteristic of the Eleatic intellect he
asks, "Ma chi può arrestare quelle immagini quando si mettono a fug-
gire traverso quel tempo che giammai somigliò tanto allo spazio?"
(Who can stop those memory pictures once they have taken flight
through time, which never before seemed so much like space?) (446–7;
391). He *is* his past, just as the engine is the train, and to stop puffing in
order to look back over the past, to refuse to follow the cigarette track,
is indeed to begin a new life:

Copler col suo rantolo, dal ritmo tanto esatto, misurava il suo ultimo tempo. La sua respirazione rumorosa era composta da due suoni: esitante pareva quello prodotto dall'aria ch'egli ispirava, precipitoso quello che nasceva dall'aria espulsa. Fretta di morire? Una pausa seguiva ai due suoni ed io pensai che quando quella pausa si fosse allugata, allora si sarebbe iniziata la nuova vita.

Copler, with the death-rattle in his throat, was measuring out his last hours of breath. His noisy breathing consisted of two sounds; one hesitating, as if produced by the air he breathed in; one hurried, when he expelled the air from his lungs. Was he in a hurry to die? A pause always followed these two sounds, and I thought that when the pause grew longer the new life would have begun.

*Coscienza* 265; 206

The moralists tell us that a pause is necessary, that the beginning of knowledge is to know one's self. But how can one reconstitute the self if it does not as yet exist except as an end term? How can one justify the belief in one's identity? Bergson seems to have dismissed the problem: "all we have to do, in fact, is to give up the cinematographical habits of our intellect."[3] But these habits are all that the *persona* Zeno possesses as he is himself the product of an intellectual exercise. Hence, he must struggle simply to survive:

Zoppicavo e lottavo anche con una specie di affanno. Io ne ho di quegli affanni: respiro benissimo, ma conto i singoli respiri, perché devo farli uno dopo l'altro di proposito. Ho la sensazione che se non stessi attento, morrei soffocato.

I limped along, trying in vain to contend with my bodily distress. I sometimes have attacks like these; I can breathe perfectly well, but I count each breath I draw, because each requires a special effort of the will. I have the feeling if I were not careful I should die of suffocation.

*Coscienza* 302; 243

Zeno is a rational construct, the justification of the historical Zeno, with *being* but without life. Small wonder if he must be on his guard against the spontaneity of the vital force. If he were to apply the mathematician's solution of Zeno's paradox to his own life, $S\infty = A / (1-r)$, he might conclude that he need only place himself at the end of the series to see that the transition from point to point has indeed been a continuous trajectory aimed at the "sum to infinity." If he were to use the maxim of Hegel and of Sartre after him, he would see that *Wesen ist was gewesen ist*: being is that which has been. Essence is then simply the *raison de la série*, the mean or average of all of the successive appearances. These solutions will do for the mathematicians and for the philosophers, who have merely to dismiss Zeno's paradox, close up shop, and go home to their wives and children at the end of their day. Not so with Zeno, or, we may guess, with any man seeking to know himself. When we apply the scientific solutions to the existential problem, we see the enormity for what it is—for how can one take the sum to infinity, the *raison de la série*, unless the trajectory is finished and the series closed? When the sum means being and the series means life, we are left with the inescapable conclusion that one cannot know one's self until one is dead. The process of finding one's identity, essential to the process of justification, is necessarily spiritual suicide. And in the world of the neurotic Zeno, there can be no Augustinian resurrection.

To be delivered of his anguish, Zeno has one of three choices: He can stop living, stop thinking, or lie. If the reason and reality, thought and action, self-consciousness and health are contradictory, one must abandon either one camp or the other, the word or the flesh. Or one can create for one's self an essence, an autobiography, and present it to the reading public or the psychiatrist to make of it what they will. One can leave the rhythmic brooding of the armchair to approach the writing table, as does Zeno when he first begins to write his memoirs, in order to create literature, itself a rationalization as closely related to the truth as are Zeno's interminable vows to quit smoking. Zeno's retrospective gaze will never capture his evolution, but rather invents a story written in Tuscan from a life lived in the dialect of Trieste, and presents us with a single character who can never change and never evolve because he does not move.

In the successive chapters of the novel, to which we can only allude here, Zeno constructs mad rationalizations about his father, his marriage, his mistress, and his business. Because of the perfect logic of all of his motivations, as he recounts them, we understand them for what they are: ludicrous attempts to justify himself. We learn to suspect all of his emotions and passions, precisely because he is a shadow of a man, without the flesh and blood of which real, illogical life is composed. He seems not to exist but to know, while those around him exist and are unaware of it. Similarly, he understands freedom, but for that very reason does not possess it, whereas those around him seem unconsciously free. Thus, all normal human relationships are impossible for him, for, lacking the principle of life, he cannot communicate with the stones or the stars. He cannot give himself to the vital forces of destiny, as do the rest of society in the seance, for instance, but instead remains outside seeking to manipulate those forces with a God-like omniscience. The result is that he becomes the unwitting victim of the very destiny he tries to elude, while those around him achieve their liberty because they are unconscious of their own limitations.

Zeno is nevertheless *in* society and so much enter into relationships of various kinds with the people around him. This would be an insurmountable difficulty were it not for a variation of the technique of the lie, his *modus operandi* throughout the novel. Since he is a shadow of a man, he can only resemble other men by imitating them, by counterfeiting their movements and their gestures. Forever an outsider to the bourgeois society around him, he can at least struggle to look like them, and his mechanical efforts to fit in, to conform to the patterns about him, are the principal source of much of the humor in the book. It is the humor of the intellect imitating life's dynamism with the mechanical movement of the Chaplinesque filmstrip, composed of successive frames that move a shade too slow to look like life. When he reads newspapers, Zeno is "trasformato in opinione pubblica" (metamorphosed into public opinion) (119; 61). With a friend in a restaurant, he absently orders the same soft drink, "even though I hate lemons." He goes so far that he even chooses a wife, not logically, as he would like to have us suppose, but simply out of fascination for her father, whose "quiet strength" he envies: "Quando io ammiro qualcuno, tento immediatamente di somigliargli, Copiai anche il Malfenti. Volli essere e mi sentii molto astuto" (When I admire anyone I at once try to be like him. So I began to imitate Malfenti. I soon began to feel myself as astute as he was) (117; 59). At the same time, the people whom he imitates are also his judges before whom he must justify himself, as a perpetual performer imitating his audience, who receives howls of laughter for his clumsy efforts.

As his models, those around him stimulate his admiration and envy; as his judges, they inspire his hatred. So it was with his father, so it was with Malfenti, so too with Guido, his rival in love. Zeno's reaction to his father and all his successive father-surrogates is necessarily ambiguous, composed of love and hate, for his reaction to life itself is ambiguous. He turns to the women in his life for deliverance, just as the man from the underground in Dostoyevsky's novel turns to the prostitute for deliverance from his love-hate fascination for the officer. But the same ambiguity prevails here, for his perpetual analysis precludes love and casts the shadow of disease over every relationship. Zeno's wife offers him shelter in the present moment, which for her really exists, and he can repay his cross-eyed Beatrice only with indifference, precisely because she *is* willing to accept him.

But Zeno's mad rationalizations and his love-hate relationships will end when life, or rather life's ultimate paradox, breaks in upon his "Oedipal" microcosm with the thunderclap of the macrocosm: war. Just as his father launched him into the world with an act of violence that was at the same time his condemnation, the death-bed slap, nature's vengeance against the poison of reason, so his world (and ours) will end with the final slap that will shatter the cosmos and return us to our primal, if somewhat antiseptic, purity. The World War is at once the product of reason's conflict with life, and nature's vengeance for the schism.

The sudden shift in the novel from what has been the private world of Zeno to a universal dimension should not surprise us, for we are after all dealing with *confession*, and confession ends in apocalypse. For Zeno, "la morte era la vera organizzatrice della vita" (death was really the great organizing force of life) (131; 74), and when one approaches the great moment in one's own life, one approaches the "conversion" that will bring about an integration in society. It is then that one realizes that history too, if organized, if at all intelligible, is also directed toward death and suffers from the same malady that afflicts the individual. "Posso anzire dire che da qualche tempo," Zeno says in his old age, "io fumo molte sigarette . . . che non sono le ultime" (For a long time now I have been smoking cigarettes and have given up calling them the last) (64; 9). One can no longer believe in facile constructions of the mind when one is confronted with personal death and universal holocaust:

> La guerra mi ha raggiunto! . . . ecco che vi capitai in mezzo stupefatto e nello stesso tempo stupito di non essermi accorto prima che dovevo esservi prima o poi tutto il fabbricato con me si sarebbe sprofondato delle fiamme.
>
> The war has reach me at last! . . . I found myself right in the middle of it, and was surprised then to think I had not realized that I must sooner

or later become involved. I had lived quite peacefully in a building of which the ground-floor had caught fire, and it had never occurred to me that sooner or later the whole building, with me in it, would go up in flames.

*Coscienza* 461; 398–9

Descending from the tower of the solipsist, he realizes that self-justification is withdrawal from one's fellow man in an act of vanity, while the admission of guilt is an act of love. At last Zeno can be successful in business, the commerce between men, when he forgets his schemes and trades the resin of medicine for the incense of adoration. In the reason there is little hope, when the reason is merely a tool for setting one's self off from the rest of mankind.

"Our life," says Zeno, using that pronoun for the first time, "is poisoned to the roots." The fact is that the world's reality is not the reality of the mind:

Oggi che siamo alla metà del mese sono rimasto colpito della difficoltà che offre il nostro calendario ad una regolare e ordinata risoluzione. Nessun mese è uguale all'altro. . . . salvo il Luglio e Agosto e il Dicembre e il Gennaio non vi sono altri mesi che si susseguano e facciano il paio in quanto a quantità di giorni. Un vero disordine nel tempo.

Today we have reached the middle of the month, and I am struck by the obstacles that our calendar places in the way of carrying out a straight-forward, well-ordered resolution. All the months are a different length . . . except for July and August, December and January, there are no two successive months that have an equal number of days. Times is really very ill-ordered.

*Coscienza* 456–7; 398

It is by manufacturing their own grace, by playing God to nature, that all of men have sinned against her. By applying to nature reason in the form of the machine, man first offended her. He abstracted himself, or attempted to, from the natural evolutionary progress, which alone could guarantee health. Now man gets more and more cunning and more and more weak. His mind increased daily in its power over the elements, but his eyes begin to require thicker and thicker spectacles. The bespectacled eyes are directed in envy toward his neighbor, and his cunning directed toward theft and violence. The process in the macrocosm can end only as it does in the microcosm: universal war and death, the inevitable end of reason's struggle, of Zeno's story, and of the world itself:

> Forse traverso una catastrofe inaudita prodotta dagli ordigni ritorneremo alla salute. Quando i gas velenosi non basteranno piú, un uomo fatto come tutti gli altri, nel segreto di una stanza di questo mondo, inventerà un esplosivo incomparabile, in confronto al quale gli esplosivi attualmente esistenti saranno considerati quali innocui giocattoli. Ed un altro uomo fatto anche lui come tutti gli altri, ma degli altri un po' piú ammalato, ruberà tale esplosivo e s'arrampicherà al centro della terra per porlo nel punto ove il suo effetto potrà essere il massimo. Ci sarà un'esplosione enorme che nessuno udrà e la terra ritornata alla forma di nebulosa errerà nei cieli priva di parassiti e di malattie.

> Perhaps some incredible disaster produced by machines will lead us back to health.
>
> When all the poison gases are exhausted, a man, made like all other men of flesh and blood, will in the quiet of his room invent an explosive of such potency that all the explosives in existence will seem like harmless toys besides it. And another man, man in his image and in the image of all the rest, but a little weaker than they, will steal that explosive and crawl to the center of the earth with it, and place it just where he calculates it will have the maximum effects. There will be a tremendous explosion, but no one will hear it and the earth will return to its nebulous state and go wandering through the sky, free at last from parasites and disease.
>
> *Coscienza* 474–5; 411–12

The world of man, yoked with violence to the flesh it seeks to redeem, will justify itself with annihilation under the shadow of the God who is no longer there.

# Notes

SHIPWRECK IN THE PROLOGUE

1. György Lukács, *The Theory of the Novel* (Cambridge, Mass.: MIT Press, 1971), 29–39. The principal pages dedicated to Dante, paraphrased or cited here, are found on 68–70 and 80–3.

2. Ibid., 68.

3. See David Thompson, *Dante's Epic Journeys* (Baltimore: Johns Hopkins Press, 1974); and Winthrop Wetherbee, *The Ancient Flame: Dante and the Poets* (Notre Dame, Ind.: University of Notre Dame Press, 2008).

4. On this see also John Freccero, *The Poetics of Conversion*, 136–51.

5. Phillip Cary, *Augustine's Invention of the Inner Self: The Legacy of a Christian Platonist* (Oxford: Claredon Press, 2000).

6. On this see also Charles S. Singleton, *Dante Studies 2: Journey to Beatrice* (Cambridge, Mass.: Harvard University Press, 1958), Chapter 3.

7. Erich Auerbach, *Dante, Poet of the Secular World*, trans. Ralph Mannheim (Chicago: University of Chicago Press, 1961).

8. Charles S. Singleton, "In Exitu Israel de Aegypto," in *Dante: A Collection of Critical Essays*, ed. John Freccero (Englewood Cliffs, N.J.: Prentice Hall, 1965), 102–21.

9. Robert Lamberton, *Homer the Theologian: Neoplatonist Allegorical Reading and the Growth of the Epic Tradition* (Berkeley: University of California Press, 1986).

10. Augustine, *Confessions*, ed. James O'Donnell, 2 vols. (Oxford: Oxford University Press, 1992), 2:95–8.

11. Ernst Robert Curtius, *European Literature and the Latin Middle Ages* (New York: Routledge and Kegan Paul, 1953).

12. Hans Blumenberg, *Shipwreck with Spectator: Paradigm of a Metaphor for Existence*, trans. Steven Rendall (Cambridge, Mass.: MIT Press, 1996), 10.

13. See George Poulet, "Bergson et le thème de la vision panoramique des mourants" in *Revue de theologie et philosophie* 3, 10:1 (1960): 23–41.

14. Felix Buffière, *Les mythes d'Homère et la pensée greque* (Paris: Belles Lettres, 1956), 454–5.

15. Giovanni Reale, *Agostino: Amore assoluto e "terza navigazione"* (Milan: Bompiani, 2000). The volume contains the text and translation of the commentary *In epistolam Ioannis ad Parthos* and of *In Ioannis evangelium tractatus, Tractatus* II.

16. Translation in Giovanni Reale, *Agostino*, 495.

17. "The Delphic Oracle Upon Plotinus," written in August 1931, in *The Collected Poems of W. B. Yeats* (London: Wordsworth Editions, 2000), 230.

18. These remarks summarize a previous work of mine (see John Freccero, *Poetics of Conversion*, 15–28). Giorgio Padoan was the first critic to underscore the importance of *De beata vita* for Dante's portrayal of Ulysses: "Ulisse 'Fandi Fictor' e le vie della Sapienza," *Studi danteschi* 37 (1960): 21–61.

19. Jean Pepin, "The Platonic and Christian Ulysses," in *Odysseus/ Ulysses*, ed. Harold Bloom (New York: Chelsea House Publishers, 1991).

20. Robert J. O'Connell, *Soundings in St. Augustine's Imagination* (New York: Fordham University Press, 1992), 176–7.

21. Translation in Giovanni Reale, *Agostino*, 503.

22. For a survey of "distinguished scholarly" discussions of the simile, see Herbert D. Austin and Leo Spitzer, "Letargo (*Par.* 33.94)," *Modern Language Notes* 52, no. 7 (1937): 469–75; and Peter Dronke, "Boethius, Alanus and Dante," *Romanische Forschungen* 78 (1966): 119–25. For a more literary interpretation, see Georges Poulet, *Le Point de départ* (Paris: Editions de Rocher, 1964) and *Les Metamorphoses du cercle*, trans. Carley Dawson and Elliott Coleman (Baltimore: Johns Hopkins University Press, 1966).

THE PORTRAIT OF FRANCESCA: *INFERNO* 5

1. For the kiss, see Nicolas J. Perella, *The Kiss Sacred and Profane: An Interpretive History of Kiss Symbolism and Related Religio-erotic Themes* (Berkeley: University of California Press, 1969).

2. For a reading of Dante's construction and Boccaccio's "elaboration" of the figure of Francesca, see Teodolinda Barolini, "Dante and Francesca da Rimini: Realpolitik, Romance, Gender," *Speculum* 75, no. 1 (January 2000): 1–28.

3. The popular theme of the Annunciation in medieval and renaissance visual art is taken from Luke 1:26–38, in which the Angel Gabriel appears to the Virgin Mary to announce the forthcoming incarnation of Christ. In the later medieval visual tradition following St. Bernard's textual gloss as well as other popular theological writings of the time, the Virgin is often depicted as having been interrupted in the act of reading. In some instances, the text of Isaiah is reproduced in the image (Isaiah 7:14, "behold, a virgin shall conceive and bring forth a son, and his name shall be called Emmanuel").

4. See Patricia Parker, "Dante and the Dramatic Monologue," *Stanford Literature Review* 2, no. 2 (Fall 1985): 165–83.

5. See René Girard, *To Double Business Bound: Essays on Literature, Mimesis, and Anthropology* (Baltimore: Johns Hopkins University Press, 1978).

6. See Peter Dronke, "Francesca and Héloïse," *Comparative Literature* 27, no. 2 (Spring 1975): 113–35.

7. See György Lukács, *The Theory of the Novel*.

8. Cranes in the poem are associated with writing and its inspiration. In *Purgatorio*, after Dante's definition of his poetry, Bonagiunta says: "io veggio ben come le vostre penne / di retro al dittator sen vanno strette / che de le nostre certo non avvenne" (24.58–60). There follows a simile of cranes, suggested by the word "penne" ("quills") and the words "sen vanno strette." The allusion is possibly to a poem by Guido Guinizelli, addressed to Bonagiunta, in which different poets are said to be as varied as species of birds. Two cantos later, a particularly contrived "hypothetical" simile of migrating cranes represent the penitent lover-poets, homosexual and heterosexual: "Poi, come grue ch'a le montagne Rife / volasser parte, e parte inver' l'arene, / queste del gel, quelle delle del sole schife . . ." (*Purg.* 26.43–5).

9. Sky-writing is described in the heaven of Justice (*Par.* 18–20), where Dante executes spectacular variations on a theme from Lucan: the successive tracing and undoing of letters formed by cranes.

10. See Leo Spitzer, "The Poetic Treatment of a Platonic-Christian Theme," *Comparative Literature* 6, no. 3 (Summer 1954): 193–217.

11. See René Girard, *To Double Business Bound*.

12. See Malcolm Bowie, *Lacan* (Cambridge, Mass.: Harvard University Press, 1991), 185.

13. Hannah Arendt, *Love and Saint Augustine* (Chicago: University of Chicago Press, 1996), 21.

14. See John Freccero, *Poetics of Conversion*, 226.

15. Macrobius, *Commentary on the Dream of Scipio*, ed. and trans. William H. Stahl (New York: Columbia University Press, 1952), 132–3.

16. See also Marcelle Thiebaux, *The Stag of Love: The Chase in Medieval Literature* (Ithaca, N.Y.: Cornell University Press, 1974), and Giorgio Bàrberi Squarotti, *Selvaggia Dilettanza: La caccia nella letteratura italiana dalle origini a Marino* (Venice: Marsilio, 2000).

17. See Renato Poggioli, "Tragedy or Romance? A Reading of the Paola and Francesca Episode in Dante's *Inferno*," PMLA 72, no. 3 (1957): 313–58.

18. Jacques Derrida, *The Politics of Friendship*, trans. George Collins (London: Verso, 2005), 186.

19. Quoted by O'Donnell in Augustine, *Confessions*, ed. James O'Donnell, 2.232, along with other citations.

20. See the commentary ad. loc. by A. W. Price, *Love and Friendship in Plato and Aristotle* (Oxford: Clarendon Press, 1990), 87, who notes the resemblance to Narcissus.

21. Erwin Panofsky, *Studies in Iconology: Humanistic Themes in the Art of the Renaissance* (New York: Oxford University Press, 1967), 99.

22. See Frederick Goldin, *The Mirror of Narcissus in the Courtly Love Lyric* (Ithaca, N.Y.: Cornell University Press, 1967).

23. See John Freccero, "Moon Shadows: *Paradiso* III" in *Studies for Dante: Essays in Honor of Dante Della Terza*, ed. Franco Fido et al. (Fiesole: Cadmo, 1998), 89–101.

24. See Leo Spitzer, "The Poetic Treatment of a Platonic-Christian Theme."

25. Gianfranco Contini, ed., *Poeti del dolce stil novo* (Milan: Mondadori, 1991), 87.

26. I take the phrase from Georges Poulet's *Études sur le temps humain, II: La distance intérieure* (Paris: Plon, 1965).

27. See Philip Cary, *Augustine's Invention of the Inner Self*, 125ff. The reference to John Locke is Cary's.

28. See Peter Dronke, "Francesca and Héloïse."

29. Peter Abelard, *Historia calamitatum. The story of my misfortunes: An autobiography*, trans. Henry A. Bellows (Saint Paul, Minn.: T. A. Boyd, 1922), 14.

30. One can imagine what a "Romance of Paolo" might have been, before his damnation: brothers, thinking that they love each other, gradually become consumed with mimetic envy, vying for the hand of the fair Francesca, who is simply a pawn. Gianciotto wins, but is ultimately defeated by the adulterous love of his wife for the dashing Paolo. Together, the lovers kill Gianciotto. Such a plot would correspond to

Cervantes's novella contained within the Quixote, "El curioso imperti-nente," as read by René Girard in *Deceit, Desire, and the Novel.* Girard's first chapter deals with "external mediation" in *Don Quixote.*

31. Augustine, *Confessions,* trans. R. S. Pine-Coffin (New York: Penguin Books, 1961), 37.

32. John Freccero, *Poetics of Conversion,* esp. 1–5.

33. See René Girard, *Deceit, Desire, and the Novel.*

34. These remarks are a synopsis of the theme as represented in Book 1 of the *Confessions.*

### EPITAPH FOR GUIDO

Decades ago I wrote on the subject of Guido's disdain and now real-ize that my efforts were incomplete and, in some respects, seriously flawed. I should like to thank some of my friends and colleagues for their constructive criticism and gentle correction, which helped me to write what I hope is this more complete and satisfactory reading of canto 10: Maria Luisa Ardizzone, Peter Hawkins, Robert Hollander, Rachel Jacoff, Anthony Oldcorn, and Beatrice Sica.

1. For these and other early essays, see the bibliography of Charles S. Singleton, "*Inferno* X: Guido's Disdain," *MLN* 77 (January 1963): 49–65.

2. Antonio Gramsci, "Il Canto decimo dell' *Inferno,*" *Quaderni del carcere,* ed. Valentino Gerratana, 4 vols. (Turin: Einaudi, 1975), 1:516–30.

3. Frank Rosengarten, "Gramsci's 'Little Discovery': Gramsci's Interpretation of Canto X of Dante's *Inferno,*" *boundary 2* 14, no. 3 (Spring 1986): 71–90. I am indebted to Rosengarten's collection of scat-tered references in Gramsci's work, especially on the theme of tragedy. The ending of his article traces the influence of Gramsci's work, not only on subsequent interpretations of canto 10, but also in Italian liter-ary criticism in general.

4. See the entry "noeud" in Heinrich Lausberg's *Handbook of Liter-ary Rhetoric,* ed. David E. Orton and R. Dean Anderson (Leiden: Brill, 1998), 1246, 889, *sub voce*: "The term Plokē (*Aristotle's Poetics* 18, 3), trans-lated [by Boileau] by noeud indicates dramatic desis . . . so dénouement corresponds to the Lusis" (catastrophe).

5. See, for example, Eric Berne, *Transactional Analysis in Psychother-apy* (New York: Ballantine Books, 1975).

6. W. H. V. Reade, "The Circle of Heresy," in *The Moral System of Dante's "Inferno"* (Oxford: Clarendon Press, 1909), 367–81.

7. Maria Luisa Ardizzone, *Guido Cavalcanti: The Other Middle Ages* (Toronto: University of Toronto Press, 2002).

8. Gustav Freytag, *Die Technik des Dramas* (Leipzig: S. Hirzel, 1863); English translation by Elias J. MacEwan, *Freytag's Technique of the Drama: An Exposition of Dramatic Composition and Art* (Chicago: Scott Foresman, 1908).

9. Antonio Gramsci, "Il Canto decimo dell' *Inferno*," 1:517–20.

10. I am indebted to Winthrop Wetherbee for his discussion of "ingenium" and for the quotation from Apuleius, in *Platonism and Poetry in the Twelfth Century* (Princeton, N.J.: Princeton University Press, 1972), 94–98.

11. Bernardus Silvestris, *Commentary on the First Six Books of Virgil's "Aeneid,"* trans. and comment. Earl G. Schreiber and Thomas E. Maresca (Lincoln: University of Nebraska Press, 1974), 32–33.

12. This is the paragraph from Plotinus in the first Ennead (1.6.9) that inspired Augustine: "When you know that you have become this perfect work . . . nothing from without clinging to the authentic man . . . wholly that only veritable Light . . . when you perceive that you have grown to this, you are now become very vision: now call up all your confidence, strike forward yet a step—you need a guide no longer—strain and see" Stephen MacKenna, trans., *Plotinus on the Beautiful* (Stratford-up-on-Avon: The Shakespeare Head Press, 1914), 28–9. When Augustine in Book 7 sees this light (we might recall "che mena dritto altrui per ogni calle" *Inf.* 1.18), he is beaten back (*reverberasti*) by it and defeated.

13. Charles S. Singleton, *Commedia: Elements of Structure* (Cambridge, Mass: Harvard University Press, 1954), 133.

14. Philip Turetzky, *Time* (London: Routledge, 1998), esp. 51–3. He provides the diagram by the pseudo-Archytas, mentioned by Iamblichus. Turetzky describes the diagram: "the horizontal line represents point e1 as earlier than e2, which is earlier that e3. The inflected line presents e1 as past, e2 as present and e3 as future. The now point of the horizontal line moves from earlier to later, while participating things on the inflected line move from the future through the present and into the past" (53).

15. Analytic philosophers are divided into two different schools of thought about time. Following J. M. E. McTaggart, who set out in 1908 to prove the unreality of time ("The Unreality of Time," *Mind: A Quarterly Review of Psychology and Philosophy* 17 (1908): 456–73), these theories are commonly referred to as "A" time and "B" time. "A" time is that to which we are accustomed, made up of past, present, and future. It is the time of the tenses of most natural languages and of human interaction. In this schema, the past and the future have no ontological status, except in our memory or anticipation. The problem of dealing with a present

which is extant but not localized has seemed so intractable to some thinkers that they have resorted to "B" time, in which the only distinction in time is the distinction between "before" and "after," much as it was for Aristotle. "B" time has the advantage of setting absolute order and sequence. An event such as the first World War was, is, will always be before the second, and by the same span of time. At the cosmological level, it is literally true that the past still exists, susceptible to astronomical observation and mathematical calculation. "B" time does not depend on human consciousness, as does "A" time, but claims to be objective. It is the preferred time of scientists and of symbolic language (per Philip Turetzky, *Time*, 121).

16. Giacomo Devoto, *Studi di stilistica* (Florence: LeMonnier, 1950).

17. See John Freccero, "Ironia e mimesi: Il disdegno di Guido" in *Dante e la Bibbia*, ed. Giovanni Barblan (Florence: L. S. Olschki, 1988) or Geoffrey L. Bursill-Hall, *Speculative Grammars of the Middle Ages: the Doctrine of Partes Orationis of the Modistae* (The Hague: Mouton, 1971).

18. Charles Singleton, "*Inferno* X: Guido's Disdain."

19. Antonino Pagliaro, *Ulisse: Ricerche semantiche sulla Divina Commedia*, 2 vols. (Messina, 1976), 1: 202–9.

20. Maria Luisa Ardizzone, *Guido Cavalcanti*.

21. The paradox of a natural desire that could only be satisfied supernaturally was most famously challenged in the thirteenth century, with the rediscovery of Aristotle and his commentators, who conceived of philosophy as a comprehensive doctrine of natural knowledge that could lead to the attainment of happiness in this life. Recent scholarship suggests that the momentous condemnations of Bishop Tempier in Paris in 1277 were aimed precisely at combating this claim. Tempier condemned what he referred to as "a double truth" along with 219 theses that have been variously ascribed to Boethius of Dacia, Siger of Brabant, and even Thomas Aquinas. In one passage of the *Convivio*, Dante chooses to follow Aristotle rather than theological tradition when at the end of 3.11 he denies the existence of any natural desire to know God in his essence. Gilson reads this as a "radical" departure from Christian teaching, to which Dante was forced by his insistence on the autonomy of earthly beatitude. One point that Dante makes in his argument is directly contradicted in the *Commedia*: He says in the *Convivio*, "[a natural desire to know God in His essence is impossible because human nature] would desire always to be desiring and never to satisfy its own desire." Even the most cursory reading of the poem will confirm that this argument of the *Convivio* is soundly rejected. Augustinian theology of beatitude is based

on the acknowledgement of the "unquiet heart." To interpret the poem
in the terms of the *Convivio* with respect to the role of philosophy, as
Dante scholars often do, is to interpret the goal of the journey in terms
of its gateway and to ignore the break that occurred between the two
texts. On the contrary, interpretation is always retrospective, in literature, exegesis, and in language itself. This is the point of the supper at
Emmaus (Luke 24:13), when Christ reads scripture as foreshadowing his
coming, and of Dante's allusion to it at the beginning of *Purgatorio* 21.
For the inadequacy of philosophy suggested by the episode of Casella,
see John Freccero, *Poetics of Conversion*, 186–94.

22.  See Etienne Gilson, *L'esprit de la philosophie médiévale* (Paris:
Librairie Philosophique J. Vrin, 1944), 259, and Henri de Lubac, *Le mystere du surnaturel* (Paris: Cerf, 2000), 254.

23.  On Acts of the Apostles and Matthew 11:25–30, see Eduard Norden, *Agnostos theos* (Leipzig: Verlag B.G. Teubner, 1913) now translated
into Italian, *Dio Ignoto*, trans. Chiara O. Tommasi Moreschini (Brescia:
Morcelliana, 2002). The altar to the unknown God is extensively discussed on 161–243, and the logion on 391–418, where the distinctiveness
of Jesus's humility among the magi and prophets is also discussed.

24.  The mystery of the supernatural continues to disturb some theologians to this day. The great theologian of the last century, Henri de
Lubac, was silenced for nearly a decade after the controversy provoked by
his book, *Surnaturel*. In that work and in the later *Mystere du Surnaturel*,
he refuted the concept of a state of pure nature having as its goal a purely
human happiness, an idea that dominated Catholic theology from the
sixteenth to the twentieth centuries. De Lubac insisted on a return to the
Augustinian idea of our natural vocation to the supernatural and of the
beatific vision as the ultimate goal of human nature. He traced the roots
of what he took to be the distortion of traditional doctrine to a misunderstanding of Thomistic texts on the part of some of the saint's commentators. De Lubac's position was finally vindicated and accepted by
most theologians at the Second Vatican Council, to which he served as
an adviser. The importance to us of the debate is not only that it began
in Dante's day, but also that it mirrors the conflict within Dante's own
work between the *Convivio* and the *Divine Comedy*. To sum up our
argument, we may say that if Aristotle provided the impetus for the philosophical search for happiness, it was Augustine, the primary Christian
authority on the supernatural, who showed the way to beatitude.

25.  Giorgio Padoan, "Ulisse 'Fandi fictor' e le vie della Sapienza," 21–61.

26. The word "philosophism" is used by Gilson to describe the temptation faced by Dante in the *Convivio*. Gilson seems uncertain about the degree to which Dante succumbed to it. In *Dante and Philosophy* (New York: Harper & Row, 1963), 151–61.

27. Antonio Pagliaro, *Ulisse*, 205–9.

28. For the negative connotations of the word "magnanimo," see J. A. Scott, *Dante Magnanimo: studi sulla "Commedia"* (Florence: Olschki, 1977), 43. For the opposition between humility and magnanimity, see Maria Corti, *La felicità mentale: nuove prospettive per Cavalcanti e Dante* (Turin: Einaudi, 1983), 51–4.

29. Gianfranco Contini, "Cavalcanti in Dante," in *Un' idea di Dante: saggi danteschi* (Turin: Einaudi 1976), 143. Teodolinda Barolini, *Dante's Poets: Textuality and Truth in the "Commedia"* (Princeton, N.J.: Princeton University Press, 1984), 123–53.

30. On the terrace of avarice, Virgil explains how he came to love Statius even before meeting him: "amore, acceso di virtù, sempre altro accese" (10), directly translating in words and sentiment Augustine's affection for an orator whom he had never met: "ex amante alio accenditur alius." As if to underscore Dante's reliance on the literature of friendship, Virgil questions Statius "come amico," repeating "come amico" again in the same terzina. So too Francesca's words in canto 5, "Amor, ch'a nullo amato amar perdona" (103) echo Augustine, even to the reduplicative play on the word "amare": "Hoc est quod diligitur in amicis, et sic diligitur ut rea sibi sit humana conscientia si non amaverit redamantem aut si amantem non redamaverit," but, quite obviously, not the Augustinian corrective excluding carnal love: "nihil quaerens ex eius corpore praeter indicia benevolentiae."

31. Teodolinda Barolini, *Dante's Poets*, 123–53.

32. *La Divina Commedia*, ed. and intro. Giorgio Petrocchi (Turin: Einaudi, 1975), xx.

THE ETERNAL IMAGE OF THE FATHER

1. Bernardus, quoted and translated by David Thompson in *Dante's Epic Journeys*, 78.

2. Peter Hawkins has placed the encounter with Brunetto Latini in the context of the poem's grander theme of "staged surprise," epitomized in the pilgrim's inflected question to his teacher, "Are *You* here?" In Peter Hawkins, "Are You Here? Surprise in the *Commedia*," in *Sparks and Seeds: Medieval Literature and Its Afterlife*, ed. Dana E. Stewart and

Alison Cornish, intro. Giuseppe Mazzotta (Turnhout: Brepols, 2000), 175–97, esp. 177–9.

3. Marguerite Mills Chiarenza, "Time and Eternity in the Myths of *Paradiso* XVII," in *Dante, Petrarch, Boccaccio: Studies in the Italian Trecento in Honor of C. S. Singleton*, ed. A. S. Bernardo and A. L. Pellerini (Binghamton, N.Y.: Medieval and Renaissance Texts and Studies 22, 1983), 134.

4. Erich Auerbach, *Mimesis: The Representation of Reality in Western Literature* (Princeton, N.J.: Princeton University Press, 1953).

5. Robert Ball, "Theological Semantics: Virgil's *Pietas* and Dante's *Pietà*," *Stanford Italian Review* 2, no. 1 (Spring 1981): 59.

6. Augustine, *Confessions*, trans. R. S. Pine-Coffin (Harmondsworth: Penguin Books, 1961), 240.

### ALLEGORY AND AUTOBIOGRAPHY

1. For a twentieth-century view of the passage and discussions of its meaning, see Rudolf Bultmann, *The Gospel of John: A Commentary*, trans. G. R. Beasley-Murray (Oxford: Blackwell, 1971), 713.

2. See, among many others, Maria Corti, "On the Metaphors of Sailing, Flight, and Tongues of Fire in the episode of Ulysses (*Inf.* 26)," *Stanford Italian Review* 9 (1990): 33.

3. See Albert Ascoli, *Ariosto's Bitter Harmony* (Princeton, N.J.: Princeton University Press, 1987), 251.

4. For Dante's use of these Augustinian themes, see the first chapter ("Allegory") of Charles S. Singleton, *Dante's Commedia: Elements of Structure*, esp. 7.

5. Pierre Courcelle, *Recherches sur les Confessions de St. Augustin* (Paris: E. de Boccard, 1950), esp. 111ff.

6. Courcelle compiled a repertory of citations of Plato's "region of unlikeness" from Statesman 272 to André Gide in *Les Confessions de St. Augustin dans la tradition littéraire* (Paris: Etudes Augustiniennes, 1963), 623ff.

7. Bruno Nardi, "La tragedia d'Ulisse," in *Dante e la cultura medievale: Nuovi saggi di filosofia dantesca*, 2nd edition. (Bari: Laterza, 1949), 153–65. See also David Thompson, *Dante's Epic Journeys*.

8. Giorgio Padoan, "Ulisse 'fandi fictor' e le vie della sapienza," 21–61.

9. The conclusion of Book 2 of Rousseau's *Confessions* relates Jean-Jacques's theft of a piece of ribbon to give to Marianne, a servant girl, whom he then publicly accuses of having stolen it. The episode is obvi-

ously an imitation of Augustine's theft of pears, but with a difference: The triviality of Augustine's theft was meant to suggest that any of his readers would be capable of such an act, whereas Rousseau's virtuosity consists in transforming banal pilfering into a truly reprehensible crime.

10. Charles S. Singleton, *Journey to Beatrice: Dante Studies 2*, 5.

11. Luigi Pirandello, "La commedia dei diavoli," in *Saggi, poesia, e scritti vari*, ed. Manlio Lo Vecchio-Musti (Milan: Mondadori, 1960). Leo Spitzer is more skeptical in "Farcical Elements in *Inferno* XXI–XXIII," in *Representative Essays*, ed. Alban K. Forcione, et al. (Stanford: Stanford University Press, 1988), 172.

12. See John B. Friedman, "Antichrist and the Iconography of Dante's Geryon," *Journal of the Warburg and Courtauld Institutes* 35 (1972): 108–22.

13. A. C. Charity, *Events and their Afterlife* (Cambridge: Cambridge University Press, 1966), 35.

14. Quoted by Busnelli and Vandelli in their commentary on *Convivio* 2.1.5: *Convivio*, comment. Giovanni Busnelli and Giuseppe Vandelli, 2 vols. (Florence: Le Monnier, 1968), 1:98.

15. See the remarks of Teodolinda Barolini, *Dante's Poets*, 113. On the question of narrative truth, see Ruth Morse, *Truth and Convention in the Middle Ages: Rhetoric, Representation and Reality* (Cambridge: Cambridge University Press, 1991), who does not, however, discuss Geryon.

16. There is a serious lacuna at *Convivio* 2.1.4, emended with discussion by Busnelli and Vandelli who include a useful appendix. For an explanation, see the Ryan translation, 42–3 and note.

17. See Paul Synave, "La doctrine de St. Thomas d'Aquin sur le sens littéral des Écritures," *Revue Biblique* 35 (1926): 40–65.

18. For the applicability of the theme to *Purgatorio*, see Charles S. Singleton, "In Exitu Israel de Aegypto," in John Freccero, ed., *Dante: Twentieth Century Views* (Englewood Cliffs, N.J.: Prentice-Hall, 1965), 102.

19. Perhaps the most consistent exponent of such a theory was Bruno Nardi, who returned repeatedly to his idea of Dante as visionary prophet: "Dante profeta," in *Dante e la cultura medievale*, 265.

20. Leo Spitzer, "The Addresses to the Reader in the *Commedia*," in *Representative Essays*, 178; Erich Auerbach, "Dante's Addresses to the Reader," *Romance Philology* 7 (1954): 268–78.

21. Charles S. Singleton, *Dante's Commedia: Elements of Structure*, 84.

22. Northrop Frye, *The Great Code* (New York: Harcourt Brace Jovanovich, 1982), 60ff.

23. Erich Auerbach, "Farinata and Cavalcante," in *Mimesis*, 174–202.

24. Jacques Derrida, *De la grammatologie* (Paris: Editions de Minuit, 1967), 103.

25. Ernst Robert Curtius, *European Literature and the Latin Middle Ages*, 302.

26. Kenneth Burke, *The Rhetoric of Religion: Studies in Logology* (Berkeley: University of California Press, 1961). Regarding this, see also John Freccero, "Burke on Logology," in Hayden White and Margaret Brose, eds., *Representing Kenneth Burke*, English Institute Essays (Baltimore: The Johns Hopkins University Press, 1982), 52–67.

27. Narrative diachronicity is incompatible with a Joachistic theory of a third testament to come. However congenial triadic speculation may be for models of becoming (Hegel), the idea of conversion requires duality, just as *terza rima* requires duality in order to begin or end.

28. Kenneth Burke, *The Rhetoric of Religion*, 183.

## IN THE WAKE OF THE ARGO ON A BOUNDLESS SEA

1. Mary Reynolds, *Joyce and Dante: The Shaping Imagination* (Princeton, N.J.: Princeton University Press, 1981). See also Jennifer Fraser, *Rite of Passage in the Narratives of Dante and Joyce* (Gainesvillle: University Press of Florida, 2002).

2. Giambattista della Porta, *Della fisionomia dell'huomo: libri sei* (Venice: Christoforo Tomasini, 1644), 86–88.

3. Hugh Shankland, "Dante aliger," *Modern Language Review* 70 (1975): 764–85.

4. Michael C. J. Putnam, *Virgil's Aeneid: Interpretation and Influence* (Chapel Hill: University of North Carolina Press, 1995).

5. Pierre Courcelle, "Quelques symboles funeraire du neo-platonisme latin: Le vol de Dédale; Ulysse et les Sirènes," *Revue des etudes anciennes* 46 (1944): 65–93.

6. Neil Hertz, *The End of the Line: Essays on Psychoanalysis and the Sublime* (New York: Columbia University Press, 1985).

7. See Georges Poulet, *Les Metamorphoses du cercle*, xii ff. See also his *Le Point de depart*.

8. Anonymous, *Il Libro dei ventiquattro filosofi*, ed. Paolo Lucentini (Milan: Adelphi, 1999), 95.

9. Charles S. Singleton, "The Vistas in Retrospect," *MLN* 81 (1966): 55–80.

10. Herbert D. Austin, "From Matter to Spirit," *MLN* 38 (1923): 140–8.

THE FIG TREE AND THE LAUREL

1. See, for example, Marcia Colish, *The Mirror of Language* (New Haven: Yale University Press, 1968), 57.

2. C. S. Peirce, *Collected Papers*, ed. Arthur W. Burks, et al. (Cambridge, Mass.: Harvard University Press, 1960), 1:117.

3. Quoted in Maurice Pontet, *L'Exégèse de S. Augustin prédicateur* (Paris: Aubier, 1946), 117.

4. Yehezkel Kaufman, *Religion of Israel*, trans. M. Greenberg (Chicago: University of Chicago Press, 1960).

5. For a different, although analogous, interpretation of "idolatry" that omits the erotic dimension of meaning, see Own Barfield, *Saving the Appearances: A Study in Idolatry* (London: Faber and Faber, 1957).

6. Dante, *Rime*, ed. Gianfranco Contini (Turin: Einaudi, 1965), 159.

7. Robert Durling, "Petrarch's 'Giovene donna sotto un verde lauro,'" *MLN* 86 (1971): 1–20.

8. Petrarch's rivalry with Dante is possibly the first example in the West of what Harold Bloom has called the "anxiety" of influence, see Harold Bloom, *The Anxiety of Influence* (New York: Oxford University Press, 1973).

9. C. S. Peirce, *Collected Papers*, 1:171.

10. II Corinthians 3, where the veil hides the face of Moses; that is, where the "letter" covers the "spirit." For the veil, see also D. W. Robertson, *A Preface to Chaucer* (Princeton, N.J.: Princeton University Press, 1962), s.v.

MEDUSA AND THE MADONNA OF FORLÌ:
POLITICAL SEXUALITY IN MACHIAVELLI

1. On the history and importance of the image, see Ernst H. Kantorowicz, *The King's Two Bodies: A Study in Medieval Political Theology* (Princeton, N.J.: Princeton University Press, 1957), 193–272.

2. See J. H. Hexter, "*Il Principe* and *lo Stato*," *Studies in the Renaissance* 4 (1957): 113–38.

3. On "humors," see *Discorsi* 1.4; on "mixed bodies," see 3.1; on "disease," see *Il Principe* 3.

4. Occasional emendations to the Adams translation are marked by brackets here.

5. See Hanna Fenichel Pitkin, *Fortune Is a Woman: Gender and Politics in the Thought of Niccolò Machiavelli* (Berkeley: University of California Press, 1984). Pitkin fails to note the distinction in Renaissance Italian

between *femina* ("woman") and *donna* ("lady"). The important sociological point is amusingly recalled in a Frank Loemer song in the musical *Guys and Dolls* (1953), when a gambler prays, before shooting his dice, "Luck, be a lady tonight!"

6. See the introduction to *Discorsi*, 2.

7. Antonio Gramsci, "Note sul Machiavelli," in *Quaderni del carcere*, 3: esp. 1598–1601.

8. Sebastiano De Grazia's title, *Machiavelli in Hell* (Princeton, N.J.: Princeton University Press, 1989), suggests the connection, although the point is not made explicitly.

9. For debates on the relative dignity of law and medicine in the Quattrocento, see Eugenio Garin, ed., *La disputa delle arti nel Quattrocento* (Florence: Vallecchi, 1947).

10. Jacques Maritain, *The Range of Reason* (New York: Scribner, 1952), esp. Chapter 11, "The End of Machiavellianism."

11. J. G. A. Pocock, *The Machiavellian Moment: Florentine Political Thought and the Atlantic Republican Tradition* (Princeton, N.J.: Princeton University Press, 1975).

12. Antonio Gramsci, "La matrice," in *Sotto la mole, 1916–1920* (Turin: Einaudi, 1960), 181.

13. Translation from Niccolò Machiavelli, *Discorsi of Niccolò Machiavelli*, ed. and trans. Leslie J. Walker and Cecil H Clough, 2 vols. (Boston: Routledge and Paul, 1975).

14. Jacques Le Goff, *The Medieval Imagination* (Chicago: University of Chicago Press, 1988), 161.

15. For further discussion of Gramsci's reading of Machiavelli, see Federico Sanguineti, *Gramsci e Machiavelli* (Bari: Laterza, 1982), esp. 3–7.

16. See Nilda Guglielmi, "L'image de la porte et des enceintes d'après les chroniques du moyen âge," in *Fortifications, portes de villes, places publiques, dans le monde méditerranéen*, ed. Jacques Heers (Paris: Presses de l'Université de Paris-Sorbonne, 1985), 106. The French word *enceinte* ("enclosure") seems to carry with it the analogy between the gate and the body.

17. See the discussion of Bruce Cole in *Piero della Francesca: Tradition and Innovation in Renaissance Art* (New York: Icon Editions, 1991), esp. 77, for the etymology of "tent." For a survey of analogous images, see Gregor Lechner, *Maria Gravida: zum Schwangerschaftsmotiv in der bildenden Kunst* (Munich: Schnell & Steiner, 1981).

18. John Freccero, *Poetics of Conversion*, 119–35.

19. A. A. Barb, "Dive Matrix," *Journal of the Warburg and Courtauld Institutes* 16 (1953), esp. 108–12.

20. Roman Jakobson, "Why 'Mama' and 'Papa'?" in *Selected Writings* (The Hague; Paris: Mouton, 1971), 1:538.

21. Sigmund Freud, "Medusa's Head," in *Sexuality and the Psychology of Love*, ed. Philip Reiff (New York: Collier Books, 1963), 212–13.

22. See Neil Hertz, "Medusa's Head: Male Hysteria under Political Pressure," *Representations* 4 (1983): 27–54. With characteristic brilliance, Hertz concentrates on the Freudian reading of the Medusa as representing castration. In the subsequent discussion of his paper, Catherine Gallagher points out that the threat of Medusa/mother is also that of *generativity* (Catherine Gallagher, "More about Medusa's Head," *Representations* 4 (1983): 55–7). This is Machiavelli's Medusa, although the threat is perceived to be directed against the conspirators.

23. On several occasions, to describe Jerusalem, Rome, or Florence, Dante quotes the opening verses of the Lamentations of Jeremiah: "How solitary lies the city, once so full of people! / Once great among nations, now become a widow." See in particular the excursus of *Purgatorio* 6. See also Nancy Vickers, "Widowed Words: Dante, Petrarch, and Metaphors of Mourning," in *Discourses of Authority in Medieval and Renaissance Literatures*, ed. Kevin Brownlee and Walter Stephens (Hanover, N.H.: Published for Dartmouth College by University Press of New England, 1989), 97–108.

24. *Vita di Benvenuto Cellini* (Milan: Società Tipografica de' Classici Italiani, 1811). The editor is Giovanni Palamede Carpani. His conjecture is repeated by Mary McCarthy in *The Stones of Florence* (New York: Harcourt, Brace, 1959). For an exhaustive discussion of the statue, its pedestal, and iconography, see Kathleen Weil-Garris, "On Pedestals: Michelangelo's *David*, Bandinelli's *Hercules* and *Cacus*, and the Sculpture of the Piazza della Signoria," *Römische Jahrbuch für Kunstgeschicte* 20 (1983): 377–415 (esp. 408–15, where the iconographic tradition is surveyed). On the "tumult" in Machiavelli, see *Discorsi* 1.4.17. I would like to acknowledge the generous help of my friend Nancy Vickers with the iconographic problem.

### DONNE'S "VALEDICTION: FORBIDDING MOURNING"

1. John Donne, *The Elegies, and The Songs and Sonnets*, ed. Helen Gardner (Oxford; Clarendon, 1965), 62–4, author's edit included.

2. For an interpretation see C. S. Singleton, "*Vita Nuova* XII, Love's Obscure Words," *Romantic Review* 36 (April 1945): 89–102.

3. Georges Poulet, *Les Métamorphoses du cercle*, introduction.

4. The phrase "swerving serpentine" is from Mario Praz, *The Flaming Heart* (New York: Doubleday, 1958), 190.

5. See also 1.231: "this Divorce [death] is a new Marriage . . ."

6. See also 4.68: "In Him we more from the beginning to the end of our circle," and 8.97 for "Gods compasse."

7. See also *Physics* 3.207a8.

8. For these and other compass emblems see Filippo Picinelli, *Mundus symbolicus*, trans. A. Erath (Cologne, 1687), 176–7 (s.v. *Circinus*).

9. The madrigal is given by Picinelli. It has often been suggested as a "source" for Donne's image. See, among others, Josef Lederer, "John Donne and the Emblematic Practice," *RES* 22 (1946): 198–200; and *contra* Doris C. Powers, "Donne's Compass," *RES*, n.s. 9 (1958): 173–5, as well as D. C. Allen, "Donne's Compass Figure," *MLN* 71, no. 4 (April 1956): 256, and Mario Praz, *The Flaming Heart*, 16.

10. *Poètes du XVI^e siècle*, ed. A. M. Schmidt (Paris: Pléiade, 1959), 119. The submerged compass is meant to show that Love "Par fermeté en inconstance esproeuve" its glory. Parturier (*Délie*, ed. E. Parturier [Paris: Droz, 1916]) reproduces it under the emblem of the weather vane, to which it of course bears a certain affinity. The words *pensée* and *foi*, however, seem to suggest that the "soul's compass" is here intended, as we shall later attempt to show. For a similar submerged image of Jean de Sponde, see n. 43.

11. Plato called the two motions the "circle of the same" and the "circle of the other." See *Timaeus* 36d–37c and the remarks by A. Ölerud, *L'Idée de macrocosmos et de microcosmos dans le Timée de Platon* (Uppsala: Almqvist & Wiksells Boktryckeri, 1951), 32ff, as well as John Freccero, *Poetics of Conversion*, 70–92.

12. The diagram is not entirely accurate, for if it were a view from the pole, then the spiral would be off-center. The pole of the universe is approximately 23 degrees from the pole of the *ecliptic* (the center of our diagram).

13. This use of the word probably arises from the fact that the ecliptic intersects the equator at an angle—"obliquely"—as in *Timaeus*, where the Demiurge places one piece of "soul-stuff" at an angle to the other. The text of Théophile's "Le matin" can be found in *Oeuvres poétiques*, ed. Jeanne Streicher (Geneva: Droz, 1951), 13. For further discussion on the oblique and the figure of the compass in Donne, see Eileen Reeves, "John Donne and the Oblique Course," *Renaissance Studies* 7, no. 2 (1993): 168–83.

14. See also remarks on this passage by W. Wölker, *Kontemplation und Ekstase bei Pseudo-Dionysius Areopagita* (Wiesbaden: Franz Steine, 1958), 191, who notes that Maximus the Confessor develops the idea further. In the Middle Ages, the *Liber de Causis* is often cited for a version of the three "conversions." For Bonaventure's doctrine, see *Itinerarium mentis in*

*Deum* 1.2. The theme and its history are discussed in John Freccero, *Poetics of Conversion*, 175. For the history of the doctrine of the "circularity" of beatitude, see Bruno Nardi, "Sì come rota ch'igualmente è mossa," in *Nel Mondo di Dante* (Rome: Storia e Letteratura, 1944), 337–50.

15. See Philippe Chevallier, et. al., eds., *Dionysiaca* (Bruges: Desclée de Brouwer, 1937), 1:190.

16. Marsilio Ficino, "*Commentario Divinis Nominibus*," in *Opera omnia*, 2 vols. (Basel: Henrich Petri, 1576), 2:1062–3.

17. *Appendix Comementarium in Timaeum*, cap. 19 (*Opera* 2:1467).

18. See *Timaeus* 39d. See Cornford's notes *ad loc.* in Francis M. Cornford, *Plato's Cosmology: The* Timaeus *of Plato* (New York: The Liberal Arts Press, 1957), 116–17.

19. Quoted by Eugenio Garin, ed., in Giovanni Pico della Mirandola, *Disputationes adversus astrologiam divinatricem, Libri 6–12* (Florence: Vallecchi Editore, 1952), 537. Garin surveys the history of the doctrine from Cicero to Pico.

20. Ibid., 12. Pico describes the "astrologasters" as whispering to their followers the suggestion that *apocatastasis* and Resurrection are the same: "Quod quidam deinde astrologomistae profundius examinantes, consectaneis solent dicere in aurem: haec est illa Christianorum resurrectio, quam et Hebraei sperant et Mahumetenses." Pico refers his readers to Nicholas Oresme's refutation of the *apocatastasis*, cited by Garin as the *Tractatus de proport. proportionum*, Venice, 1505. On the controversy in Dante's day concerning the relationship of *apocatastasis* and the Second Coming, see R. E. Kaske, "Dante's 'DXV' and 'Veltro,'" *Traditio* (1961): 185–254 (esp. 241–54). One of the earliest and most famous attempts at a Christianization of *apocatastasis* was undertaken by Origen, who was condemned by the Council of Constantinople (V) for the doctrine of the pre-existence of souls and for "la monstrueuse apocatastase qui s'y rattache," as described in A. Vacant and E. Mangenot, eds., *Dictionnaire de Théologie Catholique Contenant l'Exposé des Doctrines de la Théologie Catholique Leurs Preuves et Leur Histoire*, 15 vols. (Paris: Letouzey et Ané, 1932), 11b: 1581 (s.v. *Origénisme*).

21. Marisilio Ficino, *Opera*, 1:417.

22. For the doctrine of planetary homes (variously called *klairoi, loci, domicilia*, and so on), see Franz Boll, Carl Bezold, and Wilhelm Gundel, *Sternglaube und Sterndeutung: die Geschichte und das Wesen der Astrologie* (Leipzig; Berlin: Teubner, 1926), 58ff., and Eugenio Garin, ed., *Disputationes*, 538, who cites Manilius 2:788–970 and Firmicus Maternus 2:19–20.

23. The word is translated "erect" in modern English by Thorndike: "Every planet is erect in some one sign and falls in its opposite" in Lynn

Thorndike, *A History of Magic and Experimental Science* (New York: Columbia University Press, 1923), 1:711.

24. "Fiammeggiavano vivi i lumi chiari" in *Lirici del secolo XVI* (Milan: E Sonzogno, 1879), 118–19.

25. See notes and bibliography of Eugenio Garin, ed., *Disputationes*, 544ff.

26. The passage is accepted by the variorum edition of 1669, but modern editors reject it as probably spurious.

27. Franz Boll, et al., *Sternglaube und Sterndeutung*. They translated "Erniedrigungen." Marvell's *Definition of Love* exploits astrological doctrine in a similar way. See especially the lines " . . . conjunction of the mind, / And opposition of the stars."

28. Allen Tate has shown that Donne's compass traces the "Aristotelian circle of archetypal motion" in Allen Tate, "The Point of Dying," *SR* 61, no. 1 (Winter 1953): 76–81 (76).

29. The following passage summarizes a discussion in John Freccero, *Poetics of Conversion*, 35–7.

30. The word "gigglimus" is retained by some commentators, e.g. Averroes, *In Aristotelis de anima III* 3.55. The English expression "ball-and-socket" corresponds to the words "gibbositas et concavitas" in Latin translations. For "elbow," see especially *De generatione animalium* 2.2, which Georges Rodier considers the best commentary on the passage, whether it is spurious or not. See his translation and commentary for a lucid discussion of the Aristotelian principle: Aristotle, *Traité de l'âme*, trans. Georges Rodier (Paris: Leroux, 1900), 2:547ff.

31. *Maurice Scève: Choix des textes & préface par Albert Béguin* (Paris: G L M, 1947), 57. See also François Sagon, "Le pied," *Blason du corps feminin:* "Pied qui suyt l'autre en ordre et *par compas* . . ." (A. M. Schmidt, ed., *Poètes du XVIᵉ siècle*, 345). The analogy is implicit in the word "compass": *compassare < L. com - + passus*, a step.

32. "Et attractio et expulsio . . . non est in rectitudine sed secundum lineas non rectas, magis curvas quam rectas, et ideo assimilatur giro" (*In Aristotelis de anima III* 3.55). See also Albertus Magnus: "hic autem motus est gyrantis, quando motum mebrum gyrum habet expulsionis et retractionis in eodem loco. In talibus enim motibus expulsio est sicut principium, et attraction est sicut finis ejus . . ." (*Liber III de anima* 4.8).

33. For the symbolic importance of the doctrine of the *apex mentis* or the *synderesis*, see for instance Georges Poulet, *Les Métamorphoses du cercle*, xiii ff. For Thomas Aquinas's discussion, see *Summa Theologica* 1, q. 79, a. 12. Harry V. Jaffa compares Thomas's use of the idea to Aristotelian princi-

ples in *Thomism and Aristotelianism* (Chicago: University of Chicago Press, 1952), 171–4.

34. See n. 10, and Jean de Sponde's twin powers in the sonnet cited at n. 43: "esprit" and "constance." See also Pietro Bembo's *canzone* "Quantunque in altro clima io giri il piede . . ." which distinguishes "pensiero" and "core"; Tasso's sonnet 109 similarly refers to "pensiero" and "constanza": "somiglia il mio pensiero / . . . / stella in ciela errante / per la costanza mia fatta incostante" in *Lirici del cinquecento*, ed. Carlo Bo (Milan: Garzanti, 1945), 388. Finally, see Jonson's "Epistle to Master John Selden": "And like a Compasse keeping one foot still / Upon your Center, doe your Circle fill / Of general knowledge" in *Ben Jonson: The Poems / The Prose Works*, ed. C. H. Herford, Percy Simpson, and Evelyn Simpson (Oxford: Clarendon Press, 1947), 8:159.

35. Poulet remarks that Guy Le Febvre da la Boderie was in the "entourage" of Plantin. For the possible influence of the device on Donne's poem see the articles of Lederer and Powers cited earlier, who, however, exaggerate its importance.

36. Cesare Ripa, *Iconologia* (Venice: N. Pezzana, 1669), 496.

37. Probably the most influential statement of the allegory is in Augustine's *De Trinitate* 12.2.

38. For the *congé* and relevant bibliography, see Italo Siciliano, *François Villon et les thèmes poétiques du moyen âge* (Paris: Colin, 1934), 332.

39. Merritt Hughes, "Some of Donne's 'Ecstasies,'" *PMLA* 75, no. 5 (December 1960): 509–18. Hughes's discussion of the use of Plotinian ecstasy as an epistolary conceit provides an excellent background for an understanding of Donne's verse "Inter-assured of the mind," which might be interpreted as "participating in the *Mens*," which transcends both the lovers. Such an affirmation would be the normal way for a neoplatonist to explain the fact that two souls are in fact one.

40. *Dialoghi* (Venice: Paolo Manuzio, 1544), 29: "TUL. Il conforto della partita del Tasso sia la mia morte: che essendo tra lui et me la medesima proportione, ch'è tra il corpo, e l'anima mia; partendo esso partirà l'anima, che mi tien viva . . . GRA . . . Perchioche non sempremai, che l'anima nostra si discompagna dal corpo, noi cessiamo di vivere . . . adunque s'altrettanto in voi, e ne vostri amori vi mostrerò poter fare la partita del Tasso: onde viene che voi ve ne vogliate ramaricare? . . ." This is one citation among many. In poetry, the theme of *congé* as "ecstasy" is often repeated by Serafino dall'Aquila, with whom Parturier compares Scève's famous *dizain* 144: "En toy je vis, où que tu sois absente: / En moy je meurs, où que soye presente . . ." (E. Parturier, ed.,

244 Notes to pages 186–88

*Délie*, 108). Cf. Petrarch, "Mira quell colle . . ." For Ficino, see "Commentarium in convivium Platonis: De amore 2.8" in *Commentaire sur le Banquet de Platon*, trans. R. Marcel (Paris: Belles Lettres, 1956), 156: "In reciprocal love, there is only one death, but two resurrections . . ." See also the remarks on the passage by Giuseppe Saitta, *La Filosofia di Marsilio Ficino* (Messina: G. Principato, 1923), 263–4. The passage is translated almost verbatim by Gilles Corrozet, *Le Sophologe d'Amour* (Paris: Gilles Corrozet, 1542), fol. 15r. Parturier, who does not seem to be aware of the source, calls this "un exemple, entre mille, du galimatias amoureux à la mode sous le règne de François I" (101).

41. A serious use of the theme can be found in Scève's *Délie*, "Asses plus long qu'un Siecle Platonique" (E. Parturier, ed., 367).

42. See, for instance, Serafino dall'Aquila's dialogue between the body and the soul: "Anima, su.—Che c'è?—Disgombra e vola [cf. Donne's ". . . and whisper to their soules, to goe."]. —Dove?—A madonna.—A che? Ch'io son in via.—Tu mori?—Non.—Da te chi me desvia?—Quel crudo amor, che tutto el mondo invola—" (*Le rime di Serafino de'Ciminelli dall'Aquila*, ed. Mario Menghini [Bologna: Romagnoli-Dall'Acqua, 1894], 1:132). The first lines of Louise Labé's *Elégie 6* are a classic example of the "body's lament for its soul": "On voit mourir toute chose animee, / Lors que du corps l'ame sutile part: / Je suis le corps, toy la meilleure part: / Où es tu donq, o ame bien aymee? / Ne me laissez par si long tems pamee: / Pour me sauver apres viendrois trop tard. / Las! ne mets point ton corps en ce hazart: / Rens lui sa part et moitié estimee" (A. M. Schmidt, ed., *Poètes du XVIe siècle*, 283). For Béguin's terminology, see *Maurice Scève: Choix des textes*, 16. Dante was, of course, the first to use this pattern of the mystics to celebrate his love for his Lady.

43. The simile of the lady as pole-star is a tired topos, often found in combination with the "ship of love" or the mariner's compass motifs. Two passages from sixteenth century French poems seem particularly suggestive for establishing an affinity between Donne's "Valediction" and Petrarchan currents (see Mario Praz, *The Flaming Heart*, 186–203). In Jean de Sponde's *Amours* 18, a submerged compass image is combined with the topos (A. M. Schmidt, ed., *Poètes du XVIe siècle*, 905–6). Philippe Desportes specifically mentions zodiacal movement in a similar context: *Le cours de l'an* (A. M. Schmidt, ed., 811).

44. For the history of the doctrine, see Gerard Verbeke, *L'évolution de la doctrine du Pneuma du stoïcisme à saint Augustin* (Louvain: Editions de l'Institut supérieur de Philosophie; Paris: Desclée de Brouwer, 1945).

45. See also, Albertus, *Liber VIII Physicorum* 3, and Aristotle's definition of "aither," *De caelo* 1.3 (270b).

46. The "layetie" who do not understand love's mystery are compared to those who do not know when the soul leaves the body in a number of Renaissance poems. We may cite: Philippe Desportes, *Les Amours d'Hippolyte* 12.7: "[Celuy] qui ne sçait quand l'ame est du corps divisee . . . Qu'il s'arreste pour voi . . . ma Deese" (A. M. Schmidt, ed., *Poètes du XVI<sup>e</sup> siècle*, 791); Scève 278.4: "Comment du corps l'Ame on peult deslyer . . ." (Ibid., 167), derived from Lodovico Martelli, *Rime* (Venice, 1533) f. A iiii v, cited by E. Parturier, ed., *Délie* 192, n. 2: "Come dal corpo l'anima si svia."

47. The association between breathing and speaking and the importance of both as symbols of the soul are as old as the Bible. Augustin Calmet notes that, although "mors corporis designatur emblemate spiraculi vitae," nevertheless the "breath" of Genesis 2:7 ("inspiravit in faciem ejus spiraculum vitae") indicates the "inspiration" of the soul. He notes that "Chaldaeus vertit: *Factus est spiritum loquentem*" for the words, "factus est homo in animam viventem," since "Spirare et loqui vitae functiones sunt, quae non raro pro vita ipsa usurpantur." *Commentarius literalis*, trans. Giovan Domenico Mansi (Lucca: S. et J. D. Marescandoli, 1730), I.1.20. On the matter of the Biblical variant, see Earl Wasserman, "Pope's Ode for Musick," *ELH* 28, no. 2 (June 1961): 163–86 (170–86).

48. Marisilio Ficino, *Opera*, 2.1605.

49. The "planetary home" of the soul is, of course, a Platonic theme. Plutarch speaks of the pure soul reaching the sphere of the Moon, which is possibly a Poseidonian innovation. See Cherniss's note to *Moralia* 12 in Plutarch, *Moralia*, trans. Harold Fredrik Cherniss (Cambridge: Loeb, 1957), 209ff. The expansion and contraction of *spiritus* is the principle underlying the neo-platonic doctrine of the "pneumatic" body with which the soul "clothes" itself in its descent to earth. The doctrine is found as early as the *Pistis Sophia*. For its history in neoplatonism, see the appendix of E. R. Dodds, *Proclus: Elements of Theology* (Oxford: The Clarendon Press, 1933); for a survey of the history of the idea in the Middle Ages and Renaissance, see Robert Klein, "L'Enfer de Ficin," in *Umanesimo e Esoterismo*, Archivio di filosofia, ed. Eugenio Garin, et. al. (Padua: CEDAM, 1960), 64–7.

50. Luigi Tansilla compares love's despair to a man dying of a "grave mal" who "giace e piange lungamente . . . " *Sonnet 19* in Carlo Bo, ed., *Lirici del Cinquecento*, 248. The traditional identification of a peaceful death with virtue and a violent death with vice explains the association here of "virtuous men" and passing "mildly away."

51. Charles M. Coffin, *John Donne and the New Philosophy* (New York: Columbia University Press, 1937), 98: "Of the new astronomy, the 'moving of th'earth' is the most radical principle."

52. See A. J. Festugière, *La révélation d'Hermès Trismégiste* (Paris: Gabalda, 1950), 1:110 for the pseudo-Orphic *peri seismon*, a typical treatise on earthquakes and their interpretation.

53. "Access and Recess" is an alternate name for the movement of "trepidation." See, for example, Lynn Thorndike, *The Sphere of Sacrobosco and its Commentators* (Chicago: University of Chicago Press, 1949), Index, s.v. "Access and Recess."

54. "The path of the pole among the stars is a slightly sinuous curve." *Encyclopedia Brittanica* 11, 18th edition, 431 (s.v. *Precession*).

55. Leone Ebreo explains earthquakes by his theory of universal love; *pneuma* strives to return to its natural place in *Dialoghi d'amore*, ed. S. Caramella (Bari: Laterza, 1929), 70.

56. For the importance of *pneuma* as a principle of alchemy, see F. Sherwood Taylor, *The Alchemists: Founders of Modern Chemistry* (New York: Schuman, 1949), 11–16.

57. Quoted in ibid., 14. Albertus Magnus notes the traditional association but disagrees: "quidam dixerunt spiritus esse de natura quinti corporis: quod tamen non est verum." *Summae de creaturis* 2.2.78; cf. *Summa* 11.51.1, where Costa ben Luca is cited, and Gerard Verbeke, *L'évolution de la doctrine du Pneuma*, 148.

58. *Meteorologica* 3.6 (378c): "The vaporous exhalation is the cause of all metals, fusible or ductile things, such as iron, copper, gold," quoted in F. Sherwood Taylor, *The Alchemists*, 13, where he explains the importance of the passage.

59. For alchemical allegory in general, see F. Sherwood Taylor, *The Alchemists*, 145–61 ("Alchemical Symbolism"). See especially Plate VI.7 (156): "Their souls depart: i.e., volatization begins." For the principles of attraction, repulsion, and circularity, see Mary Anne Atwood, *Hermetic Philosophy and Alchemy*, rev. ed. (New York: Julian Press, 1960): "Attraction is the first principle of motion in nature . . . Repulsion is the second principle and a necessary consequence of the first by reaction. Circulation is the third principle, proceeding from the conflict of the former two" (154). The comparison of gold to the glorified body is not restricted to the Alchemists; theologians use the comparison as well. See, for example, Aquinas (*Summa Theologica*, *Supp* 3a, q. 83, a.1) who discusses the *subtilitas* of the glorified body: "thus we speak of subtlety in the sun and moon and like bodies, just as gold and silver. . . ." He goes on to remark that some "heretics" have suggested that the glorified body "will be like air on the wind," but of course rejects the idea. He says that gold also resembles the glorified body by its "claritas" and quotes Gregory the Great in support (ibid., ad 2.; cf. Gregory, *Moralia in Job* 18.44 and 48).

60. Joseph A. Mazzeo, "Notes on John Donne's Alchemical Imagery," *ISIS* 48, pt. 2, 152 (June 1957): 113–14.

61. Nicholas Flamel, "The Glory of the World" in *The Hermetic Museum, restored and enlarged . . .*, ed. and trans. Arthur Edward Waite (London: J. Elliott and Co., 1893), 1:47.

62. See, for example, Albertus Magnus, *Mineralium* 3. Cf. F. Sherwood Taylor, *The Alchemists*, 148: "The second great symbol of alchemy is that of a marriage." See also Nicholas Flamel, *His Exposition of the Hieroglyphical Figures . . .* , trans. Eirenaeus Orandus (London, 1624), 84: "in this . . . operation [are] two *natures* conjoyned and married together, the *Masculine* and the *Foeminine*"; again, the anonymous *Golden Tract . . .* "they [husband and wife] fell to embracing each other so passionately that the husband's heart was melted with the excessive ardour of love, and he fell down broken in many pieces" (Arthur Edward Waite, ed., *The Hermetic Museum*, 1:1); and finally, Nicholas Flamel, *His Exposition*, 78: "This dissolution is by the envious *Philosophers* called *Death . . .* Others have called it . . . *Liquefaction . . .*"

63. For the remarks of Lacinio, see *The New Pearl of Great Price*, trans. Arthur Edward Waite (London: J. Elliott and Co., 1894), 133. See also p. 331 for "tempestuous conditions." My quote is from Thomas Norton, "The Ordinal of Alchemy" in Arthur Edward Waite, ed., *The Hermetic museum*, 2:148. Basil Valentine remarks that "too much rain spoils the fruit" (ibid., 2:336). Tears enter into the allegory of the *Golden Tract* cited earlier: "[she] covered him with overflowering tears, until he was quite flooded . . ."

64. "The Sophic Hydrolith or, Water Stone of the Wise" in Arthur Edward Waite, ed. *The Hermetic Museum*, 1:110.

65. "A philosophic fire never described by any philosopher but only whispered by the adept on his death bed is a tremendous secret." Lynn Thorndike (describing a ca. 1605 work by Joachim Tanckins), *A History of Magic and Experimental Science*, 8:106.

66. W. A. Murray, "Donne's Gold-Leaf and His Compasses," *MLN* 73, no. 5 (May 1958): 329. Murray's argument may be supported by the venerable but legendary tradition that Origen believed the glorified body would be perfectly spherical in shape (*Dict. Théol. Cath.* s.v. "Origénisme"), and it would therefore be a living symbol of gold. The association of gold and the glorified body with two lovers is reinforced by Aristophanes's whimsical comparison of the body of the Hermaphrodite to a sphere in Plato's *Symposium*.

67. Murray remarked on the "integral" relationship of center and circumference and reproduced a text in support which will serve admirably

to illustrate our point: "In puncto enim non minus circulus existit, ac in ipso cyclo. Iam quanto maior est cyclus respctus punti? Et tamen utrique integri sunt. Sicut ergo fieri potest, ut circini pes immobilis circulum ducat, alter autem mobilis spatiosam peripheriam: sic aequale ac simile incrementum est magnitudinis hominis respectu coeli. Similiter etiam in decremento a coelo versus hominem veluti radii ab ambitu in punctum suum redeuntes." The so-called Arabic *Theology of Aristotle* explains that because God is the point upon which all of nature depends (cf. Dante, *Par.* 14.1–3 and *Par.* 28.14: "Da quel punto / depende il cielo et tutta la natura," echoing Aristotle *Metaphysics* 30.7) we can never stray from him: "Auch wir bestehen fest nur durch den ersten Schaffer; an ihn hängen wir uns, zu ihm sehnen wir uns, ihm neigen wir uns zu und kehren zu ihm zurück, wenn wir auch von ihm fern und weit ab sind. Denn unser Gang und unsere Heimkehr geht nur zu ihm, gleichwie die Linien (Radien) des *Kreises*, wenn sie auch fern und weit ab sind, zum Mittelpunkt gehen." *Die sogenannte Theologie des Aristoteles aus arabischen handschriften zum ersten mal heratisgegehen*, ed. and trans. Friedrich Dieterici (Leipzig: J. C. Hinrichs 1882–83), 133. The first chapter of Poulet's book (see n. 3) deals fully with this theme of the mystics. Donne's innovation on the theme is to place his beloved at the center to which all radii must return.

68. See n. 56. Since *pneuma* was believed to be the constituent of the fifth essence, then it also had to be the constituent of the heavenly bodies. This homologous composition was what accounted for their similar movement, according to Costa ben Luca, quoted by Albertus (see n. 57).

69. For the figures concerning exaltations and domiciles, see the table provided by Boll, Bezold, and Gundel, *Sternglaube und Sterndeutung*, 59 and also Eugenio Garin, *Disputationes* (quoting the Arabs), 545 for confirmation. Sexes were assigned to all of the planets; the higher planets were considered to be male and the lower female, except that Mercury was hermaphrodite. See A. J. Festugière, *La révélation d'Hermès Trismégiste*, 1.97.

70. Thorndike traces two separate theories concerning Mercury and the "tincture"—one was that earthly mercury had to be combined with a small measure of gold and silver in order to produce Heavenly Mercury; the other was that mercury alone would suffice (Lynn Thorndike, *A History of Magical and Experimental Science*, 3.58ff, 88ff, and Index, s.v. Mercury). A typical example of the production of tincture from mercury is given by Paracelsus, who distinguishes two different kinds of mercury: "Take Philosophers' Mercury, prepared and purified to its supreme

degree. Dissolve this with its wife, that is to say, with quick mercury, so that the woman may dissolve the man, and the man may fix the woman. Then, just as the 'husband loves his wife and she her husband, the Philosophers' Mercury purses the quick mercury with the most supreme love . . . [so that] . . . they have no difference . . . For this reason, the woman is united to the man in such a way that she dissolves the man, and he *fixes* her and renders her *constant in every consideration* as a consequence" (Arthur Edward Waite, ed., *The Hermetic Museum*, 1:85–6).

71. Joseph A. Mazzeo, "Notes on John Donne's Alchemical Imagery," 105, n. 5.

72. Quoted from the *Turba Exercitationum* I by Mary Anne Atwood, *Hermetic Philosophy and Alchemy*, 72. She quotes Geber as saying "All is made of Mercury" (77), a saying which is echoed by Arnold of Villanova (Lynn Thorndike, *A History of Magical and Experimental Science*, 3:76).

73. For the generic principle of "circulations," reflux condensation, and so on, see F. Sherwood Taylor, *The Alchemists*, 118ff and 142ff. The spherical container might also be a limbeck. Mazzeo says: "In 'spiritual alchemy' the tortuous curvings of the retort tube was analogous to the hard path traveled by the soul in the process of its purification" (Joseph A. Mazzeo, "Notes on John Donne's Alchemical Imagery," 110). For the use of the term "refinement," see Benedictus Figulus, *A Golden and Blessed Casket of Nature's Marvels:* "A refined spirit cannot appear except in a body suitable to its nature . . . ," trans. Arthur Edward Waite (London: James Elliott and Co., 1893), 42.

74. Albertus says that "animalia mutant voces et sunt in motu tempore coitus et exclamant se invicem," and quotes Aristotle (*De hist. animal.* 5.14.544b22) in support (*Quaestiones super de animalibus* 5.3). Thus the *strepitus* of coitus is bestial.

75. Albertus also describes the role of the *spiritus spumosus* in coitus and describes the debilitating effects of a lack of moderation. Leone Ebreo (*Dialoghi d'amore*, 80–1) speaks of the relationship between the earth (female) and "il suo maschio" (the heavens) in sexual and alchemical terms. One line in particular is reminiscent of Donne's "makes no show / To move, but doth, if the other doe": "Ella [i.e., the earth], se ben è quieta, si muove pur un poco per il movimento del maschio."

76. A résumé of a typical form of the *Timaeus* analogy is given by Festugière, where the head is said to be equivalent to the heavens and the "ventre" to the earth (A. J. Festugière, *La révélation d'Hermès Trismégiste* 1.92). It is because of this analogy that Renaissance theoreticians of love

distinguished between rational and carnal love with the terms "celestial" and "terrestrial."

77. Translation taken from Baldessare Castiglione, *Book of the Courtier*, trans. Charles S. Singleton (New York: Doubleday, 1959).

78. *The Midrash Rabbah*, trans. Louis Isaac Rabinowitz (London: Soncino Press, 1939), 187 (Deuteronomy 2:10). Pico takes issue with Ficino's interpretation of the kiss of Agathon in the *Convivium* and suggests that the real significance is the ecstatic *binsica* (bensiqah) or "death by the kiss." Castiglione's remarks paraphrase the long passage in *the Commento . . . sopra una Canzona de Amore . . . composta la . . . Girolamo Benivien* 3, stanza 4 (in Giovanni Pico della Mirandolda, *De hominis dignitate; Heptaplus; De ente et uno; e scritti vari*, ed. Eugenio Garin [Florence: Vallecchi, 1942], 557ff.).

79. For the kiss as the recapitulation of a whole life, see Giovanni Battista Guarini, *Il Pastor fido* 2.1: "La mia vita, chiusa / in così breve spazio, / non era che un bacio," quoted by Nicholas Perella, "Fate in the *Pastor fido*," *Romantic Review* 49, no. 4 (December 1958): 262 and note. See also Perella's monograph on the kiss, *The Kiss Sacred and Profane*. Giambattista Marino's *Baci* (*La Lira* 2.4) provides an example of scientific and sensual virtuosity on the subject. Echoing Guarini, he gives a scientific basis to the ecstasy of the kiss: "*spiriti* rugiadosi, *sensi* d'amor *vitali*, che 'n breve *giro* il viver mio chiudete" (italics mine). Another verse echoes Castiglione's (and Donne's) conceit: "e più d'un'alma in una bocca asconde!" Again, he recalls the ecstasy in a purely erotic sense: "quel bacio, che mi priva di vita mi raviva." Finally, he combines sigh, whisper, smile, and kiss: "un sol bacio beve sospir, parole e riso." In *Marino e i marinisti*, ed. Giuseppe Guido Ferrero (Milan: R. Ricciardi, 1954), 37:352–5. In another poem, Donne refers to the ecstatic kiss of rational love as a banality, which he rejects in favor of the epistolary ecstasy popularized by Ficino (Cf. Merritt Hughes, "Some of Donne's 'Ecstasies,' "): "Sir, more than kisses, letters mingle Soules . . ." (*Verse epistle: To Sir Henry Wotton*).

### ZENO'S LAST CIGARETTE

1. Fyodor Dostoyevsky, *Notes from Underground*, trans. Constance Garnett, rev. Ralph E. Matlaw (New York: Dutton, 1960), 35.

2. Henri Bergson, *Creative Evolution*, trans. Arthur Mitchell (New York: Henry Holt and Company, 1911), 312.

3. Henri Bergson, *Creative Evolution*, 312.

# Bibliography

Abelard, Peter. *Historia calamitatum. The story of my misfortunes: An autobiography.* Translated by Henry A. Bellows. Saint Paul, Minn.: T. A. Boyd, 1922.

Albertus Magnus. *Convivio,* comment. Giovanni Busnelli and Giuseppe Vandelli, 2 vols. Florence: Le Monnier, 1968.

———. *La Divina Commedia.* Edited and with an introduction by Giorgio Petrocchi. Turin: Einaudi, 1975.

———. *Opera omnia.* Edited by Augustus Borgnet. Paris: Apud Ludovicum Vives, Bibliopolam Editorem, 1890.

———. *Opera Omnia.* Edited by B. Geyer. Monasterii Westfalorum, Westphalia: Aschendorff, 1955.

Allen, D. C. "Donne's Compass Figure." *MLN* 71, no. 4 (April 1956): 256–7.

Anonymous. *Il Libro dei ventiquattro filosofi.* Edited by Paolo Lucentini. Milan: Adelphi, 1999.

Aquinas, Thomas. *Summa Theologiae.* Translated by Fathers of the English Dominican Province. 3 vols. New York: Benziger, 1948.

Ardizzone, Maria Luisa. *Guido Cavalcanti: The Other Middle Ages.* University of Toronto Press, 2002.

Arendt, Hannah. *Love and Saint Augustine.* Chicago: University of Chicago Press, 1996.

Aristotle. *Du ciel (De caelo).* Translated by Paul Moraux. Paris: Les Belles Lettres, 1965.

———. *Generation of Animals.* Translated by A. L. Peck. Cambridge, Mass.: Harvard University Press, 1942.

———. *Meteorologica.* Edited by H. D. P. Lee. London: Loeb, 1952.

————. *Physics*. Edited and translated by P. H. Wicksteed and F. M. Cornford. 2 vols. Cambridge, Mass.: Harvard University Press, 1934.

————. *Traité de l'âme*. Translated by Georges Rodier. Paris: Leroux, 1900.

Ascoli, Albert. *Ariosto's Bitter Harmony*. Princeton, N.J.: Princeton University Press, 1987.

Atwood, Mary Anne. *Hermetic Philosophy and Alchemy*, rev. ed. New York: Julian Press, 1960.

Auerbach, Erich. *Dante, Poet of the Secular World*. Translated by Ralph Mannheim. Chicago: University of Chicago Press, 1961.

————. "Dante's Addresses to the Reader," *Romance Philology* 7 (1954): 268–78.

————. *Mimesis: The Representation of Reality in Western Literature*. Translated by William R. Trask. Princeton, N.J.: Princeton University Press, 1953.

Augustine. *Confessions*. Edited by James O'Donnell. 2 vols. Oxford: Oxford University Press, 1992.

————. *De Trinitate*. In *Corpus Christianorum, Series Latina*. Turnhout: Brepolis, 1953–2013.

Averroes. *Aristotelis Opera cum Averrois Commentariis*. 11 vols. Venice: Junctas, 1562–74.

————. *Commentarium magnum in Aristotelis de anima libros* 6. Edited by F. Stuart Crawford. Cambridge, Mass.: Harvard University Press, 1953.

Austin, Herbert D. "From Matter to Spirit," *MLN* 38 (1923): 140–8.

Austin, Herbert D. and Leo Spitzer. "Letargo (*Par.* 33.94)," *MLN* 52, no. 7 (1937): 469–75.

Ball, Robert. "Theological Semantics: Virgil's *Pietas* and Dante's *Pietà*," *Stanford Italian Review* 2, no. 1 (Spring 1981): 19–36.

Barb, A. A. "Diva Matrix," *Journal of the Warburg and Courtauld Institutes* 16 (1953): 193–238.

Barblan, Giovanni, ed. *Dante e la Bibbia*. Florence: L. S. Olschki, 1988.

Barfield, Own. *Saving the Appearances: A Study in Idolatry*. London: Faber and Faber, 1957.

Barolini, Teodolinda. "Dante and Francesca da Rimini: Realpolitik, Romance, Gender," *Speculum* 75, no. 1 (January 2000): 1–28.

————. *Dante's Poets: Textuality and Truth in the "Commedia."* Princeton, N.J.: Princeton University Press, 1984.

Bergson, Henri. *Creative Evolution*. Translated by Arthur Mitchell. New York: Henry Holt and Company, 1911.

————. *Essai sur les données immédiates de la conscience.* Edited by Frédéric Worms. Paris: Quadrige, 2007.

Bernardo, A. S., and A. L. Pellerini, eds. *Dante, Petrarch, Boccaccio: Studies in the Italian Trecento in Honor of C. S. Singleton.* Binghamton, N.Y.: Medieval and Renaissance Texts and Studies 22, 1983.

Berne, Eric. *Transactional Analysis in Psychotherapy.* New York: Ballantine Books, 1975.

Bloom, Harold. *The Anxiety of Influence.* Oxford: Oxford University Press, 1973.

————, ed. *Odysseus/Ulysses.* New York: Chelsea House Publishers, 1991.

Blumenberg, Hans. *Shipwreck with Spectator: Paradigm of a Metaphor for Existence.* Translated by Steven Randall. Cambridge, Mass.: MIT Press, 1996.

Bo, Carlo, ed. *Lirici del cinquecento.* Milan: Garzanti, 1945.

Boll, Franz, Carl Bezold, and Wilhelm Gundel, eds. *Sternglaube und Sterndeutung: die Geschichte und das Wesen der Astrologie.* Leipzig; Berlin: Teubner, 1926.

Bowie, Malcolm. *Lacan.* Cambridge, Mass.: Harvard University Press, 1991.

Brownlee, Kevin and Walter Stephens, eds. *Discourses of Authority in Medieval and Renaissance Literatures.* Hanover, N.H.: Published for Dartmouth College by University Press of New England, 1989.

Buffière, Felix. *Les mythes d'Homère et la pensée greque.* Paris: Belles Lettres, 1956.

Bultmann, Rudolf. *The Gospel of John: A Commentary.* Translated by G. R. Beasley-Murray. Oxford: Blackwell, 1971.

Burke, Kenneth. *The Rhetoric of Religion: Studies in Logology.* Berkeley: University of California Press, 1961.

Bursill-Hall, Geoffrey L. *Speculative Grammars of the Middle Ages: the Doctrine of Partes Orationis of the Modistae.* The Hague: Mouton, 1971.

Cary, Phillip. *Augustine's Invention of the Inner Self: The Legacy of a Christian Platonist.* Oxford: Clarendon Press, 2000.

Castiglione, Baldessare. *Book of the Courtier.* Translated by Charles S. Singleton. New York: Doubleday, 1959.

Cellini, Benvenuto. *Vita di Benvenuto Cellini.* Edited by Giovanni Palamede Carpani. Milan: Società Tipografica de' Classici Italiani, 1811.

Charity, A. C. *Events and Their Afterlife.* Cambridge: Cambridge University Press, 1966.

Chevallier, Philippe, ed. *Dionysiaca.* Bruges: Desclée de Brouwer, 1937.

Chiarenza, Marguerite Mills. "Time and Eternity in the Myths of *Para-diso* XVII." In *Dante, Petrarch, Boccaccio: Studies in the Italian Tre-cento in Honor of C. S. Singleton*, edited by A. S. Bernardo and A. L. Pellerini. Binghamton, N.Y.: Medieval and Renaissance Texts and Studies, 1983.

Ciminelli, Serafino dei. *Le rime di Serafino de'Ciminelli dall'Aquila.* Edited by Mario Menghini. Bologna: Romagnoli-Dall'Acqua, 1894.

Coffin, Charles M. *John Donne and the New Philosophy.* New York: Columbia University Press, 1937.

Cole, Bruce. *Piero della Francesca: Tradition and Innovation in Renaissance Art.* New York: Icon Editions, 1991.

Colish, Marcia. *The Mirror of Language.* New Haven: Yale University Press, 1968.

Contini, Gianfranco, ed. *Poeti del dolce stil novo.* Milan: Mondadori, 1991.

———. *Un' idea di Dante: saggi danteschi.* Turin: Einaudi, 1976.

Cornford, Francis M. *Plato's Cosmology: The "Timaeus" of Plato.* New York: The Liberal Arts Press, 1957.

Corrozet, Gilles. *Le Sophologe d'Amour.* Paris: Gilles Corrozet, 1542.

Corti, Maria. *La felicità mentale: nuove prospettive per Cavalcanti e Dante.* Turin: Einaudi, 1983.

———. "On the Metaphors of Sailing, Flight, and Tongues of Fire in the episode of *Ulysses* (*Inf.* 26)," *Stanford Italian Review* 9 (1990): 33–47.

Courcelle, Pierre. *Les Confessions de St. Augustin dans la tradition lit-téraire.* Paris: Etudes Augustiniennes, 1963.

———. "Quelques symboles funeraire du neo-platonisme latin: Le vol de Dédale; Ulysse et les Sirènes," *Revue des etudes anciennes* 46 (1944): 65–93.

———. *Recherches sur les Confessions de St. Augustin.* Paris: E. de Boccard, 1950.

Curtius, Ernst Robert. *European Literature and the Latin Middle Ages.* New York: Routledge and Kegan Paul, 1953.

De Grazia, Sebastiano. *Machiavelli in Hell.* Princeton, N.J.: Princeton University Press, 1989.

De Lubac, Henri. *Le mystere du surnaturel.* Paris: Cerf, 2000.

Derrida, Jacques. *De la grammatologie.* Paris: Editions de Minuit, 1967.

———. *The Politics of Friendship.* Translated by George Collins. London: Verso, 2005.

Devoto, Giacomo. *Studi di stilistica.* Florence: LeMonnier, 1950.

Dieterici, Friedrich, ed. and trans. *Die sogenannte Theologie des Aristoteles aus arabischen handschriften zum ersten mal heratisgegehen.* Leipzig: J. C. Hinrichs, 1882–83.

Dodds, E. R. *Proclus: Elements of Theology*. Oxford: Clarendon Press, 1933.

Dostoyevsky, Fyodor. *Notes from Underground*. Translated and with introduction by Jessie Coulson. New York: Penguin, 1972.

Dronke, Peter. "Boethius, Alanus and Dante," *Romanische Forschungen* 78 (1966): 119–25.

———. "Francesca and Héloïse," *Comparative Literature* 27, no. 2 (Spring 1975): 113–35.

Durling, Robert. "Petrarch's 'Giovene donna sotto un verde lauro,'" *MLN* 86 (1971): 1–20.

Ebreo, Leone. *Dialoghi d'amore*. Edited by S. Caramella. Bari: Laterza, 1929.

Ferrero, Giuseppe Guido, ed. *Marino e i marinisti*. Milan: R. Ricciardi, 1954.

Festugière, A. J. *La révélation d'Hermès Trismégiste*. Paris: Gabalda, 1950.

Ficino, Marsilio. *Commentaire sur le Banquet de Platon*. Translated by R. Marcel. Paris: Belles Lettres, 1956.

———. *Dialoghi*. Venice: Paolo Manuzio, 1544.

Fido, Franco, P. Parker Fido, and Rena Syska-Lamparska, eds. *Studies for Dante: Essays in Honor of Dante Della Terza*. Fiesole: Cadmo, 1998.

Finerman, Joel, Catherine Gallagher, and Neil Hertz. "More about Medusa's Head," *Representations* (Fall 1983): 55–7.

Flamel, Nicholas. *His Exposition of the Hieroglyphical Figures . . .* Translated by Eirenaeus Orandus. London, 1624.

Fraser, Jennifer. *Rite of Passage in the Narratives of Dante and Joyce*. Gainesville: University Press of Florida, 2002.

Freccero, John. "Burke on Logology" in *Representing Kenneth Burke*, edited by Margaret Brose and Hayden White. Baltimore: Johns Hopkins University Press, 1982. 52–67.

———, ed. *Dante: A Collection of Critical Essays*. Englewood Cliffs, N.J.: Prentice Hall, 1965.

Freud, Sigmund. "Medusa's Head." In *Sexuality and the Psychology of Love*, edited by Philip Reiff. New York: Collier Books, 1963.

Freytag, Gustav. *Die Technik des Dramas*. Leipzig: S. Hirzel, 1863.

Friedman, John B. "Antichrist and the Iconography of Dante's Geryon," *Journal of the Warburg and Courtauld Institutes* 35 (1972): 108–22.

Frye, Northrop. *The Great Code*. New York: Harcourt Brace Jovanovich, 1982.

Gallagher, Catherine. "More about Medusa's Head," *Representations* 4 (1983): 55–7.

Garin, Eugenio, ed. *La disputa delle arti nel Quattrocento*. Florence: Vallecchi, 1947.

Gilson, Etienne. *Dante and Philosophy*. New York: Harper & Row, 1963.

———. *L'esprit de la philosophie médiévale*. Paris: Librairie Philosophique J. Vrin, 1944.

Girard, René. *Deceit, Desire, and the Novel: Self and Other in Literary Structure*. Translated by Yvonne Freccero. Baltimore: Johns Hopkins University Press, 1965.

———. *To Double Business Bound: Essays on Literature, Mimesis, and Anthropology*. Baltimore: Johns Hopkins University Press, 1978.

Goldin, Frederick. *The Mirror of Narcissus in the Courtly Love Lyric*. Ithaca, N.Y.: Cornell University Press, 1967.

Gramsci, Antonio. *Quaderni del carcere*. Edited by Valentino Gerratana. 4 vols. Turin: Einaudi, 1975.

———. *Sotto la mole, 1916–1920*. Turin: Einaudi, 1960.

Gregory the Great. *Moralia in Job*. In *Corpus Christianorum, Series Latina*. Turnhout: Brepolis, 1953–2013.

Guglielmi, Nilda. "L'image de la porte et des enceintes d'après les chroniques du moyen âge." In *Fortifications, portes de villes, places publiques, dans le monde méditerranéen*, edited by Jacques Heers. Paris: Presses de l'Université de Paris-Sorbonne, 1985.

Guzzo, A. and R. Amerio, eds. *Opere di Giordano Bruno e di Tommaso Campanella*, in *La Letteratura Italiana: Storia e testi* vol 33. Milan: Ricciardi, 1956.

Hawkins, Peter. *Dante's Testaments: Essays in Scriptural Imagination*. Stanford: Stanford University Press, 1999.

Hertz, Neil. *The End of the Line: Essays on Psychoanalysis and the Sublime*. New York: Columbia University Press, 1985.

———. "Medusa's Head: Male Hysteria under Political Pressure," *Representations* 4 (1983): 27–54.

Hexter, J. H. "*Il Principe* and *lo Stato*," *Studies in the Renaissance* 4 (1957): 113–38.

Hughes, Merritt. "Some of Donne's 'Ecstasies,'" *PMLA* 75, no. 5 (December 1960): 509–18.

Jacoff, Rachel, ed. *The Cambridge Companion to Dante*. Cambridge: Cambridge University Press, 2007.

Jakobson, Roman. *Selected Writings*. Edited by Stephen Rudy. 6 vols. Paris: Mouton, 1971–85.

Jonson, Ben. *Ben Jonson: The Poems / The Prose Works*. Edited by C. H. Herford, Percy Simpson, and Evelyn Simpson. Oxford: Clarendon Press, 1947.

Kantorowicz, Ernst H. *The King's Two Bodies: A Study in Medieval Political Theology*. Princeton, N.J.: Princeton University Press, 1957.

Kaske, R. E. "Dante's 'DXV' and 'Veltro,'" *Traditio* (1961): 185–254.

Kaufman, Yehezkel. *Religion of Israel*. Translated by M. Greenberg. Chicago: University of Chicago Press, 1960.

Klein, Robert. "L'Enfer de Ficin," in *Umanesimo e Esoterismo*, Archivio di filosofia, eds. Eugenio Garin, et. al. Padua: CEDAM, 1960.

Lacinio. *The New Pearl of Great Price*. Translated by Arthur Edward Waite. London: J. Elliott and Co., 1894.

Lamberton, Robert. *Homer the Theologian: Neoplatonist Allegorical Reading and the Growth of the Epic Tradition*. Berkeley: University of California Press, 1986.

Lausberg, Heinrich. *Handbook of Literary Rhetoric*. Edited by David E. Orton and R. Dean Anderson. Leiden: Brill, 1998.

Lechner, Gregor. *Maria Gravida: zum Schwangerschaftsmotiv in der bildenden Kunst*. Munich: Schnell & Steiner, 1981.

Lederer, Josef. "John Donne and the Emblematic Practice," *RES* 22 (1946): 182–200.

Le Goff, Jacques. *The Medieval Imagination*. Chicago: University of Chicago Press, 1988.

*Lirici del secolo XVI*. Milan: E Sonzogno, 1879.

Lukács, György. *The Theory of the Novel*. Translated by Anna Bostock. Cambridge, Mass.: MIT Press, 1971.

MacEwan, Elias J. *Freytag's Technique of the Drama: An Exposition of Dramatic Composition and Art*. Chicago: Scott Foresman, 1908.

MacKenna, Stephen, trans. *Plotinus on the Beautiful*. Stratford-up-on-Avon: The Shakespeare Head Press, 1914.

Macrobius, *Commentary on the Dream of Scipio*. Edited and translated by William H. Stahl. New York: Columbia University Press, 1952.

Mansi, Giovan Domenico, trans. *Commentarius literalis*. Lucca: S. et J.D. Marescandoli, 1730.

Maritain, Jacques. *The Range of Reason*. New York: Scribner, 1952.

Martelli, Lodovico. *Rime*. Venice, 1533.

Mazzeo, Joseph A. "Notes on John Donne's Alchemical Imagery," *ISIS* 48, pt. 2, 152 (June 1957): 103–23.

McCarthy, Mary. *The Stones of Florence*. New York: Harcourt, Brace, 1959.

McTaggart, J. M. E. "The Unreality of Time," *Mind: A Quarterly Review of Psychology and Philosophy* 17 (1908): 456–73.

*The Midrash Rabbah*. Translated by Louis Isaac Rabinowitz. London: Soncino Press, 1939.

Morse, Ruth. *Truth and Convention in the Middle Ages: Rhetoric, Representation and Reality*. Cambridge: Cambridge University Press, 1991.

Murray, W. A. "Donne's Gold-Leaf and His Compasses," *MLN* 73, no. 5 (May 1958): 329–30.

Nardi, Bruno. *Dante e la cultura medievale: Nuovi saggi di filosofia dantesca*. Bari: Laterza, 1949.

———. *Nel mondo di Dante*. Rome: Storia e Letteratura, 1944.

Norden, Eduard. *Agnostos theos*. Leipzig: Verlag B.G. Teubner, 1913.

———. *Dio Ignoto*. Translated by Chiara O. Tommasi Moreschini. Brescia: Morcelliana, 2002.

O'Connell, Robert J. *Soundings in St. Augustine's Imagination*. Fordham: Fordham University Press, 1992.

Ölerud, A. *L'Idée de macrocosmos et de microcosmos dans le Timée de Platon*. Uppsala: Almqvist & Wiksells Boktryckeri, 1951.

Padoan, Giorgio. "Ulisse 'Fandi Fictor' e le vie della Sapienza," *Studi danteschi* 37 (1960): 21–61.

Pagliaro, Antonino. *Ulisse: Ricerche semantiche sulla Divina Commedia*. 2 vols. Messina: G. D'Anna, 1976.

Panofsky, Erwin. *Studies in Iconology: Humanistic Themes in the Art of the Renaissance*. New York: Oxford University Press, 1967.

Parker, Patricia. "Dante and the Dramatic Monologue," *Stanford Literature Review* 2, no. 2 (Fall 1985): 165–83.

Parturier, E., ed. *Délie*. Paris: Droz, 1916.

Peirce, C. S. *Collected Papers*. Edited by Arthur W. Burke, Charles Hartshorne and Paul Weiss. Cambridge, Mass.: Harvard University Press, 1960.

Pepin, Jean. "The Platonic and Christian Ulysses," in *Odysseus/Ulysses*, ed. Harold Bloom. New York: Chelsea House Publishers, 1991.

Perella, Nicolas J. *The Kiss Sacred and Profane: An Interpretive History of Kiss Symbolism and Related Religio-erotic Themes*. Berkeley: University of California Press, 1969.

Petrarch. *Prose*. Edited by G. Martellotti, et. al. Milan: Ricciardi, 1955.

Picinelli, Filippo. *Mundus symbolicus*. Translated by A. Erath. Cologne, 1687.

Pico della Mirandola, Giovanni. *Disputationes adversus astrologiam divinatricem, Libri 6–12*. Edited by Eugenio Garin. Florence: Vallecchi Editore, 1952.

Pirandello, Luigi. "La commedia dei diavoli." In *Saggi, poesia, e scritti vari*, edited by Manlio Lo Vecchio-Musti. Milan: Mondadori, 1960.

Pitkin, Hanna Fenichel. *Fortune Is a Woman: Gender and Politics in the Thought of Niccolò Machiavelli*. Berkeley: University of California Press, 1984.

Plutarch. *Moralia*. Translated by Harold Fredrik Cherniss. Cambridge, Mass.: Loeb, 1957.

Pocock, J. G. A. *The Machiavellian Moment: Florentine Political Thought and the Atlantic Republican Tradition*. Princeton, N.J.: Princeton University Press, 1975.

Poggioli, Renato. "Tragedy or Romance? A Reading of the Paola and Francesca Episode in Dante's *Inferno*," *PMLA* 72, no. 3 (1957): 313–58.

Pontet, Maurice. *L'Exégèse de S. Augustin prédicateur*. Paris: Aubier, 1946.

Poulet, George. "Bergson et le thème de la vision panoramique des mourants" in *Revue de theologie et philosophie* 3, 10:1 (1960): 23–41.

———. *Études sur le temps humain, II: La distance intérieure*. Paris: Plon, 1965.

———. *Les Metamorphoses du cercle*. Translated by Carley Dawson and Elliott Coleman. Baltimore: Johns Hopkins University Press, 1966.

———. *Le Point de départ*. Paris: Editions de Rocher, 1964.

Powers, Doris C. "Donne's Compass," *RES*, n.s. 9 (1958): 173–5.

Praz, Mario. *The Flaming Heart*. New York: Doubleday, 1958.

Price, A. W. *Love and Friendship in Plato and Aristotle*. Oxford: Clarendon Press, 1990.

Pseudo-Dionysius. *De divinis nominibus*. In *Corpus Dionysiacum I*, edited by B. R. Suchla. Berlin: De Gruter, 1990.

Putnam, Michael C. J. *Virgil's Aeneid: Interpretation and Influence*. Chapel Hill: University of North Carolina Press, 1995.

Reade, W. H. V. *The Moral System of Dante's "Inferno."* Oxford: Clarendon Press, 1909.

Reale, Giovanni. *Agostino: Amore assoluto e "terza navigazione."* Milan: Bompiani, 2000.

Reeves, Eileen. "John Donne and the Oblique Course," *Renaissance Studies* 7, no. 2 (1993): 168–83.

Reynolds, Mary. *Joyce and Dante: The Shaping Imagination*. Princeton, N.J.: Princeton University Press, 1981.

Ripa, Cesare. *Iconologia*. Venice: N. Pezzana, 1669.

Robertson, D. W. *A Preface to Chaucer*. Princeton, N.J.: Princeton University Press, 1962.

Rosengarten, Frank. "Gramsci's 'Little Discovery': Gramsci's Interpretation of Canto X of Dante's *Inferno*," *boundary 2*, 14, no. 3 (Spring, 1986): 71–90.

Saitta, Giuseppe. *La Filosofia di Marsilio Ficino*. Messina: G. Principato, 1923.

Sanguineti, Federico. *Gramsci e Machiavelli*. Bari: Laterza, 1982.

Scève, Maurice. *Maurice Scève: Choix des textes & préface par Albert Béguin.* Paris: G L M, 1947.

Schmidt, A. M., ed., *Poètes du XVIᵉ siècle.* Paris: Pléiade, 1959.

Scott, J. A. *Dante Magnanimo: studi sulla "Commedia."* Florence: Olschki, 1977.

Shankland, Hugh. "Dante aliger," *Modern Language Review* 70 (1975): 764–85.

Siciliano, Italo. *François Villon et les thèmes poétiques du moyen âge.* Paris: Colin, 1934.

Silvestris, Bernardus. *Commentary on the First Six Books of Virgil's "Aeneid."* Translated and commentary by Earl G. Schreiber and Thomas E. Maresca. Lincoln: University of Nebraska Press, 1974.

Singleton, Charles S. *Dante's Commedia: Elements of Structure.* Cambridge, Mass.: Harvard University Press, 1954.

———. *Dante Studies 2: Journey to Beatrice.* Cambridge, Mass.: Harvard University Press, 1958.

———. "*Inferno* X: Guido's Disdain," *MLN* 77 (January 1963): 49–65.

———. "The Vistas in Retrospect," *MLN* 81 (1966): 55–80.

———. "*Vita Nuova* XII, Love's Obscure Words," *Romantic Review* 36 (April 1945): 89–102.

Spitzer, Leo. "The Poetic Treatment of a Platonic-Christian Theme," *Comparative Literature* 6, no. 3 (Summer 1954): 193–217.

———. *Representative Essays*, edited by Alban K. Forcione, et al. Stanford: Stanford University Press, 1988.

Squarotti, Giorgio Bàrberi. *Selvaggia Dilettanza: La caccia nella letteratura italiana dalle origini a Marino.* Venice: Marsilio, 2000.

Stewart, Dana E. and Alison Cornish, eds. *Sparks and Seeds: Medieval Literature and Its Afterlife.* Introduction by Giuseppe Mazzotta. Turnhout: Brepols, 2000.

Streicher, Jeanne, ed. *Oeuvres poétiques.* Geneva: Droz, 1951.

Synave, Paul. "La doctrine de St. Thomas d'Aquin sur le sens littéral des Écritures," *Revue Biblique* 35 (1926): 40–65.

Tate, Allen. "The Point of Dying," *SR* 61, no. 1 (Winter 1953): 76–81.

Taylor, F. Sherwood. *The Alchemists: Founders of Modern Chemistry.* New York: Schuman, 1949.

Thiebaux, Marcelle. *The Stag of Love: The Chase in Medieval Literature.* Ithaca, N.Y.: Cornell University Press, 1974.

Thompson, David. *Dante's Epic Journeys.* Baltimore: Johns Hopkins Press, 1974.

Thorndike, Lynn. *A History of Magic and Experimental Science.* New York: Columbia University Press, 1923.

————. *The Sphere of Sacrobosco and Its Commentators*. Chicago: University of Chicago Press, 1949.

Turetzky, Philip. *Time*. London: Routledge, 1998.

Vacant, A. and E. Mangenot, eds. *Dictionnaire de Théologie Catholique Contenant l'Exposé des Doctrines de la Théologie Catholique Leurs Preuves et Leur Histoire*. 15 vols. Paris: Letouzey et Ané, 1932.

Verbeke, Gerard. *L'évolution de la doctrine du Pneuma du stoïcisme à saint Augustin*. Louvain: Editions de l'Institut supérieur de Philosophie; Paris: Desclée de Brouwer, 1945.

Waite, Arthur Edward, ed. and trans. *The Hermetic Museum, restored and enlarged* . . . London: J. Elliott, 1893.

Wasserman, Earl. "Pope's Ode for Musick," *ELH* 28, no. 2 (June 1961): 163–86.

Weil-Garris, Kathleen. "On Pedestals: Michelangelo's *David*, Bandinelli's *Hercules* and *Cacus*, and the Sculpture of the Piazza della Signoria," *Römische Jahrbuch für Kunstgeschicte* 20 (1983): 377–415.

Wetherbee, Winthrop. *The Ancient Flame: Dante and the Poets*. Notre Dame, Ind.: University of Notre Dame Press, 2008.

————. *Platonism and Poetry in the Twelfth Century*. Princeton, N.J.: Princeton University Press, 1972.

Wölker, W. *Kontemplation und Ekstase bei Pseudo-Dionysius Areopagita*. Wiesbaden: Franz Steine, 1958.

Yeats, William Butler. *The Collected Poems of W. B. Yeats*. London: Wordsworth Editions, 2000.

# Index